Just a Thought

by

Aaron Linford

Published by
Aleph Publishers
Preston, Lancashire

Published by
Aleph Publishers
5 Southlands Avenue, Lostock Hall
PRESTON, Lancashire PR5 5XB

Printed by Sharon Press
Bolton

ISBN 0 9530530 1 6

Further copies are available from the Publishers
at the above address

Prologue

God's counsellors

"Thy testimonies also are my delight; and my counsellors" (lit. men of counsel) Psalm 119:24

Counselling is a current form of helping sufferers from trauma - possibly overdone these days. The Psalmist states that God's word, His "testimony" to His own nature, purposes and activities, is counsel from Heaven. And so it is - the Bible "speaks to our condition, ministers to our moods, interprets the mysteries of life, and points to solutions of its problems. Social and personal, domestic or economic, political or practical - all issues receive not only mention, but also explanation. The Bible is God's life-plan for all His creatures. To accept and obey His word is life: to disregard it is disaster.

The following **'JUST A THOUGHT'**, brief daily homilies, are intended to act as a primer to set the pump of ideas flowing, a pointer to direct courses of moral and spiritual investigation.

They are not intended to supplement regular reading or devotional studies, but to add **"just a thought"** to help in each days pilgrimage. May they help you to tread more lightly the Christian way.

Language of the heart

"My heart said unto Thee"   Psalm 27:8

The trouble with us is that we often use words as a cloak to conceal our real self. But before God only honesty and sincerity count. He does not hear the veiled utterance, He sees the heart - the inner sentiment, the true nature, the real self - and only responds to this deeper prayer.

"Seek ye My face". God longs to hear our voice, He seeks our worship. It was for this He made us, not for His personal gain or glory, but because our souls can only find rest and fulfilment in Him. We were created with a capacity for fellowship with our Maker; lacking this leaves a vacuum that nothing else can fill.

"Thy face, Lord, will I seek". This is the only rational response to God's invitation, as Romans 12:1 says, it is "our spiritual service" (NIV). The face of God, His nature and His favour, is "lifted upon us" as we humbly look toward Him. His smile of acceptance is sunshine to our hearts, making them glow with joy. Our lips are loosened, we respond with praise, glory be to the God or our salvation for ever and ever. Amen!

The here and now God

"Which is, and which was, and which is to come, the Almighty" Rev 1:8

This statement seems out of keeping with the usual temporal and grammatical order of PAST, PRESENT and FUTURE. But it is correct in God's order. To Him, and therefore to us, "now is the accepted time".

It is present experience of God that matters most. History and prophecy take second place to immediacy. If God is not "now" to us, He is "never". He certainly is the eternity that was and the eternity to come: but our present consciousness and appreciation of Him is of primary worth.

His past ways and works reinforce our faith, His future prospects endorse our hope, but it is His immediate presence that enthuses our love. He is our eternal contemporary, "with us alway, even to the end of the world. Amen" (Matt 28:20).

Two Hebrew names for God express His "here-ness" and "now-ness" - JAH and JEHOVAH. The former is not a mere contraction of the latter, it contains a different concept JAH is God the eternal. JEHOVAH is God the everlasting. "Eternity" is timeless, "everlasting" is time-fraught: It represents infinite Deity condescending to be thought of in terms of time: past, present and future rolled into one. No longer remote but near: accessible, amenable, gracious the "here - and - now" God.

3 January

God is not dead

"For I know their sorrows" (Exodus 3:7)

Israel groaned under the afflictions of Egypt. The faint glimmer of hope as Moses made an abortive attempt to relieve them was snuffed out: they suffered in turgid darkness. Full forty years their agony was extended, while Moses pined in Midian. Had God forgotten them? Worse still, had he forsaken them? They must have felt abandoned.

But God's delays are not denials. The time was not ripe for their release. They had still more to learn in the school of adversity. Their schoolmaster may have been sorrow, but their curriculum was ordered by God. When the time was ripe their faith would procure their graduation, they would receive their degree in the art of living.

<u>God's silence does not mean that He is insolvent</u>, that He has lost the power to save. Not only was He preparing their deliverance, He was also perfecting their deliverer - Moses. In the silences of shepherd-life, God was bringing to moral and spiritual maturity the one who was to lead the flock of God from the prison of Egypt to the Paradise of Canaan.

<u>God was not dead, though to suffering saints He may seem dormant</u>. "I know their sorrows", He said "and I am come down to deliver them". The redemptive event was to become an epoch. Their woes were swallowed up in a wonderful salvation.

The rationale of faith

"In the beginning God ....." (Genesis 1:1)

Christians are often charged with having mighty sentiments but meagre sense, possessing misty ideals rather than concrete ideas. But Christian beliefs and behaviour have rock-like foundations, as we will see.

<u>The logic of faith</u>. Posit God - and the rest follows. "In the beginning God" introduces, without controversy "the mystery of Godliness". If we believe these words we have a God who precedes and dominates time, occupies and fills space ("the heavens") and forms and directs matter ("the earth"). What are miracles to such a God? They are simply the way He decides to work; not only possible, but inevitable.

<u>The reasonableness of hope</u>. With such a God, hope becomes a rational expectation of future good. He made us, He sustains us. More than that, when we fall He lifts us, when we sin He saves us. His purposes were not defeated by Adam's involvement of the human race in ruin, He had already planned our redemption through the sacrifice of His son, our Lord Jesus Christ."

<u>The radicality of love</u>. "God is love" - the most radical statement of God. And if we accept this basic premiss, the conclusion is assured. His love has bought redemption through the shed blood of Christ; His love gives life and sustenance through the gift of His Spirit. Accept the Bible's concept of God - and life has meaning, salvation reality and fulfilment completion.

The worst can be the best

"Yet I will rejoice in the Lord" Habakkuk 3:18

It is not easy to live the Christian life - but by the grace of God it is possible. The gate to God's life is open always, and access is easy, but, as Jesus said, "Narrow is the way that leadeth unto life". Nevertheless, He who saves us, keeps us, His pardoning grace is followed by His providential care.

<u>Faith Rampant</u>. Things could not have been worse for the prophet. Figs, vines and olives, three staple comestibles, had failed. Flocks and herds had succumbed, lack of fodder - Times were had. But faith is triumphant through all bad times, under all dire circumstances and in all difficult cases. In fact, faith flourishes by trial, hope brightens in black nights of test, and love defeats all bouts of gloom.

<u>Joy Triumphant</u>. If we believe God we overcome the world, doubts are dispersed, questionings quietened, and mourning dispelled. We rejoice in the Lord, for He who permitted our troubles will either remove them or give us strength to overcome them. In any case we joy in God. On the high and slippery slopes of life He gives us a safe footing. Like the stormy petrel we can sing while the tempest blows; for God is our salvation.

I can do it - with God's help

"Our sufficiency is of God" 2 Cor 3:5

Paul was under great stress. Persecuted by his fellow-Jews, puzzled by the strange ways of Providence, pressed by concern for his favourite church, he asks the question,

"Who is sufficient for these things?"

Have you ever felt totally inadequate to meet the situation, wondering if you can cope with the problems of life, or maintain your equilibrium in a disordered world? You're not the only one. Even apostles and prophets sometimes found things just too much to manage. But don't stop there.

Paul had two answers to the demands laid upon him. The first was negative -

"Not that we are sufficient of ourselves"

The psychologist bids us realise our resources. Paul had a better approach. His positive answer was, "Our sufficiency is of God, who has made us able". We can draw on the resources of God, whose limitless grace can "supply all your need according to His riches in glory by Christ Jesus" (Phil 4:19). Inexhaustible means are at our disposal as we put our faith not in ourselves, but in God.

7 January

The last "Amen"

"Amen, even so come, Lord Jesus ..... Amen" Rev 22:20,21

The last "Amen" of the bible is not the end of God, He is bigger than the Book. No, this oft-used word that terminates so many prayers, simply expresses here the end of history, not the finality of Jehovah. Let us look at this word from three aspects.

It is a soteriological "Amen". The doctrine of salvation culminates with this final word. The witness to the atonement of Christ is so complete that to take away from it is dangerous as to add to it is devastating. The blood of the Lamb that was slain is sufficient for the cleansing of all the sins of all mankind.

It is an eschatological "Amen". The doctrine of the last things has been fully expressed. The Second Advent is the blissful hope set before us. Beyond that is an eternity of rapture as the world to come takes shape and reality.

It is a theological "Amen" The doctrine of God has been clearly expounded, the Biblical record is complete. This "Amen" is a consent to Holy Scripture, not a suggestion of finality in Deity. God continues when time shall cease to be. To trust in Him is to enjoy His life now as a foretaste of His life to come. "But while God and I shall be, I am His and He is mine". Glorious thought!

Joseph triumphant

"Ye thought evil .... but God meant it unto good" Gen 50:20

The dreams of Joseph turned out to be visions of God. So many of his experiences seemed to deny their reality, but when God gives dreams they become part of the divine drama of life. Acts and scenes may vary, but the plot proceeds relentlessly to its predestined denouement.

"Ye thought evil" - was a mild expression for the torment and distress fomented by his jealous and unprincipled brothers. Now Joseph triumphs, while they cringe at his feet. But does he take revenge on these miserable miscreants? Not at all.

"God meant it unto good", he concludes. It Is remarkable that the words "thought" and "meant" are the same in the original Hebrew text. In a bad sense it means to hatch a plot, in a good sense it means to devise a plan. But what a thought! The very hurtful plots of men were used to fulfil a divine purpose. The instruments of hate became the tools of Providence. And so the love and purposes of God can transmute the lead of evil into the gold of triumph. "He will turn what seems to harm us into everlasting joy". Hallelujah!

9 January

When heaven and earth agree

"Also they saw God and did eat and drink" Ex 24:11

What a privilege to join Moses in this mountain-top banquet! God and man met in holy convocation. What can we learn from this?

<u>Some do not see God, they only "eat and drink</u>". Their lives are wholly absorbed in secular activities. They feed the "flesh" - and are satisfied.

<u>Others see only God, and do not "eat and drink</u>". They are the super - spiritual, so heavenly minded that they are of little earthly use. This "righteous overmuch" coterie live an unbalanced life. They are really selfish. They forget that others need them. In their "head-in-the-clouds" mentality they fail their more "down-to-earth friends".

<u>A third group "see God and eat and drink</u>". They are the well-balanced believers who enjoy mountain-top blessings and minister to those in the valley below.

If ever you feel like Peter who wished to stay on the Mount of Transfiguration in permanent joy of heavenly fellowship, remember that Jesus went down from the mountain to minister blessing to sin-tormented folk. Be spiritual; but let your vision of God be matched by a vision of gracious ministry to men.

God gives wings

"They shall mount up with wings as eagles" Is 40:31

As we wait expectantly and patiently for God we rise above our troubles. This source of spiritual strength removes our fears and sustains our energies. No one can fail if faith prevail.

<u>The Bird on the Bough</u>
Like the bird on the bough
That is ready to break,
She feels the bough tremble
But gaily she sings.
What is it to her?
She has wings!
She has wings!

An eagle's wings go in pairs:

Our wings are faith and prayer. When both are exercised we soar into higher reaches of spiritual experience.

And the flying eagle seems to be suspended on nothing, like the Christian whose invisible means of support is God Himself. The pull of earth is conquered as we flap our spiritual wings in joyful trust in the Lord who saves and keeps us.

God's seconds are best

"The second man is the Lord from heaven" 1 Cor 15:47

Milton's Paradise Lost is a far greater piece of literature than his later Paradise Regained. That literary gem Robinson Crusoe showed the genius of Daniel De Foe far better than its sequel describing Crusoe's return to his former island home. And John Bunyan in his Pilgrim's Progress is more gripping in the first part than the latter. Man hits his best - and cannot rise above it.

But God can. The "second man", our Lord Jesus, is far greater than the first man, Adam. What the father of the human race relinquished by his fall is more than restored by the Lord.

> "In Him the tribes of Adam boast
> more blessings than their father lost"

So sang Charles Wesley - and so sing we, God's covenant with Israel was rich, but not fully enjoyed. God's second covenant - the New Testament - in Christ is far richer, its blessings sealed and purchased by the blood of His Son. And all to be enjoyed by those who through faith in Christ receive a second birth - a life that knows no death.

12 January

To the end of time

"The grace of our Lord Jesus Christ be with you all. Amen"
Rev 22:21

The last "Amen" of the Bible is not the end of God. The narration ceases but the reality proceeds. God is greater than any book; though He fills the Bible to running over, yet the untold tale of Deity is yet to be unfolded. Will eternity itself suffice to expound the vastness of the Infinite Lord?

When time has ceased to be, the riches of the wisdom and knowledge of God will continue to fascinate and feast His wondering saints. "How unsearchable are His judgements, and His ways past finding out!" (Rom 11:33).

We may use the term "Amen" in two ways - first in affirmation, "I believe it to be true", of statements made. Secondly, in acclamation - "It shall be so!" in vibrant faith of petitions offered.

Our Lord is called "The Amen" (Rev 3:14) in that He is the last word in God's purposes, there is nothing beyond Him or outside of Him. He also Is the dependable One whose fidelity to His own word can be absolutely trusted. He is the key to all the promises of God, which in Him are "yea and Amen". Trust Him! He is worth it. He'll never let you down.

A timeless word in a time-fraught world

"But the word of the Lord endureth forever" 1 Pet 1:25

Time exudes meaning but eludes definition. It is the warp on which is woven the web of life, the essence of being, the substance of existence.

It can be measured but not made, experienced but not excluded, passed but not recalled. Is it a creature or an illusion? Sometimes its leaden feet drag slowly along, each hour seemingly endless and heavy; again, it skips forward as days seem but frolicking minutes.

Time issues from eternity, for its source is God. It flows through life to a destiny determined by Him, to whom past, present and future are one everlasting NOW.

Time can be lost: it can be redeemed. He values time most who loads its presence with significance, who makes moments momentous. Time's richest enjoyments are spent in the presence of God. Fellowship with Him gives time its ultimate accolade. All that time is intended to be, is realised in fellowship with the divine.

" ---- Not Iscariot" John 14:22

Judas was a respected name at the time of Christ. It is the Greek form of "Judah", designation of the leading tribe of Israel. There are several Judas's in the New Testament, one of them, the brother of Jesus (Mathew 13:55).

But this once good name has become a hateful epithet. Judas Iscariot betrayed his Lord; his cognomen is now a term of loathing. In his lifetime other Judas's disdained him; since his suicide no one will burden his progeny with this name; it is the tag of a traitor.

That is life! We can besmirch a good name by bad behaviour. The converse is also true. An ordinary name can exude fragrance when it calls to mind the sweetness, the honesty, the kindness, the liberality of its bearer.

Let us so live that the memory of our name may be "as ointment poured forth", repeated with respect, its possessor dubbed as a knight of noblest worth, by the accolade of good reputation. Such a name is of infinite value, a diadem of beauty, a crown of rejoicing.

15 January

Why he got up early

"And Abraham rose up early in the morning" Gen 22:3

If any man had an excuse for staying in bed, it was Abraham. He could have pleaded his age. He was well over 100 years old; a many-miled journey lay before him; and worst of all, the dire demands of duty were severe.

God had asked him to sacrifice his only son, a seemingly preposterous request. But Abraham had heard that voice too often to mistake it. The response? "God has said it: I must do it!"

The Patriarch acted with alacrity. God had given; God could take away. the Almighty is sovereign. His will in final. But He is also wise and good. He had given His word that Isaac would continue the covenantal relationship. God does not change His mind, He is immutable, His promises are sure.

On this ground Abraham believed that if his son was slain, God would raise him from the dead, "from whence also he received him in a figure" (Heb 11:19). Neither life nor death, nor time, nor circumstance can impede the fulfilment of divine promises.

Aromatherapy

"Thy name is as ointment poured forth"
Song of Solomon 1:3

A Japanese firm has devised a method of infusing sweet smells into offices and hospitals by injecting perfumes into the air-conditioning. It is claimed that this treatment improved productivity and reduces stress. Experiments show that lavender and rosemary have a soothing effect, while lemon and eucalyptus keep the mind alert. This is called aromatherapy - healing by aromas.

But this is no new thing. Solomon discovered it ages ago, likening the name of a lover to a delightful aroma - "ointment poured forth". So did John Newton when he wrote:

> "How sweet the name of Jesus sounds
> In a believers ear;
> It soothes his sorrows, heals his wounds
> and drives away his fear".

Fragrance often evokes fond memories; so the name of Jesus calls to mind countless benefits and blessed experiences derived from knowing Him. The mention of His precious name drives gloom and fear away, speaks peace to our troubled mind, heals our deep-seated traumas and solves our deepest dilemmas.

When Mary broke her box of spikenard "the house was filled with the odour" (John 12:3). So the redolence of His name fills our hearts with joy, our minds with peace.

17 January

Reverence

"Ye shall .... reverence My sanctuary" Lev 19:30

While God does not dwell in temples made with hands as if to adorn men's work, yet wherever His presence is manifested that place is holy.

Humble chapel or mighty cathedral, marble pile or mud-and-wattle hut is made sacred when He is there. And His presence calls for reverence and holy fear.

Rev Mackey, minister of a Boscombe church, wrote this verse and placed it at the entrance of a new Youth Chapel:-

"Enter this door
As if the floor
Within were gold,
And every wall
Of jewels, all
Of wealth untold,
As if a choir
In robes of fire
Were singing there
No shout, no rush
But hush .....
For God is near."

Indeed, in those precious places devoted to divine service, rush, racket and revelry are out of place. We do not worship bricks and mortar, but we do respect the place where God reveals Himself, whether it be the great outdoors or the glad indoors. We reverence His sanctuary because we revere Him.

18 January

Inner Power or dynamic living

"I can do all things" Phil 4:13

Charles B Williams, in his lively translation of the New Testament, gives in a footnote the literal rendering of the above text. He puts it: "I have power for all things through Him <u>who puts a dynamo in me</u>".

Like a remote farm that draws its power from its own electrical motor, so may we live independent of circumstances by the divine dynamic within us. "I know how to live in lowly circumstances and I know how to live in plenty", boasted Paul by the grace of God. Ups and downs could not disturb the holy contentment he felt in Jesus.

This same inner power can be ours by faith in Christ. It has three effects. First, it gives us <u>A BURNING HEART</u>, inflamed with love for Christ (cf Luke 24: 32); secondly, it bestows <u>A SHINING FACE</u>, reflecting the glory of God (cf Exodus 34:29); thirdly, it produces <u>A WORKING FAITH</u> that not only speaks good things but also performs good actions (cf James 2:24, 1 John 3:18). Heat, light and energy.

The Holy Spirit can become within us a source of spiritual energy that will enable us to be master of every situation, "more than conquerors" indeed. Faith is the victory (cf Acts 9:22 and Heb 11:34).

19 January

Refer it all to God

"They .... asked not counsel at the mouth of God" (Jos 9:14)

Or, as the LIVING BIBLE so aptly puts it: "They did not bother to ask the Lord".

The story is old. The conquest of Canaan is in full spate. City after city is falling before the onslaught of God's army. The town of Gibeon sought safety in subterfuge. An elaborate pretence deceived Joshua and his compatriots. They made a league with this wily deputation, only to discover that they were a nearby folk under the divine ban. But God's people must keep faith with their own word. Gibeon was let off under penalty of becoming "hewers of wood and drawers of water" to their captors: but better conscripts than corpses.

The matter was serious but it was salutary. To be so taken in at the beginning of this mighty enterprise boded danger and possible defeat. It did not happen again, Joshua learned from his mistake to consult God at all times.

Are we any wiser than they? Do we not make our plans as if God was not there, or was not interested? James advises us always to bring the Lord into our daily living. "ye ought to say, If the Lord will, we shall live, and do this or that" (James 4:15). Deo Volenté (DV) is a good motto to apply to our engagement calendar.

The message of events

"When ye see these things come to pass" Luke 21:31

Jesus is speaking of His second Advent. His coming is certain; the time is uncertain. How wise God is! If a date had been given, we would have ignored intervening days for the Day. He rather chose to have us note the signs of the times, and let them speak to us. The emphasis is thus placed not on chronology but on preparedness.

But when we consider the events our Lord emphasised as tokens of the grand climax of time, the consummation of the ages, we cannot help but feel that the present moral and spiritual scenario portends the raising of the curtain on the last act of the divine drama of redemption.

Devastating ecological disasters, national and international perplexity, mighty natural disturbances, fearful occurrences - are all part of the genesis of "the last days". To the world this is demoralising - the prevalence of "heart failure" (a corroding sympton of modern stress-fraught humanity) is plainly indicated. But to the children of God, the worse the times, the brighter their hope. "And when these things begin to come to pass, then look up, and lift up your heads, for your redemption draweth nigh". It's better on before, my brother, cheer up!

21 January

Just a bit, but not a lot

"I shall not be moved" Psalm 62:2,6

Bishop J C Ryle has a splendid comment on this text - he says: "The ships at anchor in Spithead may swing too and fro with the tide, and pitch heavily in a south easterly gale, but so long as their anchors hold the ground they ride safely ...." The hope of the Christian is the anchor of his soul, sure and steadfast. His heart may be tossed to and fro sometimes, but he is safe in Christ.

Later in the same Psalm the writer states, "I shall not be moved". Firmer in God, richer in experience, deeper in grace, he is now not moved at all. The storms of life are beaten, the winds of temptation conquered, the pull of cross-currents mastered. He rides stately and serene, master of the elements. His hidden anchor holds. So we, in God, can find a cable so strong, and an anchor so true that our lives though shaken a bit at times prove it to be "not a lot". We proudly but humbly sing:

"We have an anchor that keeps the soul
Steadfast and sure while the billows roll,
Fastened to the rock which cannot move,
Grounded firm and deep in the Saviour's love"

Our lives may never become storm-free but they can become storm-proof as we link the cable of faith to the Rock of Ages, the anchor of our souls.

A merry Gospel

"Good tidings of great joy" Luke 2:10

The term "gospel" comes from the Anglo-Saxon "God-spell", or the God-story. Tyndale, early translator of the English Bible. defines the term thus: "It signifies good, merry, glad and joyful tydinges that maketh a mannes heart glad, and maketh hym synge, dance and leape for joye".

The angels told it well. The good news of Jesus is a joy-producing message. It truly is God's "spell", casting its magic over our lives. When Jesus came a new day dawned, the Sun of Righteousness rose with healing in His wings.

And what a salvation He brought! It dealt with our past - the PENALTY of sin that we should have borne, He bore for us. It deals with our present - the POWER of sin is broken, we are no longer slaves but free men. Nay, more, we are sons of God, soldiers of Christ, and servants of His grace. It deals also with our future - we shall one day be delivered from the very PRESENCE of sin. Happy days are here, happier days are yet to come.

When the Prodigal son came home "they began to be merry". Even so our return to God is cause of a feeling of great joy. Truly we have in Christ a merry Gospel.

23 January

The vocabulary of faith

"If thou canst believe, all things are possible to him that believeth" Mark 9:23

The Authorised Version needs a little correcting here. the word "believe" is omitted by some ancient versions, a stance taken up by the Revised Version and the NIV. Another point; the words of Jesus are a question, almost an expostulation.

Look at it like this. The father of the demon-tormented boy cries out desperately: "If thou canst do anything". Jesus takes his words: "If thou canst?" He says, as if to make it clear that there is no such word in the vocabulary of faith.

"IF!" faith knows no such term. "IF!" the Christian's dictionary does not admit it. "IF!" The thesaurus of Gospel theology does not recognise it. If it was once there, now the space is blank. Faith and "if" cannot exist together, they are mutually exclusive.

There is no "if" in godly prayer life. The hymn-writer puts it!

> Unanswered yet! Faith cannot be unanswered.
> Her feet are firmly planted on the rock.
> Amid the wildest storm she stands undaunted
> Nor quails before the loudest thunder shock.
> She knows Omnipotence has heard her prayer
> And cries "It shall be done sometime, somewhere!"

But should we be sometimes constrained to say with the father, "Lord, I believe, help Thou my unbelief", give that deadly "if" a mighty kick. It is out of place.

"I'm bored ...... "

"Vanity of vanities; all is vanity" *Eccles 1:2*

Bored? so was Solomon. "There is no new thing under the sun", he moaned. The same old environment, the same old activities, scenes and events. What a bore!

How surprising this is. Solomon had wealth and learning, status and reputation, palace and plenty. But was he satisfied? Generations pass - life stumbles on. The sun rises - the sun sets. The wind blows its endless course; the rivers empty into the sea without filling it. What a footless round!

It is true that life can be a treadmill, a persistent meaningless passage of time, of activity, of phenomena - a daily and monotonous cycle - round and round and round. But Christ can add to our lives a plus element. We still go round, but life is no longer a circle, it is a spiral. With every round we are a little higher, a little further on the road, a little nearer our Heavenly home.

And my dear King Solomon, your God-given wisdom should have shown you the cure for boredom. It is to forget yourself and be lost in the service of others. Never mind sporting with your 300 wives, forget the pleasures on which you dispense so much time and money, rise above your vaunted philosophy and spend yourself for the needy, the disconsolate, the weak. You could have been Israel's greatest king, instead you died of self-indulgence. And so will we unless we find true happiness in making others happy. Bored? No time for it.

25 January

Tomorrow is another day

"Sufficient unto the day ..... " Matt 6:34

Don't overload today with tomorrow's agenda. "Manyana" may seem a way out of trouble, but we cannot debit today's grace to tomorrow's account. "As thy days so shall thy strength be", promises all we need to fulfil each day's demands. Delay not to fulfil the "now" routine, then we may sincerely and deservedly enjoy the "then" rest. Be like Longfellow's Village Blacksmith.

> "Each morning sees its task begun
> Each evening sees its close"

On the other hand, do not burden today with tomorrow's demands. Careful planning may often be necessary but carking care that loads us with woes to come, will destroy our peace. Anxiety is a killer, worry is lethal. More people have died under tomorrow's load than those that have borne the heat and burden of today. Tomorrow is another day. Let its cares rest until a new dawn arrives, then we meet it fresh with grace that is renewed to us every morning - sufficient unto the day is the evil thereof. Don't knock the scales of life off balance by a surplus of tomorrow's demands.

26 January

All our yesterdays

"The former days ..... " Eccles 7:10

Don't underrate the past, for without it there would be no present. The sturdy oaks of strong tradition emerge from acorns of foregone years. Pioneers, now fond memories, were in their day bold entrepreneurs. They blazed trails through trackless forests that are now highways of industry and progress. Their ways seem crude to us, and their resources primitive but by their sturdy endeavours they built the civilisation we now enjoy. Life has proved that what is morally right endures; yesterday's virtues are needed today.

But do not overrate the past. Memory is often selective, forgetting the morbid and grosser episodes and dwelling on the highlights. Life must progress. Some well established social and spiritual tranditions sometimes need adjustment. We cannot live on the past, and it is foolish to try and live in the past.

But all our yesterdays can still minister to us, God does not change with the passing years. What He was, He is, and ever will be. Resting in Him, past, present and future, have all their significant contribution to life's enlargement.

27 January

The long look

"Demas ..... loved this present world" 2 Tim 4:10

The "now-world" is all around us: "Vanity Fair" (Bunyan's eponomy for this passing scene) has it attractions, it appeal, its aspirations. Pilgrim's are tempted to linger there. But all its enjoyments are temporal, it is part of "this world which passeth away" (1 John 2:17).

Demas felt its pull. Like gravitation, the world's attraction is always downwards. It takes an outside power to break us free. Man has done it by rocketry: wo do it by the power of the Holy Spirit, who gives us vision of a brighter world-to-come, ambition to attain to it, and inner dynamism to seek it. We do not settle for "this present" because we expect a bright tomorrow.

"It is the wise person who takes the long look", says John R Rise. "How foolish it is to think only of today with its passing pleasure or profit!" He then cites for example Esau, who sold his birthright for a mess of pottage. His present appetite was met, but his future blessing was lost.

When tempted to think that Christianity is loss, couple Heaven with it, brother. "Now" is but a phase, our future is eternal bliss.

Have a go!

"Whatsoever thy hand findeth to do Eccles 9:10

Don't wait for opportunities, make them, "find" them by seeking. So advises the Old Testament preacher: but his advice is as modern as it is ancient. Have a go!

Do it wisely. Whatever you are handy at, pursue it. It is not sense to attempt the impossible, but the possible should be grasped.

Do it willingly. don't let it overtake you, be ready for it. To be prepared is half the battle. Lethargy can kill the tardy soul, but a constant availability, like fertile loam, can embrace the seed of opportunity and provide it with the elements of fruition.

Do it well - "with all thy might". If we tackle problems half-heartedly, we must not complain if results are meagre. In sacred, as will as secular, affairs, we only get out what we put in.

Romans 12 teaches us that if we are living in a state of consecrated readiness, the will of God will become clear to us, good, acceptable and perfect. Having by sober assessment discovered our propensities we will then pursue them to the perimeter of possibility making a meaningful contribution to the living Church of God.

29 January

Enthusiasm

"..... with thy might" Eccles 9:10

Nothing great was ever accomplished without enthusiasm. The very word itself means. "God in you" and describes that burning passion that drives us on to attempt great things for God. We are not to be like barges that are to be dragged into service, or like yatchs that only move when the wind blows, but like a steam-ship that carries "fire in its belly" - driving it on.

What an example of enthusiasm David was. Visiting his soldier-brothers, he "shouted for the battle". Too young to join the forces, he cheered on those who stood in the ranks. And when he faced Goliath "David hasted and ran ..... to meet the Philistine". A skilful harpist, he attacked the strings with fury. He even invented an "instrument of ten strings" so that all his digits might be employed in holy music-making. The Psalms he wrote are alive with God-given inspiration. When the Ark was brought to Jerusalem he danced with all his might as he led the procession up Mount Zion. Even in his defection he slumped hard, but in repentance he was deeply sorry. He was not allowed to build the Temple, but he deposited his vast wealth in a fund to make its erection possible. What a man! May I be as wholehearted as he was!

God's army

"A good soldier of Jesus Christ" 2 Tim 2:3

Every Christian is a member of God's salvation army. This fighting force is supplied with heavenly munitions - "the whole armour of God" (Eph 6:11-17) and is sustained in morale by "exceeding great and precious promises" (2 Pet 1:4). Empowered by the Spirit (Acts 1:8) each soldier is able to withstand the enemy of souls (the devil) and make victorious advances into his kingdom of darkness.

The manoeuvres of this great host are directed by "the Captain of our salvation" (Heb 2:10) whose superb strategy and tactics outclass "the wiles of the devil" (Eph 6:11) and enable us to storm his gates (Matt 16:18). Thus the movement of God's army is ever forward: the Church of Jesus Christ is marching on to victory.

The warfare is as wide as the cosmos, but by discipline and zest the Christian soldier marches on, keeping step with his fellows and faith in his Commander in Chief.

There are no medals to celebrate heroism and service, but there are crowns - stephanos - victors' crowns (Rev 2:10) which the overcomer will wear forever in honour of his Leader and in praise of Jehovah God.

God of mystery

"Verily Thou art a God that hidest Thyself" Isaiah 45:15

Moffatt translates: "Yours is indeed the God of Mystery, a God who saves". And the Living Bible paraphrases "Truly, O God of Israel, Saviour, you work in strange mysterious ways". And so He does! The record states how the Lord would raise up Cyrus, a heathen king, to deliver Israel, which he did, for it was under his direction that this captive nation were freed from bondage and enabled to return to their own land.

> "God moves in a mysterious way
> His wonders to perform"

So penned William Cowper, whose own deliverance from suicide was living testimony to God's wonderful ways. Driven by despair, he hailed a cab to take him to London Bridge, where he thought he could end his woes in the murky waters of the Thames. A fog came down. The cabby lost his way and landed at the doorstep of Cowper's own home. Struck with awe and thanks, he wrote his famous hymn, a testimony to a wonder-working God.

God's thoughts are higher than our thoughts, and His way often mystify us. But when we are baffled by life's strange twists, then we must trust in God. If he hides Himself from us, He is still working for us, and will ultimately make all things clear and plain. He loves us.

1 February

Jesus saves

"He is able also to save them to the uttermost" Heb 7:25

What a Saviour! His salvation extends to the uttermost point of time and to the uttermost degree of experience.

A brief scan of the New Testament will reveal the all-embracive salvation our Lord provides, as battalions of converted sinners parade before our mental gaze.

Here they come! Fishermen and lawyers, Rabbis and taxmen, bourgeoisie and proletariat, aristocracy and commoners, doctors and solicitors, business-women and fortune-tellers, jailer and jail-birds, intellectuals and illiterate, black and white, youths and maidens, housewives and householders, seamstress and solicitor, soldier and civil servant, old and young - what a motley crew, yet all finding in Jesus Christ a Saviour and Lord. All nations find forgiveness in Him.

And in all stages of life the Lord shows Himself as Redeemer. A raging persecutor is smitten to the ground and converted, a dying thief promised a paradise, a prostitute is relieved of her infamous trade, a rich tax-inspector transformed into a liberal philanthropist, a Gentile convert changed into a flaming evangelist. And more!

All this is meant to show us that no case is too hard for God to change.

> <u>The vilest offender who truly believes</u>
> <u>That moment from Jesus a pardon receives</u>

What a wonderful Saviour is Jesus!

2 February

From pillow to pillar

"Jacob ..... took the stone that he had put for his pillows, and set it up for a pillar" Gen 28:18

The hymn-writer puts it beautifully:

> "Out of my stony grief's
> Bethel I'll raise"

The night before had been hectic for Jacob. Forced by his brother's threats to run away from home he rests "weary, worn and sad" on the green sward, with a stone for his pillow. Hard luck! But God visits him in his dreams, the world of reality is transformed. He is shattered and over-awed by the divine Presence. He went to sleep sad and lonely: he woke glad and free.

The morning after. Jacob discovered three things that night. First, that you cannot escape God. He is not confined to any sacred spot, He is everywhere. Secondly, that where God is becomes holy ground. His awesome presence transforms the lowliest place into a temple. That lonely spot became to him Bethel - house of God, threshold of Heaven. Thirdly, that God's purposes are bigger than our plans. Even when we make a mess of our lives, and find our plans frustrated, He can take over and turn even our mistakes into miracles and our devious paths into divine perfection. No wonder he "lifted up his feet", rejoicingly pressing on to his goal and God's destination for him! Pillows of woe can become pillars of gladness.

Admiration

"He shall come ..... to be admired in all them that believe 2 Thes 1:10

The Greek word for "admired" (thaumazõ) implies incredible surprise, baffling astonishment, spontaneous admiration, amazement and wonder. None of this is exaggeration. We see Jesus now by the eye of faith, and are filled with wonder. When we see Him as He is at the Second Advent we will be overwhelmed with His beauty.

The Queen of Sheba visited Solomon, and when she saw the glory of his kingdom and how magnificently he managed it "there was no more spirit in her" (1 Kings 10:5) - she was breathless with wonder. So will the revelation of the Son of God fill us with admiration as we gaze on His glorious face.

Wonder is the essence of worship. When we approach God we bow before an excellence above all earthly concepts: His glory is brighter than the sun in its meridian strength, His wisdom greater than human learning, His love transcends all human affection.

And it is this God who has provided "so great salvation" through Jesus Christ - a bountiful life, a sin-cleansing atonement, a fruit-bearing experience. If we, who have not seen, yet love Him, are filled with "joy, unspeakable and full of glory", what will it be when we meet Him on that perfect day of His appearing?

4 February

God's signature

"With signs following" Mark 16:20

It has been pointed out that "the Word" often followed "the signs", as with Peter at Lydda and Paul at Lystra - But the Greek akalouthõ can also mean accompany, as Charles Williams renders: "the Lord kept on working with them confirming their message by the signs that attended it".

Moulton and Milligan point out a contemporary use of this term "following". "Another development of meaning is 'to ratify', or to verify an account as in the signatures to a series of receipts. This usage throws an interesting sidelight on Mark 16:20. The signs did not merely follow, they act as a kind of authenticating signature to the word". So miracles are God's signature. Peter, in different words asserts the same idea concerning the ministry of our Lord. "A man approved of God among you by miracles and wonders and signs, which God did by Him in the midst of you" (Acts 2:22). Jesus was "God-endorsed".

We need this divine endorsement today. Jesus said signs would "follow them that believe" (Mark 16:17). It is not dispensational restriction that prevents their happening, it is unbelief. If the church believes God, signs will emerge. And who cares whether they occur before, with or after the preaching! God is the same as ever; if we will trust Him we may still see "signs" endorsing His Word.

Search for God

"Canst thou by searching find out God? Job 11:7

These words of Zophar the traditionalist to Job the tormented still ring a bell in the troubled mind. Where is God? Is He near or far? why can't I find Him?

<u>It is impossible to intellect</u>. How can finite mind embrace infinite majesty? God lives in a realm so remote from human reason that He is unembraceable. Logic cannot frame premisses from which to reason conclusions; experience cannot break from the limitations of earthly conditional notions; emotion cannot lift us into the ethereal realms of divine presence.

Science is helpless. Limited to sensuous experiment, tied up with weights and measures, dealing with controllable materials, their basic concept of cause and effect cannot procure knowledge of God, guarantee His presence or reveal His will. God's realm no human mind can reach.

<u>It is possible to faith</u>. "He that cometh to God must believe that He is" Heb 11:6. Not that faith produces God, but belief enables us to detect His presence, hear His "still, small voice", and feel His love and grace.

Groping fingers of philosophy fails to find Him, and sensitive instruments of human inventiveness cannot prove He is there. But to seeking hearts He reveals Himself. They discover, "He be not far from everyone of us .... for in Him we live, and move, and have our being" (Acts 17:27,28). Faith breaks the barrier of sense and finds that God is always there. Believe, and the elusive God will discover Himself.

6 February

The tangible and the intangible

"Ye are not come unto the mount that might be touched" Heb 12:18

Old Testament worship was fraught with tangibles, it was a religion of SENSE. The sacrifices were solid objects - animals, cereals, silver and gold. the sense of smell was titillated with incense; sight was regaled with elaborate rites and priests decked in special garments; their ears presented with tinkling bells and sounding trumpets. Even its laws were accompanied by trembling of mountains, flashing light and peels of thunder. All was tangible, audible, visible.

Not so is New Testament worship. Christianity is basically a religion of SPIRIT. Its ceremonies are simple, its sacraments few - just two, water baptism and the Breaking of Bread. Even the glory of God is felt rather than seen. But, though "mickle" in display, Christianity is "muckle" in dynamic (with respect to my Scottish brethren).

It is this spirituality that gives our faith its, other-worldly essence. The world sees to believe, we believe to see. Science is based on tangibles, dealing with what can be weighed and measured. But the quality of life cannot be subjected to, or assessed by, laboratory experiment, or field observation. Love, joy and peace are beyond computation; faith and hope do not fit scale or tape-measure. "The things which are seen are temporal; but the things which are not seen are eternal" (2 Cor 4:18). "They that worship Him (God) must worship Him in spirit and in truth" (John 4:24) for when we touch God we touch reality.

The petrine penumbra

"That at the least the shadow of Peter passing by might overshadow some of them" Acts 5:15

In time of revival supernormal things happen. Here the sick are healed and blessed by the lightest of touches, the shadow of Peter - powerful penumbra!

But all who live in God's light cast a healing shadow. Every child of God exerts an influence for good on society.

An unplanned element. Peter was just "passing by". And so our daily walk can exert a forceful power on others. It is not only our spoken testimony that affects our neighbours, it is our unplanned mode of behaviour that, like a lambent aura, makes, our presence felt. As salt quietly infuses its appetising qualities into our culinary preparations, so society benefits from the presence and prayers of God's people. Ten good men could have saved Sodom, what, then, is the sanctifying energy of a lively group of godly people on their locality?

An unknown effect. Peter did not know what effect his overshadowing presence had on the line if sick and needy folk. He just passed by - and left a blessing behind him. And we can never know what help and inspiration we are to those who observe our Christian behaviour. "Moses wist not that the skin of his face shone" (Exodus 34:29), and the sincere saint of God will never know here effective his consistent life affects those in darkness.

8 February

Air-borne saints

"Be filled with the Spirit" Eph 5:18

The park near where I lived was a centre for hot-air ballooning. I once watched a balloon laid out, a colourful mass, but inert and lifeless. Then, by means of a propane-burner, hot air was directed into its recumbent form. It filled up, reared its frame, and tugged against its earth-ties. When released it rode proud and high into the sky.

Then I thought of Pentecost, when the Spirit came as wind and flame - hot air indeed. Into the spiritually inert lives of the waiting 120 came a new force that lifted then above their normal propensities. Earth-ties broken, they soared into realms of heavenly experiences. The gravity of a sinful world sought to ground them, but fresh bursts of holy flame kept them "in heavenly places in Christ Jesus."

by the indwelling Spirit we can live above the earthly plane. "Filled with the Spirit", our personal life is enriched, we worship more meaningfully; our domestic life is made sweeter; our educational life becomes fuller; our social life is expanded; our occupational life is adjusted; and our spiritual life is empowered as we wrestle with and overcome our Satanic and demonic foes.

In the spirit we break with earthly ties, cease to gravitate to earthly things, live and triumph in higher realms of spiritual experience. To live life at its best, "be filled with the Spirit".

Superfluous energy?

"The glory of young men is their strength" Prov 20:29
"You, young men, ... are strong" 1 John 2:14

Both Old and New Testaments emphasise one of the characteristics of youth - STRENGTH: boundless energy, audacious endeavour, brave (though at time brash) enterprise. It is the "glory" - that is, the superb quality - of youth. Vibrant youth attempts the impossible and achieves the incredible. There is no horizon to the vision and venture of this active age.

But this surplus energy needs guidance and control. Just as water needs channels to flow through, so the mental and physical potential of youth needs direction and discipline to achieve its best ends and fullest exploitation. Sport, exploration, adventure are all areas that give scope to full-blooded youth.

John gives a different emphasis to adolescent achievement. An old man of great experience, and apostle of rich inspiration, he makes it clear that there are excursions into spiritual realms that Spirit-equipped youth can excel in. Their innate strength can launch them into spheres of divine experience and enable them to accomplish great things for God. Their zeal for spiritual things can drive them, like cataracts of power, down channels of service. And the source and sustenance of this inner energy is "the word of God (that) abideth in you". This dynamic agency gives victory over Satan's attacks and all the temptations the world imposes. Youths surplus energy thus becomes absorbed in noble deeds, in godly living, in performing great things for God.

10 February

Temptations threefold urge

"All that is in the world, the lust of the flesh, and the lust of the eyes, and the pride of life" 1 John 2:16

The essence of all temptation to evil is expressed in these words. PASSION - "the lust of the flesh" issues from the basic instincts of our human make-up. Natural but neutral, essential but existential, these fundamental elements can be drawn out by Satanic suggestion into areas that are sinful. Those same instincts, under Holy Ghost discipline, can regulate our whole spiritual life to the glory of God.

Possession "the lust of the eyes". To see is a natural exercise of vision, to want what we see is a vicious extension of acquisitiveness. Covetousness wants more and more. It diverts our energies from helping others to satisfying self. It can become a mode of worship, a bowing at the altar of gold - and all worship distracts from God, the only true object of devotion.

Prestige - "the pride of life". How we love ourselves! And so we should within the limits of spiritual love-law. But when we take an ego-trip, or seek self-display we go beyond what Christian personality demands. In doing so, our puffed-up selves miss true happiness when capital 'I' sits on the throne of our heart, we are usurping the position only Jesus should hold. The secret of real and lasting joy is **J**esus first. **O**thers next; **Y**ourself last. To those who accept this simple creed temptation loses its power. Try it! It works!

War of the roses

"I am the Rose of Sharon" Song of Solomon 2:1

I am a Yorkshireman, our emblem is a white rose, symbolic of the ancient struggle between the houses of York and Lancaster. Sad for me, for my favourite rose-colour is red. But the war of the Roses is over. It ended in a marriage. But roses remind us of a higher realm of action. The lover in Solomon's song calls himself a rose. We are led from this to think of Jesus, the love of our heart, and the Lover of our Soul.

Fragrant beauty. A rose, especially as cultivated by skilful horticulturists, is a thing of beauty. But its presence is not only a feast of the eyes, its pefume is an olfactory delight. So our Lord: He is beautiful in character, blameless in reputation. His very name is sweet to our hearing, precious to our contemplation.

Fearful battles. And yet the red and white roses of Lancaster and York were symbols of furious conflict. So with our Lord. His conflict with Satan and sin on our behalf was costly and cruel: He died to save us. But He won through, and now lives, our glorious Victor, in Heaven, where one day we shall join Him.

Fantastic bravery. No earthly rose is without a thorn. Our Lord was associated with the thorn of conflict, but with courage and strength he faced the pains of suffering and death on our account. And now our Heavenly Rose is the only one without a thorn. The Rose of Sharon is the symbol of love that gives, love that lives, for us sinners, love that triumphs over evil.

12 February

Just like a man!

"Answer me speedily" Psalm 102:2

The Psalmist can't wait. Just like a man - not so much in the sense of gender as common human nature. We are all impatient with God at times. We pray, and nothing happens. "Give me speedy answers" we cry, "I can't wait!"

But God is not in a hurry. In fact the time element is often submerged in an eternal element - the purpose and the glory of God. Prayer does not put God at our disposal. In fact, true prayer puts us at the disposal of God. But we are creatures of time, and unanswered prayer becomes a painful problem.

But is there such a thing as "unanswered prayer". Not really. God hears us when we cry; His delays are not denials; His timing can turn an event into an epoch. Some answers are immediate, for the need is dire; some answers are more remote, we often have to be prepared to benefit fully from God's gracious response.

And it is by "faith and patience" that we inherit the promises. Faith never doubts God's ultimate answer; faith bears with fortitude the intermediate inaction; Faith finally receives the divine solution to the desired end. God's will is done when our will corresponds to His. So Jesus found.

Pentecostal hypocrites

"Laying aside all ..... hypocrisies 1 Peter 2:1

Peter is writing to seasoned Christians, to established saints, to Pentecostal believers - and he uses that shocking word, "hypocrisies".

Is it possible that Christians are tempted to hide their true selves behind a mask of make-belief? The apostle admits this danger. Under pressure of persecution some tended to hide their faith behind a screen of fear. But this will not do. Such hypocrisy is an impediment to spiritual growth. Together with malice, guile envy and evil speaking, it acts like a weed, robbing the useful plant of light above and sustenance beneath.

Spiritual babes may not feel strong enough to maintain innocence in a wicked world, but there is one source of nourishment that will promote growth with its accompanying energy to withstand the evil of hypocrisy, it is "the spiritual" milk of the word".

MILK: the nourishing food of babes, a providential provision awaiting their coming into the world. As imbibed from the mothers' breast it is at the right temperature and sweetness for instant absorption. It contains fats, protein, carbohydrates - plus other essential ingredients - and even holds in its liquid stream antibiotics to prevent infant ailments: all the essentials to promote healthy growth. Such is the Word of God to our souls. Rid of the impediment of pretence, we can in sincerity and faith, continue in the way of truth as we "grow thereby".

Soft pedal

"Ahab ..... went softly" 1 Kings 21:27

Wicked Ahab was shattered - judgement, decreed by God and pronounced by Elijah scared him stiff. He had gone too far - and he knew it. Shaking with fear he "went softly", tip-toeing in the presence of God, walking humbly before the Lord. God did not cancel his due punishment, but He delayed it. So does God respond to penitence, however late.

But should we not always go softly before God, walking in submission to His will?

Our walk displays our character or condition. A proud autocrat struts along in haughty disdain, a senseless minx minces along in provocating dainty steps, a labouring ploughman "homely plods his weary way", a marching soldier makes disciplined strides, a babe totters hesitatingly, a healthy youth strides manfully, an aged pensioner shuffles weakly. And a child of God, in a higher sphere, shows his devotion by keeping step with God in joyful humility.

Ahab's unwonted humility affected his behaviour. Hitherto he had been the pitiful tool of his unscrupulous wife. Jezebel wrapped him round her little finger, using her royal prerogative as queen to degrade Israel into idolatrous practices. But now judgement looms, and Ahab is scared into better ways. But to Christians, the fear of the Lord is not torment, it is an inspiration to piety. We "go softly" because we believe soundly - we tip-toe in God's presence because we reverence Him deeply.

Jesus is the key

"In my name.." Mark 16:17, Luke 24:27, Jn 14:13, 3 Jn 6

Life presents many problems. Many locked-in situations baffle and impede us, many conflicting ideologies puzzle and perplex us, many-practical and essential duties find us impotent and useless. But in Jesus we have a key to unlock every door -to let us in, or let us out.

Key to prayer-success. "Ask in My name". Our Lord directs. And when we "Whisper Jesus only, wide will ope the pearly gate". Like an Aladdin's cave, the name of Jesus is an "Open Sesame" to the fulfilment of our petitions.

Key to penetrating Scriptures. When Jesus opened up the scriptures to His disciples after His resurrection, they saw God in a new way. The Bible is redolent of our Lord. As "all roads lead to Rome", so Jesus is a highway of truth. Philip "began at the same Scripture" to preach Jesus to a perplexed aristocrat, so we may find that the whole Bible has but one basic message. In Jesus we have the key to open the treasure chest of Scripture.

Key to potent service. "In my name they shall cast out devils". This precious name imparts power to the servants of God. This Peter found when accosted by a crippled beggar. "Silver and gold have I none", he said to the expectant man, "but such as I have give I thee. In the name of Jesus ....." and at that name the paralysed limbs received life. And all our service can be empowered to success by that name. Like a switch that turns on electricity so the name of Jesus, used in faith, releases God's power.

Play dead

"Reckon ye also yourselves to be dead indeed unto sin" Romans 6:11

A superintendent of an American National Park instructed visitors how to act in the rare case of an attack by a grizzly bear. "Don't run or it will chase you. Stand still or play dead and he will go away". One couple failed to do this. they ran, were chased and mangled by the savage creature.

I thought of Paul's words: "Reckon yourselves dead". When sin, like a ferocious animal, waylays us, we must not try to fight it in our own strength, but in the strength of Christ. How? we are to consider ourselves dead to the appeal of instinctive urges, natural lusts, carnal appetites. We are "dead in Christ". When He died on the Cross, we died with Him. Such is the power of our union with Him that though we are still subject to temptation, it has as little effect as a call for response from a dead man.

Supposition? Unreality? Not at all. For just as much as we died in Christ, so much do we live in Him. Crucifixion slays human nature with its feckless foibles and feeble frailty, but resurrection gives us new life in Christ, divine life that gives us power over evil. We become alive to God in such a way that victory over all evil is ours constantly.

But "playing dead" is no mere charade. As we follow Christ "death worketh in us" so that sin fails to harm us. And the life of Christ enables us to conquer life's evils, as we live to God we die to self.

17 February

Don't you believe it

"Hath God forgotten to be gracious" Psalm 77:9

The Psalmist was in deep distress. In his trouble he sought the Lord in night-long prayer. But God did not seem to be there. "Has He forgotten to be gracious?" is the querulous complaint.

Don't you believe it! God cannot deny Himself, He does not change, He is the only totally stable Being in the vast universe. The scenes of life may change, the seasons of time do change, human nature is subject to change. But "I am the Lord, I change not" (Malachi 3:6). He cannot change, for to grow less would make Him lower than perfection, to grow greater is impossible for He is already great beyond increase. He is still the same loving, merciful, just, wise and gracious God. As ever he was.

But sometimes He hides Himself to test us. If we cannot trust God in the dark, can we really trust Him in the light? Temptation would seek to obscure our vision, but faith, whether it be dark or light, summer of winter, bitter cold or boiling heat, holds firm. True faith is more than rational consent or emotional content, it is gripping God like wrestling Jacob, and not letting go. "Lay hold on eternal life".

The Psalmist found help in remembering what God had done, and was assured that He would do it again. Rain may be unpleasant, but it fructifies the earth, so dark clouds of trouble are often fraught with blessing. "God forgotten to be gracious?" Don't you believe it!

18 February

Wonderful Jesus

"His name shall be called Wonderful" Isa 9:6

In Jesus two worlds unite: He is the "child born" and the "Son given", the God-man, incarnate deity: the wonder of the ages. His name is "wonderful" in seven respects.

He is wonderful in admonition, "a wonder of a counsellor" (Moffatt). His words are the essence of wisdom. He is wonderful in action. "God the Mighty One", as Matthew Henry puts it. This Jesus whose words are oracles, also shows that His works are miracles. He is wonderful age-wise. He is "the Father of eternity", Potentate of Time, ageless in being, timeless in becoming. He is wonderful in alleviation, "Prince of Peace" who settles man's affairs, banishes man's sins, secures man's future - and all by "the blood of His cross". He is wonderful in authority Moffatt translates, "Great is His authority". When Christ rules, evil is restrained and good promoted. All "principalities and powers" are subject to Him. He is wonderful in administration. In His kingdom and under His sway both the principles and practices of justice will prevail. Righteousness is a vital element of kingdom-life (Romans 14:17). He is wonderful in achievement. All chose promises cherished by Israel, "the sure mercies of David" will be realisable in Jesus Christ.

So Isaiah. But the greatest wonder is that He should die for sinful humanity. As the hymn-writer has it. "But countless acts of pardoning beyond Thy other wonders shine". Jesus is indeed wonderful.

"Thou fool ....." Luke 12:16-21

How strong and direct are the words of Jesus in His scathing attack on covetousness. The inordinate lust for possessions, the worship of things, the materialistic attitude robs life of its real meaning. Jesus tells a story to emphasise His point. A rich farmer has a profitable harvest. He packs his produce into enlarged barns and then sits back in hope of enjoying the rest of his days. He dies by a stroke the very night of his proposed retirement. God calls him a fool, or, to give the modern sense of this strong word, "A mindless idiot"

<u>He was a fool because he lived without God</u>. In his soliloquy the rich man has no mention of God. The Giver of all good is the One whose bountiful munificence granted him a bumper crop of corn. But was he thankful to the Creator of this benefit? Not at all! The name of God is ominously unmentioned.

<u>He was a fool because he lived for self</u>. He was already rich, why should he fill bigger barns when the empty bellies of the poor cried of satisfaction. Note his use of "I" (six times), "my" (five times), and "Thine", in reference to self (once). And all within sixty words. He was wholly absorbed in self, and so missed that happiness that comes from giving to meet the needs of others.

<u>He was a fool because he misread the future</u>. As one writer puts it: "He was forgetful of the insecure tenure of life" All his plans were for this life. His vision could not see beyond the grave. Wise men and women put their trust in Jesus, who gives promise of this life and of that which is to come.

20 February

Keep your word

"He that sweareth to his own hurt, and changeth not"

So states Psalm 15:4 of the man that God appreciates and blesses.

Stability. Society benefits from a man who keeps his word. Business is safer if you can trust a man's word. "White lies" to satisfy customers or cover discrepancies are self-defeating. Goodwill, a valuable commodity of public service, is destroyed by falsehood. A person whose word can be trusted is a pillar of society.

Spirituality. Not only do human relationships benefit from this basic honesty, but also divine fellowship is established on this praiseworthy element. The Tabernacle of God is open to men of truth, the Hill of the Lord is accessible to the man of integrity. Keeping one's word is a spiritual quality, a Christian should be noted for being dependable. His "yes" is a firm affirmative, his "No" a positive negative. God likes that.

Strength. But it often takes moral courage to keep one's word. But, says the Psalm (in modern parlance), "He keeps his word even if it kills him". A disciplined mind does not make rash promises, and certainly makes no thoughtless vows. His conversation is not loaded with lurid expletives, his speech is guarded with reason and restraint, his way with words is uncomplicated and straightforward. He is admired by men, approved by God and accepted by his own conscience: a man of worth.

Inspired - and inspiring

"All scripture is given by inspiration of God" 2 Tim 3:16

What a treasure is the Bible! Without it we would know little of God, but He has chosen to reveal Himself by His word. The Bible is the voice of God, when I read it I feel that it speaks to me.

The Bible is a FULL Book: It is replete with history and mystery, doctrine and deeds, high ideals and deep incentives, absolutes and relatives, counsels and consolations, demands and directives. It is so complete that to add or take away is a sin.

The Bible is a FRAGRANT book. It exudes sweetness as a rose its perfume. Dr David Smith affirms that the word for "inspired by God" (Greek, theopneustos) means not only that the Scriptures are "God breathed", but also that they "breathe God". This holy Book is redolent of deity. The Bible is like Mary of Bethany's alabaster box, when broken open by scriptural insight and sound exegesis, exudes a heavenly aroma gladdening the heart, thrilling the mind.

The Bible is the FINAL book. It is the last word on all that matters. It is God's mind in verbal expression, and so is infallible. If infallible, it is immutable: if immutable, it is eternal. Never to pass away, as eternal as God Himself.

God's eternal purposes - embodied in His word, tell how Jesus, His only begotten Son, was ordained before the foundation of the world to be our Saviour. Or ever man fell the safety-net was provided, all of us, by trusting in Him are forgiven for past failures, granted new life to enjoy present benefits, and given a lively hope of a glorious eternal future.

The will of God

"Thy will be done" Matt 6:10

The will of God is a didactic entity, it must be known before it can be done; a dynamic energy; it can be known and done; a deliberative economy, it links earth with heaven. Angels do it, so should we.

But this term "will of God" may be understood in five different ways. First, it is God's sovereign plan in creation. His will is absolute; as Augustine wrote: "Nothing, therefore, happens, unless the Omnipotent wills it to happen". Secondly, God's supreme piloting of His creation. His providential care foresees and orders the course of all things in the Universe. He not only made the world, He pilots it to its ultimate destiny. Thirdly, God's saving purpose in Christ. He predestined the salvation of saints "according to the good pleasure of His will" (Eph 1:5). He arranged for its proclamation to all men, for He would have all men to be saved (1 Tim 2:4). Fourthly, God's sanctifying principles in the Bible (1 Thes 4:3, 5:18). Both the negative prohibitions and the positive enjoyments of holiness are laid down the the Book of God. And as Isaac Walton declared: "Every time I read you kills a sin or lets a virtue in to fight against it". Fifthly, God's superb pattern for the individual, that is, for me. God's part is to reveal His plan for my life. "Cause me to know the way wherein I should walk. My part is to respond to Him. "Teach me to do Thy will" (Psalm 143:10). "The foundation of Christian ethics is complete surrender to God", says Peak's Commentary. And so say I: and so may I do.

What is Christian charity?

"Follow after charity" 1 Cor 14:1

Christian charity is all that is implied in the term "love", the essence of benevolence and care. Let us put it into verse:

CHRISTIAN CHARITY:-
It is silence - when your words would hurt;
It is patience - when your neighbours curt;
It is deafness when a scandal flows;
It is thoughtfulness for another's woes;
It is promptness when duty calls;
It is courage when misfortune falls;
It is support when means run dry;
It is comfort when sufferers cry;
It is action when deeds avail;
It is diction when words prevail;
It is giving when poverty mounts;
It is living when experience counts;
It is praying when burdens press;
It is moving to meet another's distress;
It is loving the unloved and unlovable;
It is girding the distraught and the gullible;
It's setting exemplary behaviour;
It is following the steps of the Saviour.

HOW CAN I TREAD SUCH A NOBLE WAY?
I CAN TRUST, I CAN TRY, I CAN PRAY.

But our Christian charity must not be merely poetic, it must be firmly pragmatic. Deeds must never be lost in words, or action smothered by sentiment. True charity never fails to respond to the needful care of and attention to others.

For preachers only

"Lift up thy voice like a trumpet" Isa 58:1

In the parish church of Newport (IoW) there is a carved pulpit on which is engraved the above text: What a word for a preacher!

There is a certain amount of attack in a trumpet-sound. "sounding brass" projects its message boldly to all. And all good preaching has this out - speak; what one preacher called "oomph"!

A warning to Tokyo motorists some years ago read like this: "When passengers of the foot heave in sight, tootle the horn. Trumpet at him melodiously at first, but if he still obstacles your passage, then tootle him with vigour". In other words "Blast him awake!" Effective preaching "tootles with vigour".

But also preaching is more than sound it is articulation: "If the army bugler doesn't play the right notes, how will the soldiers know that they are being called to battle?" (1 Cor 14:8 Living Bible). I once asked Donald Gee (Himself a preacher of no mean ability) what was the most important element in preaching. "To be heard", was his instant response, "and the next essential thing is to be understood". So it is. Preacher, make yourself heard; but above all, be sure you are understood.

Christians are different

"You must not do as they do in Egypt" Lev 18:2 (NIV)

We are redeemed by the blood of Jesus, bought out of the slavery of sin by a great price, "therefore glorify God in your body, and in your spirit, which are God's" 1 Cor 6:20.

The world (our Egypt) presses in on all sides, but we are not to be conformed to its ideologies, its practices or its indulgences. Christians are called "saints" in the Bible, that is "somebody different". Our actions, our attitudes; our words and ways; our concepts and convictions should evidence that we are on a higher plane of living.

Such difference may not necessarily exhibit the eccentricity of a Quaker, the rigid behaviour of a puritan or the outlandish expressions of a fanatic, but the sober, solemn and sanctified determination to do the will of God at all costs, even if that means I am thought mad by the world.

Is such a life possible in this modern hectic age? Yes, writes John, "This is the victory that overcometh the world, even our faith" (1 John 5:4). Egypt must not rule us, we are under the domination of the laws of Heaven.

26 February

The King's view

"In Thy light shall we see light" Ps 36:9

On one of her visits to the Highlands of Scotland, Queen Victoria paused briefly to take in the sight of Loch Tummel. since then the beautiful vista has been called "The Queen's View": What a link with royalty to see as the queen sees.

But Christians can do even better, we can see as the King of Kings sees. From our vantage point of "the heavenly places" into which Christ has lifted us (cf Eph 1:3). We see life differently. In the light of God's presence dark things become plain, obscure things clear and distorted things brought into focus.

As we "seek those things which are above" (Col 3:2) our emotions are sanctified, our desires modified, our thoughts clarified. We learn from Christ what we ought to do and how we ought to do it. Our whole aspect of apprehension and appreciation is enhanced. Just as light makes all colours glow with greater intensity, so the light of God enables us to distinguish things that differ, enjoy more fully what is good and eschew more readily what is evil. His light is life, a fountain of understanding and joy.

A date with destiny

"Accounted worthy to escape" Luke 21:36

An American scientist warns of a possible collision with the earth of a comet over 6 miles across, a mass of cosmic dust and sub-zero ice. It is suggested that such a collision in the earth's earliest ages killed off the dinosaurs by the catastrophic shock to the earth's climate.

This epochal event is timed to take place 11th July 2126. Will this be the end of the world? Not really; for three reasons.

First, the date of the earth's demise is hidden in the counsels of God. So said Jesus (Mark 13:32). And what is hidden from saints and angels is unlikely to be revealed to experts in astrophysics.

Secondly, the earth will ultimately be destroyed by fire, not by ice (2 Peter 3:7). Scriptural truth is more reliable than scientific fiction.

Thirdly, though the end of time is sure, the offer of an escape (which science does not concede) is made to all who will believe in the Lord Jesus Christ. This vital event will come as a snare on a surfeiting world who will be taken unawares. But just as Noah escaped the destruction of the Flood, and Lot the fiery judgement of Sodom and Gomorah, so those who are born again Christians will be raptured to safety before this "curtain-fall" on earth's history.

Pigeon post

"The dove returned ..... " Gen 8:12

Pigeons have a remarkable homing instinct, difficult to explain but factually present. My grandfather was a pigeon-fancier. Two of his successful fliers were, on their demise, stuffed and preserved in a glass case. They had won races from the continent in important competitions.

Noah may well have so preserved for posterity the famous dove had it returned from its final release. It did a great job. From its second release it returned with a message of assurance - the plucked-off olive leaf in its mouth told Noah that the flood waters had greatly receded. In another week the intrepid crew of the ARK stood on dry ground. The Flood was over; the wild and turbulent waters were still; the olive-leaf was a symbol of peace.

When explorer Nansen was lost to civilisation in the arctic wastes (1895) his worried wife received a welcome visitor, a homing pigeon brought a message of his safety. Even so when our Lord ascended to the Throne of God, the heavenly Dove, the Holy Spirit came ten days later to signal His arrival. Peter said exultantly: "Christ ..... being at the right hand of God exalted ..... He hath shed forth this (ie the Holy Spirit)" (Acts 2:33).

And today we know that Jesus is exalted, for the Holy Spirit is with is - messenger of assurance and peace.

29 February

Afterglow

The summer sun sets, leaving a soft radiance in the western sky - it is the afterglow.

Life's experience can be like that. "They looked unto Him, and were lightened", wrote David (Ps 34:5), their faces became radiant in that holy glow.

Moses spent 40 days alone with God. When he came down from the holy mountain, his countenance shone with divine glory. So may our lives (and indeed our faces) become luminous with divine love as we absorb God's presence.

Anointed preaching can leave us with an "afterglow" that fills us with a deep, deep peace. When we fellowship together in our services, a sense of divine nearness can bestow on us a blessing that lasts long after the benediction.

May our "afterglow" be often and intense - to God's honour.

No go area

"Touch not Mine anointed" Ps 105:15

The reference is to the experience of Abraham and Sarah, founders of the dynasty of pilgrims - God "reproved kings for their sakes"; instance Pharaoh (Gen 12:17) and Abimelech (Gen 20:1-8).

The divine anointing was their protection. Though sometimes weak and fearful, Abraham was kept from harm by the God who had said, " I am thy shield" (Gen 15:1). The pilgrim's path led him through alien lands; but he was safe. His tent was a "no-go" area to opposing elements.

And so with modern pilgrims, those who believe in Jesus and are on the way to Glory, whom Peter calls "strangers and pilgrims" (1 Pet 2:11). God, by giving us His Spirit, has sealed us "unto the day of redemption" (Eph 4:30). The seal is a proof of identification, as the hymn writer puts it :

> "Then on each he setteth His own secret sign,
> They that have My Spirit, these saith He are Mine"

But the Holy Spirit not only establishes our identity as Christians, He also guarantees our safe passage through time to eternity. We are "sealed unto the day of redemption". No power on earth or in hell can keep us from reaching our desired and determined destination. Satan may impeach our passage, but he can never stay our ultimate progress. Our lives are to him "a no-go area".

Blank cheque

"Ask what I shall give thee" 2 Chron 1:7

Here is a blank cheque signed by God Himself to Solomon, the young king who succeeded David his father.

What a test! No other person in Scripture was presented with such a carte blanche. Even the proclamation to Messiah was limited to kingdoms. But here is an offer with no horizons. What a test for a youth with all his future before him!

What a token of humility was the answer! "Give me wisdom", asked Solomon, "I want to serve your people well". He sank self into service. God was so delighted that He promised him what he did not ask for - riches and honour.

What would I have requested? In find it difficult to know. But this I learn from the experience of Solomon, that prayer that is absorbed with self often fails of an answer, but when the needs of others and the will of God take precedence the answer is sure.

It is impossible completely to erase ego from our service to God, but we may join the Baptist in his resignation to the purpose of God. "He (that is, Christ) must increase, but I must decrease" (John 3:30) he said; and it is only as we become less that Christ can become more.

Alas, Solomon's early promise was later overshadowed by his defection. Devotion to God is a daily necessity, not a passing phase.

Surprise! surprise!

"Suddenly" Acts 2:2, Mark 13:36

It is surprises that make life exciting. To have some happy event burst into our humdrum lives adds a new dimension to our experience. The commonplace is lit up for a moment by a lightning-flash of the unexpected.

Alexander Gammie, in his <u>Preachers I Have Heard</u>, said of the renowned Joseph Parker, "There was always the element of the unexpected in what he said and how he said it". In preaching or writing it is the surprise element that arrests the mind. It is also true of experience:

> "<u>Sometimes a light surprises</u>
> <u>the Christian while he sings;</u>
> <u>It is the Lord Who rises</u>
> <u>With healing in His wings</u>"

So penned Cowper - and He is right!

The Christian era is bound by surprises; it opened with a sudden Pentecost, it will close with a sudden Parousia. And in-between what rich blessings may come to us by a spiritual incursion of grace as "the Lord whom ye seek suddenly comes to His temple" (cf Malachi 3:1).

In the light of this, the "sudden fear" that Satan stirs up does not result in panic. The grace of God is stronger far, even in its surprises, than any and all of Satan's attacks.

Blessings in passing

"By the way" Luke 24:32

Catastrophe had smitten the disciples of Jesus. He was dead: their hopes died with Him. Returning home from the scene of tragedy Cleophas and his wife drag their weary feet along the path to a life now emptied of meaning, their talk as solemn as a dirge.

A stranger (?) draws near, to whom they unfold their tale of woe. With quiet grace He gently applies the balm of Scripture truth. Their numbed hearts begin to glow. They invite him to an evening meal and discover that their guest is Jesus - alive and well. They race back through the night to spread the message to His disciples.

And it happened "by the way". What seemed an incidental approach turned out to be a divine visitation.

Does your path seem thorny, each step an effort, each stride a pain? Do not despair, you, too, can have a "by-the-way" experience as Jesus draws near. His presence will banish gloom, His assurance destroy despair. Your Emmaus will become a sanctuary. Your familiar "downsittings and uprisings" brightened with the light of His presence. You don't have to go to church to find Jesus, it can happen "by the way".

Just a smile

Moffatt's translation of Job 29:24 is "when I smiled it encouraged them, my cheerful gaze put heart into the hopeless".

How much joy a smile of appreciation or approval can inspire. It seems so little, yet can mean so much. A mother smiles at her babe, it chuckles with delight; a father smiles at his child's feeble efforts and he glows with glee, a friend smiles a greeting and we feel warm inside. Best of all, when the Lord "makes His face shine upon us", we are inspired, strengthened and blest.

Romans 12:8 counsels, "He that showeth mercy with cheerfulness". To visit the sick or afflicted calls for a tender approach. A S Way put it thus: "If you come with sympathy to sorrow, bring God's sunlight in your face".

The "cheerfulness" spoken of is not thoughtless hilarity, but a face radiant with grace and compassion, and words of understanding. Not like Job's friends whose morose and argumentative approach made Job's gloom more gloomy. "Miserable comforters are ye all", he complained (Job 16:2). He needed sympathy, not ill-constructed syllogisms, compassion, not criticism. What a tender smile would have done for him! Just a smile yes, but a means of comfort to the distressed.

6 March

The parchments

"But especially the parchments" 2 Tim 4:13

It is interesting to note that Paul took books with him on his travels. With all his inspiration he felt a need of mental stimulation provided by the writings of gifted men.

The common writing material was papyrus (from which we get our "paper"), but valuable works, such as the Scriptures, were written on more expensive and durable vellum.

Paul, at his first hearing, had been released. He continued his missionary work, but was suddenly arrested at Troas. He was dragged off without a chance to collect his goods. Fearing a long term of imprisonment, he asks Timothy to bring his cloak (Roman prisons were cold), his books, (for he could not bear to waste time), and "especially" the parchments, his Bible. He was prepared to freeze, he could manage without books - but his very spiritual life depended on the word of God.

The Holy Scriptures was the most treasured possession he owned. It was his most blessed acquisition. From it he gained moral strength, by it he acquired divine wisdom, through it his mind was informed of vital truth and his spirit fed on the bread of God.

Is the Bible special to you? If you love the Lord you cannot help but love His word. A knowledge of its contents will enlighten you, faith in its statements will encourage enrich and elevate you. The Bible should have priority over all other reading.

7 March

Bless you

"We bless you in the name of the Lord" Ps 129:8

The word "bless" means to express good wishes to a person, or as we say, "All the best". It is an expression of goodwill. But when it is done in the Name of the Lord it takes on a new dimension. It becomes more than pious patter, it invokes the favour of God, "the blessing of the Lord, it maketh rich, and He addeth no sorrow with it" (Prov 10:22). Faith turns a wish into a solid reality. Such a blessing is a word charged with power.

And this realm of faith extends to even greater things. "By faith Isaac blessed ..... Joseph blessed ......", and their good wishes became prophetic promises.

The pronouncement of blessing over Israel by the High Priest became their morning cordial and their good-night sedative. What precious words! "The Lord bless thee and keep thee: the Lord make His face shine upon thee, and be gracious unto thee: the Lord lift up His countenance upon thee, and give thee peace". And "in the name the Lord we too can bless others.

Psalm 129 recites the vicissitudes of life wherein many dangers and difficulties oppose. But God is greater than circumstances and with His blessings we triumph.

So when you say, "God bless you" do it in faith, and it will surprise you and the one you bless how God responds.

Heartfelt prayer

"They never put their heart in their prayers" Hosea 7:14

So translates James Moffatt. So then, prayer is not just words, a kind of magic formula to invoke God, it is a cry of the heart.

What matters most to God is not the grammar of our prayers, how correct they are; the logic of our prayers, how reasonable they are; the arithmetic of our prayer, how often they are offered; the chronology of our prayers, how long they are; or even the passion of our prayers, how forceful they are. All those may be essential elements, more or less, but the vital feature is our "hearts", that deep inner yearning for, looking for and trusting in the living God.

James gives a living example of effective prayer in Elijah's experience on Mount Carmel (James 5:17,18). He prayed for fire - it fell; he prayed for rain - it came. He was not special intimates the writer, but "a man of like passions as we are".

The 400 prophets of Baal "called on the name of Baal from morning even until noon". Goaded by Elijah they lashed themselves into fury, but no answer came. Their prayers were but words, windy and empty. Then God's prophet prayed simply, briefly and believingly. Heaven responded. And so for us, God will always respond to faith. No heartfelt petition will ever be denied.

Wider vision

"The same afflictions are accomplished in your brethren that are in the world" 1 Pet 5:9

In times of trial, affliction or depression we tend to feel isolated. We become introspective and wonder "Why me?"

God's scattered and persecuted flock felt thus in New Testament times. Peter presents to them a salutary fact. "You're not the only ones", he states, "there is a world-full of you". Don't let the devil isolate you, widen your vision. Your post may be under heavy fire, but we are winning all along the line.

Elijah complained that, "I, even I only, am left". "You're not", answered the Lord, "there are 7,000 more of you".

Sometimes our local situation seems hopeless our endeavours fruitless. We feel alone, but a puny patrol in a major campaign. Revival seems remote, our cause feeble and futile.

Widen your vision. In the church at large millions are accepting Jesus as their Saviour. In this 20th Century the Christian witness is advancing more than at any time in history. Use wider lenses and gain a wider vision.

"The same afflictions" - we do not suffer alone, neither do we triumph alone. A sweeping wave of power is coming our way. Believing, we will see it arrive.

The thirteenth devil

"Why art thou cast down, O my soul" Ps 42:5

Dante, in his DIVINE COMEDY names twelve devils - the allurer, the malicious, the grace-scorner, the snarler the tusked boar, the fell-dragon, the scandalmonger, the doggish, the ill-tempered, the red with rage, the baneful, the fidgets (Brewer's dictionary of Phrase and Fable). He missed one out. The thirteenth devil is the Demon of Discouragement.

"Where is thy God?" taunted the enemies of the psalmist. How many souls, burdened with oppression, have caved in under the added load of discouragement. And the opposite is true; not to speak a kind word to a struggling neighbour is a sin.

When David was at the end of his tether Jonathan "strengthened his hand in God". His gracious words were as cold water to a thirsty soul. David cheered up, and went on to win through. A regular member of his congregation said to Dr John Watson ("Ian Maclaren"), "your best work in the pulpit has been to put heart into men for the coming week". That is true ministry.

Chief among the vocal gifts of the Spirit is Prophecy, which "speaketh unto men to edification, and exhortation, and comfort" (1 Cor 14:3). The message of this charismatic gift is "Cheer up, carry on, God is with you!"

Lord help us to cast out the demon of discouragement by a kindly word, a gentle hand shake, a friendly visit.

11 March

Why limit God?

"They limited the Holy One of Israel" Ps 78:41

Or, as Dr Faussett paraphrases: "They circumscribed Him with bands". But God is without bounds, He is infinite. It is our unbelieving minds that reduces to us the dimensions of God. Lack of faith is like looking through the wrong end of a telescope, it makes big things little.

Maisie came in from school crying exultantly, "I know all my tables, even the 12 times". With a twinkle in his eye, Grandpa asked, "what is 13 times 13?" "Don't be silly, Grandpa, there's no such thing", she replied petulantly. Her apprehension of the boundless extensions possible to Mathematics was indeed limited.

And so our disbelief often reduces God to a circumscribed view of reality. "How great is the ocean and how tiny the shell with which we dip", wrote one philosopher. God can do anything but deny Himself.

Our tiny concept of God will not diminish Him, He is exhaustless but it will lessen our spiritual life, impeding our prayers, affecting our whole attitude. Israel failed to please God and conquer their allotted benefits because their limited vision sapped their faith, sullied their hope and stultified their endeavours.

God is great

"Now unto Him that is able to do exceeding abundantly above all that we ask or think" Eph 3:20

I was meditating in prayer one day, when I felt I heard God speak to me - "My answers are greater than your petitions". I was thrilled. When God answers prayer He does not confine Himself to the limits of our vocabulary or vision, He goes beyond our words and our unspoken wishes. We bring to Him our empty cup, He sends us away with a cask of blessings.

Look at the text. "He is able to do what we ask" .... ALL that we ask ABOVE ALL that we ask; ABUNDANTLY ABOVE ALL that we ask: EXCEEDING ABUNDANTLY ABOVE ALL that we ask. And to all this perceptual petition is added the inexpressible conceptions of imagination. God is bigger than our thoughts, greater than our actions (Is 55:8), therefore we are encouraged to ask largely:

> "Thou art coming to a king,
> Large petitions with thee bring:
> For His grace and power are such,
> Non can ever ask too much"

So sang John Newton: so sing we.

And this is "according to the power that worketh in us" - the Holy Spirit, who inspires our prayers, gives us the wisdom to know what to pray for, the faith to pray for it, and the joy to anticipate the answers of God.

Pray for the preacher

"Praying .... for me .... that I may open my mouth boldly .... as I ought to speak" Eph 6:18-20

Spurgeon came to Aberdeen to give a lecture. In the vestry the great man was besieged by expectant friends. A deacon who had travelled with him told Dr Brown (cf the Jamieson, Faucett and Brown Commentary) that if Spurgeon could not have a few quiet minutes his lecture would be a failure. The room was cleared, but the great preacher seemed in distress of mind. Even on the platform he was manifestly out of sorts. Dr Brown leaned towards him; "I will hold up your hands in prayer" he said quietly. "Thank you for that", was the cordial reply, and again, "thank you for that, thank you for that". The lecture turned out a brilliant one. Friends came to express their thanks and admiration. Mr Spurgeon, turning to Dr Brown, remarked "You owe it all to him".

You see, preaching is more than a concatenation of words or a concentration of thoughts, under God it is a confluence of divine truth and consecrated personality. Every effective preacher needs the anointing of the Spirit of God.

That is why our prayers are needed. Don't blame the preacher for a poor sermon, blame yourself for not praying victoriously for him. Such praying will not only bring liberty of utterance to God's messenger, it will also prepare your heart to receive God's message.

A great conclusion

"Fear God .... the whole duty of man" Eccles 12:13

Ecclesiastes is a record of a vital experiment. "How can you know life unless you live it?" contested the preacher. Fortified by wealth and opportunity he embarked on an excursion that ended in disaster.

The man endowed with superb wisdom became the greatest fool in sacred history. You don't have to sin to feel its power or to murder to experience contrition, or to worship idols to test the power of evil.

Solomon investigated all that the world could offer - pleasure, philosophy, religion, ethics, science even a touch of agnosticism. He probed everything "under the sun" (a phrase he uses 29 times). He found it all vanity, futility, emptiness, disappointment.

How could he, who started so well, deviate from God's clear purpose so drastically. The writer of Chronicles blames it on his wives. But there was more than that. The Lord gave guiding principles to a future king in Deuteronomy 17:16,17. This warning against PASSION, POWER and PELF was disregarded.

He ended up burdened with regrets, a cynical failure. But he ended his "sermon" with a great conclusion - FEAR GOD. This is the only element that produces worthwhile living. Why did he not keep his own word: "the fear of the Lord is the beginning of wisdom"? (Prov 9:10). Let us begin there, and we will not end feeling that life has been wasted. Reverence God - and succeed.

God's surprises

"We have seen strange things today" Luke 5:26

The Greek word for "strange things" is paradoxes - things contrary to opinion or expectation, unexpected. Hence seemingly absurd or contradictory. Better still, holy surprises, strange but wonderful.

God does not always move according to our expectations. His ways are often paradoxical, puzzling but profound. But is not paradox the essence of wisdom? God's thoughts are higher than our thoughts. He is unpredictable. He can produce the impossible. No situation can exhaust His creative ability. He is always consistent, but often incomprehensible. He baffles us - but He blesses us; He answers us but he astonishes us; He is ever with us, but His presence may burst upon us suddenly and unexpectedly in greater glory and meaningfulness.

As William Cowper expresses it:

> "Sometimes a light surprises
> The Christian while he sings;
> It is the Lord who rises
> With healing in His wings".

And so "the even tenor of our way" may know divine incursions into our mundane path. The secret of surprise in that holy incident recorded by Luke is that Jesus was there. "The power of the Lord was present to heal" because the Lord of life was there to dispense His benefits. May God surprise you today with a rich blessing.

16 March

A day at a time

"Take therefore no (anxious) thought for tomorrow"
Matt 6:34

"Live in day-tight compartments", advised our Lord. Why clutter our lives with regrets from the past and fear for the future. Live today free from care. And we may do so if our priorities are right. Set Christ on the throne of our hearts, and He will put all things under our feet, even that arch-tormentor, the devil himself (Romans 16:20).

Was this the lesson God taught His ancient people when He gave them Manna? It came daily (all but the Sabbath). As they left their tents to gather God's provision, they needed faith to believe it would be there. But it was, and for 40 years they gathered a harvest they did not sow. And they had to scoop it up before sun-up. Lazy bed-lovers lost their rations. Early rising was a key to their health. And it came in measured but sufficient supply, so that none lacked the essential daily sustenance.

If we put God first, all other things will fall into place. We will live the daily round in confidence and contentment. Each passing day can prove a spiritual feast.

17 March

Vicarious faith

"When Jesus saw their faith" Mark 2:5

The healing of the paralytic let down through the tiles by friends who brought him to Jesus is full of remarkable suggestions re the power of faith.

Faith is <u>discernible by action,</u> augmented by co-operation and immovative in motion. Above all, faith can be <u>vicarious in operation</u>: "Jesus saw <u>their</u> faith": the paralysed man may have been beyond helping himself but believing friends brought him to Jesus.

Faith not only puts itself about for others but it is also accepted by God on another's behalf: vicarious faith! This opens up a tremendous concept of service. I can believe for my brother, gain the attention of God by proxy. What a revelation! But what a responsibility! Do not charge your weak brother with lack of faith if he is not blessed or healed; believe for him.

James echoes this idea when he says, "And the prayer of faith (by the elders) shall save the sick" (James 5:15). We can maintain each other, bless each other, protect each other by faith. If four men could effect a miracle, what of a whole congregation?

This <u>principle of proxy</u> is a redemptive verity. "Christ died for our sins according to the Scriptures" (1 Cor 15:3). He took our load of sin so that we might be forgiven. May we not also take the burden of others, and so believe for their deliverance that they are saved? God accepts vicarious faith.

18 March

"God bless you"

Ps 129:8

How often we use these words! But are they more than pious platitude? If done "in the name of the Lord" they can become words charged with power that bestow a benediction.

The Hebrew word here means to wish a person health and prosperity. But faith can make these words more than a wish, they can actually bestow a positive feeling of well-being upon those we bless in God's name.

But more than this: "By faith Isaac blessed Jacob and Esau concerning things to come" (Heb 11.20). Their destiny was influenced by this paternal benediction. And what of the children Jesus took up in His arms and blessed? (Mark 10:16). How this affected their lives we may never know. And what of the priestly "Goodnight and God bless you" of Aaron high priest of Israel? (Num 6:22-27) I like a service to finish with a benediction: it leaves me with a sense of peace so when you say, "God bless you!" mean it, and spread a little sunshine.

> "Make me a channel of blessing today;
> Make me a channel of blessing, I pray;
> My life possessing, my service blessing;
> Make me a channel of blessing today"

God bless you!

19 March

Say "Amen"

"Say Amen at thy giving of thanks" 1 Cor 14:16

One of the most common words in the Bible is "Amen". It is used in two senses.

First, it is an affirmation of prayer. We close our own intercession with "Amen" in firm trust that God will answer. It implies, "I mean it, Lord; please do it".

We use it in response to the prayers of others. Our text above shows how important this is. By its sincere use we not only imply our assent to what has been said, we also (and this is the nub) iterate the petitions made. This one word gathers up our wholehearted agreement and our confident hope. One such prayer, with its implied "Amens", brought a breath-taking response (Acts 4:31).

Secondly, it is an acceptance of God's Word. In Ezra's day a great crowd assembled in a public square in Jerusalem to hear readings from the Scriptures. Men, women and children stood for hours listening to God's holy word. As Ezra opened the ancient scroll, he thanked God for His word: "And all the people answered, "Amen, Amen" (Neh 8:6). The double "Amen" implied that they really meant it. They were ready to receive God's word as His voice to them. Still more, they were ready to appropriate and apply it. May we ever say "yes!" to God.

20 March

God's map

"I am but a pilgrim here on earth: how I need a map - and your commands are my chart and creed" Ps 119:19 (Living Bible)

Have you ever felt lost, wondered what life is about, bewildered by events? Don't despair; consult God's oracle - the BIBLE.

The Bible tells me where I am. A guide to visitors in some towns will display a map with an arrow pointing YOU ARE HERE. The Bible will show you where you are morally and spiritually. You needn't feel lost, the Holy Book will dictate your position. What a vital day when God told me I was a sinner - "you are here!" he said. He then led me to the Cross. I was saved.

The Bible tells me where I've been. By its help. I can trace the mystery of His dealings with me: the past can become a guide for the present, for God never changes.

The Bible tells me where to go. The recreational activity called orienteering calls for its participants to make their way in unknown terrain by map and compass. So the Bible is our "map and compass" through the unknown path of life. Guided by the Word of God our pilgrimage becomes a spiritual adventure discovering to us the glorious ways of God and the delights of the "heavenly country" through which the Lord is leading us to Glory. Bunyan called it "Beulah Land".

21 March

Curtains!

"There should be time no longer" Rev 10:6
"There will be no more delay" (NIV)

When Paul speaks of "the fashion of this world passeth away" (1 Cor 7:31) he uses a word borrowed from the theatre. Scene upon scene passes by as the drama of existence is unfolded. Yet "through all the changing scenes of life" a redemptive purpose unfolds. History is not merely a record of events, it is a revelation of God's saving purpose: salvation history.

God invaded time in the Incarnation of His Son to perfect His eternal plan. Jesus lived, died and rose again according to "the determinate council and foreknowledge of God". And now He patiently waits to give all men time to repent and be converted.

But there is an end to this human pantomime. The curtain must fall. God will soon cry, "Time, gentlemen please", and the drama of life will end. The last act is in process, "for the time is at hand" (Rev 1:3). It will end in "sudden destruction" upon the ungodly, but sudden salvation for these who love and serve the Lord.

If we fulfil our role in life with faith, hope and love, we will receive our destined reward from the Author of all good. For those who trust in Jesus, "curtains!" will be a welcome home-call.

The paradox of freedom

"The law of liberty" James 2:12

This seems a contradiction of terms: but it is true. All true liberty is based on law. Morally, the Ten Commandments stamp liberty on life. Sin, the essence of which is self-choice, is bondage. Materially, freedom is based on natural law. The freest creature, so we say, is a bird. But how can an heavier-than-air object float in the sky? By instinct it obeys the rules of aerodynamics, and is thus able to perform at pleasure aerial gymnastics. It obeys the law of nature, and is free.

And so spiritually. As Elton Trueblood avers: "We have not advanced very far in our spiritual lives if we have not encountered the basic paradox of freedom, to the effect that we are most free when we are bound".

The hymn-writer, George Matheson, confirms this in his well-known words:

"Make me a captive, Lord,
And then I shall be free;
Force me to render up my sword,
And I shall conqueror be".

To submit to the will of God brings joyful freedom; the chains that bind us to Him are fetters of delight. The yoke of Christ brings sweetest rest to our souls.

Keeping in tune with the spirit

"And the Spirit and the Bride say come" Rev 22:17

One of the last clauses of the Bible story contains a vital principle of service for "God" - "the Spirit and the Bride":

First, the primacy of the Holy Spirit. It is God first in all my work from him. His plan, His purpose, His potential. The Church council in Acts 15 was wound up in the terse expression: "It seemed good to the Holy Ghost, and to us" (vs 28). One godly commentator draws out the important application - "the Senior partnership of the Holy Spirit". Precious thought!

Secondly, The potency of co-operation with the Holy spirit. The invitation to sinners to "take the water of life" can only become effective as the "Bride" echoes the "Spirit". It is He who convicts the ungodly of his need of God and convinces him of the Gospel way of salvation. We may be channels, He is the "Spirit of life in Christ Jesus" (Rom 8:2).

Thirdly, the priority of the Spirit's message - "come". The call to salvation is simple, expressed in one word. Do we complicate matters by pseudo-appeals? Are our often sophisticated methods counter-productive? Paul tried philosophy at Athens - and failed. Having learned his lesson, he preached the Cross of Christ at Cornith, without oratorical finesse, but with simple appeal to trust in Jesus. He had remarkable success.

The second touch

"He put His hands again upon his eyes" Mark 8:25

This seems to be a unique occurrence. Usually, one touch was sufficient but here there is a second ministration. The first touch on this blind man restored the <u>faculty</u> of sight; the second gave <u>focus</u> to see clearly! Is this a parable?

How often the experience of those who come to Christ need a complimentary touch! We see this in the life of the Apostles of Jesus. Throughout their association with Him they learned many things. "Blessed are your eyes, for they see" (Matt 13:16); but in many things, "their eyes were holden" (Luke 24:16). But a remedy was at hand. After Jesus had departed this earth, the Holy spirit came, who "opened the eyes of their heart" (cf Eph 1:17 NIV), so that things once obscure now became clear (cf John 2:20).

We, too, need this second touch. When we first commit ourselves to Christ our eyes are opened (cf Acts 26:18) but we may still "see men as trees walking" the second touch - the Baptism in the Holy Spirit - opens to us a new world of understanding. If Calvary is the redeeming touch, Pentecost is the revealing touch.

By the Holy Spirit our grasp of spiritual things is enhanced. "We have received .... the Spirit which is of God - that we might know the things that are freely given to us of God" (1 Cor 2:12). Have you had the second touch?

25 March

Cushions for comfort

"He was ..... asleep on a pillow" Mark 4:38

This "pillow" was the steersman's cushion, a device to ease his position as he sat on the hard wooden bench directing the boat.

What a human touch is here? An exhausted Jesus pillows his head on this means of comfort - and sleeps. We conclude, then, that it is allowable to employ means of reducing discomfort in our service for God. Our devotion to him calls for self-discipline, but not for self-demolition.

Needless asceticism is no part of the demands of Christian life. "Neglecting of the body" is inimical to Christ's religion. The Bible condemns those whose ethical code is "touch not; taste not; handle not" (Col 2:21). Self-denial is indeed a Christian virtue, but to make a fetish of material discomfort is self-torture. We need to regulate our natural instincts, not punish our bodies. Rest as well as toil is our lot.

Without over-indulgence, there is a place for "cushions". It is logical and allowable for us to "nourish and cherish" our bodies (Eph 5:29). They are temples of the Holy Spirit, therefore we keep them clean and clothed, fed and fended for, preserved and prepared for holy service.

26 March

Discipline

"But I keep under my body" 1 Cor 9:27

Paul was severe with himself. He metaphorically battered his body into subjection so that there should be no impediment to his being the best for God. Normal human nature craves for indulgence, gravitates toward comfort, gives way to ease. The body must be mastered if we are to master the demands of divine service.

The apostle draws illustrations from the Olympic games, and cites running and boxing as examples of discipline and dedication. To win a laurel wreath of honour these athletes exert every particle of their being in strict exercise and determined activity. Shall we be less devoted in our work for God. There is a greater race to run, a fiercer opponent to beat, a richer prize to win - let us go for it.

Discipline is <u>essential</u> to Christian living. "Every competitor in those athletic contests practices continual self-denial" (A S Way). This virtue of loss is fed by a vision of gain.

Discipline is <u>effectual</u>. It releases potential, it brings out the best in us, it develops faculties to the full. In fact, in many spheres, discipline produces proud results. In music, "wild sounds are tamed to time and tune"; in literature, random words are marshalled into ordered battalions of ideas and emotions; in logic, thoughts are forged into sensible shape. And all by rational discipline.

To order our lives by the will of God is to achieve spiritual maturity, fit us for fruitful ministry, and gain for us the mastery of self in the service of God.

27 March

No change!

"I am the Lord, I change not" Malachi 3:6

He cannot change, or He would not be God. To change for the better would imply imperfection of the first state, to change for the worse would destroy what already is.

But human nature demands change; "variety is the spice of life", is its motto. And so man often turns his back on the stability and security of a changeless deity to wallow in the uncertainties of changeful things. Such change is charged with decay.

Even in normal natural existence, it is the changeless things that make life liveable. The majesty and mystery of a star-spangled sky is just the same as it ever was; the glory of sunrise and sunset know no change; the magic of moonlight still maintains its romantic gleam.

Some things do not change; some things we don't want to change! The essentials of life are the same "yesterday and today, and forever". A throbbing heart, breathing lungs, a thinking brain, digestion, metabolism, plus a bevy of active organs, make life stable. The things that do not change are the very essence of being.

But amazing paradox! - within this aura of sameness is a vastness of variety. Roses are one variety, but within that oneness is a multitude of tints and tinctures. And so in every mode of existence. Life is a mixture of essentials and variables: but without the essentials the variables could not exist. No change is a law of creation.

Star - struck !

"And, lo, the star ..... went before them" Matt 2:9

The "star of Bethlehem" moved into the orbit of eastern astronomers at the birth of Jesus. Their response is an example to us.

Revelation. Their sky was lit up by this divine super-nova. The Magi discerned its message: a King was born. Was this "the star out of Jacob" that Balaam predicted (Numbers 24:17)? They felt so - and rightly.

Response. At great cost and exertion, and tremendous risk, they lead their caravan over many miles of alien territory, guided by the star. It became their prompter to action, their pointer to location and their leader to worship. The technical college at which I was trained shared accommodation with a girls high school. Where they attended daily, we held our evening classes. On the wall was a banner with the stirring device: "HITCH YOUR WAGON TO A STAR". In literal form: "Let your life be guided and spurred by the noblest ideals".

I hitched the wagon of my life to the Star of Bethlehem as a young boy. My life was given direction and destiny. There followed many years of service, there awaits glad and lasting satisfaction.

Rendezvous. The star eventually "stood over where the young child was". The wise men worshipped. And our star of revelation will lead us to Jesus, the final rendezvous of the Christian experience: not to a "house" this time, but to "the Holy City".

29 March

Casket of love

"Thy word have I hid in my heart" Ps 119:11

Brewer's DICTIONARY OF PHRASE AND FABLE records: "After the battle of Arbela a golden casket, studded with jewels, was found in the tent of Darius. Alexander (the Great), being asked to what purpose it should be applied, made answer, "there is but one production in the world worthy of so costly depository?" He placed in it his treasured copy of Homer, the great Greek poet.

God did the same with the DECALOGUE. Within the sacred precinct of the Tabernacle Court was the Sanctuary of God called "The Holy Place". This was the vestibule to "the Holy of Holies", the most hallowed spot of the Hebrew camp. Enshrined in this "Holiest of All" was the most prestigious piece of sacred furniture - the ARK OF THE COVENANT. In this coffer was placed the tablets of stone on which were engraved by the finger of God the Ten Commandments given on Mount Sinai. Thus the Word of God held the central place in the lives of God's people. The very heart of the Old Covenant is this divine edict - God's prescription for life.

The psalmist goes beyond this. He hides God's word in the most sacred casket, his HEART, from that central point to instil virtue into the whole life, so that from the centre to the perimeter of his being the saving and sanctifying power of the holy word is felt.

"Let the word of Christ dwell in you", said Paul (Col 3:16). This word will cleanse us, comfort and sustain us throughout our life.

30 March

Doughty daughters

"The daughters of Zelophebad" Num 26:33, 27:1

In Israel, to be without sons was an impediment, to have daughters only was a catastrophe - until these five valiant virgins took up their case with Moses.

Inheritance endangered. The father had died leaving no son to inherit his name and his lot in the "Land of Promise". This was serious. The whole life of an Israelite was bound up in the hope of gaining a plot in Canaan - their destined eldorado. When we speak of women as "the weaker sex", it does not always apply. These Israeli maidens; weaker in physical prowess, weaker in social status, weaker in tribal influence, were strong in determination. They felt that insult was done to their sex, despite to their prospects, injustice to their rights. They speak up - as any wronged female should.

Inheritance secured. They bring their case to Moses, and Moses refers their case to Jehovah - the hightest authority of all. God is just, and finds in their favour. If they marry within the clan, they can claim their father's inheritance. And this became a law in Israel. The tenacity and audacity of these "famous five" turn a bane into a boon, not only for themselves but also for the female section of Israel. What custom could not do, God did. The lesson? Don't be afraid to stand up for justice. Persist in pressing on and laws could be changed for the better.

31 March

I'm a nobody

I recently read a book by the outstanding biblical scholar, Karl Barth. At the back was a bibliography of his works and of those who wrote about him. This latter list comprised more than forty volumes.

Something incongruous smote my sense of humour. I burst out laughing, saying to myself: "Forty books! No one ever wrote a book about me or is likely to. I'm a nobody. Outside a limited circle of friends I'm just a nonentity." I added, "Hallelujah!" for I was immediately reminded of 1 Corinthians 1:28, "God hath chosen ..... things which are not".

I may be a cipher in this world, unknown, unsought for and as far as the multitude is concerned, non-existent. But God knows me - what are men? And he often takes us the least likely folk to do a work for Him. Think of Stephen Jeffries, coalminer, and Smith Wigglesworth, plumber, and the impact they made on early Pentecostalism. The present charismatic surge owes much to the service of such men.

And God does this so that no man can boast. When nonentities are successful all the glory goes to the Lord who raised them.

Sparks fly upward - Job 5 : 7

The words of Eliphaz to job may not have given him much comfort, but they contain an arresting picture of life as it is.

It is possible that the first fire on earth was lit by God on the altar of Abel and ever since the altar-flame has sought to return to its source.

"Sparks fly upward"; the fire creates its own thermals which hurl these "sons of flame" heavenwards. The fire of God always has an uplifting effect; an aspiration to ascend. It is a law of life, both natural and spiritual.

"Sparks fly upward". But what did this mean to tormented Job? His friend implied that as trouble is the lot of mortal man, Job, who had been so prosperous, could not expect to escape this universal malady. But he could pray, thus sending up his petitions with the sparks. In fact, as fire creates this upward surge, so troubles are meant to drive us upwards to God.

"Sparks fly upward". But there is more than this. Deep in human nature is felt a need for something higher, nobler and purer. But man is bound by base instincts, by ignoble impulses, by passions and lusts. Left to himself, in spite of his better longing he gravitates to a worldly level of life. But in regeneration, especially crowned with Pentecostal blessing a fire is lit - the fire of the Holy Spirit - that creates a spiritual thermal. Sparks of dynamic experience are released that lift the soul higher and higher.

2 April

Experts are not always right

"Sirs, ye should have harkened unto me" Acts 27:21

Paul, travelling as prisoner to Rome had a premonition, inspired by the Holy Spirit that a storm would wreck the ship. Sailing was dangerous at that season, but the journey to Rome was urgent and delay costly. Paul gave advice not to leave the harbour of Fair Havens, incommodious though it was. But the centurion-in-charge consulted the captain - after all, he was the expert - and turned down the admonition of the apostle. Paul was right: the ship was eventually wrecked on the rocks of Malta - the expert was wrong.

We often benefit from expert advice, but the best of men can make mistakes; and when it comes to REVELATION versus REASON, we know what course must win.

Paul, caught up in catastrophe, did not complain, he prayed, and by faith secured the lives of passengers and crew. But he did remind them of his rejected advice, while at the same time assuring them that his prayer for their deliverance was answered. Reason wrecked them: revelation saved them.

And so it sometimes is. When Caruso's mother took her promising son for an audition to a celebrated music-master, he said that the youth would never make a singer. "His voice sounds like wind in the shutters", he observed. How wrong was he! Caruso became the greatest tenor that Italy ever produced. So don't lose hope if the experts say it can't be done. If God was spoken to you His revelation is greater than mans' reason. Go on!

True nobility

"Not many noble are called 1 Cor 1:26

The Countess of Huntingdon, friend and patron of George Whitfield, thanked God for the letter M, it changed "not any" into "not many". She was one of the few aristocrats of the day to respond to the appeal of the Gospel.

The noble (as we call this élite stratum of society) are hard to reach, and harder still to teach, for the noble are often tainted with ignoble pride. One noted divine, preaching on the Ethiopian Eunuch of Acts 8:27, marvelled that an aristocrat read the Scriptures, and more, that he admitted he could not understand them and asked for help. But there are famous exceptions.

However, true nobility is not the monopoly of those of high rank, there is a higher order, the nobility of character. Tennyson put it thus:

"Howe're it be, it seems to me,
'Tis only noble to be good;
Kind hearts are more than coronets,
And simple faith than Norman blood."

The noblest character that ever graced this planet earth was the penniless prophet from Nazareth - Jesus. Poor, unlearned, obscure, He now dominates the hearts of half the world's population. He had no titles, He held no degrees, but, even after 2,000 years, He is the greatest force in modern civilisation. And all who follow Him are among the noblest of living mortals.

4 April

The original streaker

"A certain young man ..... fled naked" Mark 14:51

The youth that fled naked from Gethsemane was undoubtedly Mark, at whose house was held the Last Supper. What was he doing there?

Two explanations. First, out of curiosity being disturbed in his sleep by the departure of the apostolic group, he had hurriedly wrapped his bed sheet around him and followed Jesus into the night. Or else the Roman posse, plus the Temple squad and directive priests, led by Judas the betrayer had called at his home to arrest Jesus. Mark went out to warn the departed band. Whatever reason, the inquisitive youth was there. One of the marauding band grabbed hold of him. He shed his sheet and ran off naked - the original streaker.

This was not the first time he would run away. Converted to Christ under the ministry of Peter, he later joined his uncle Barnabas at Antioch in Syria, and became his aide-de-camp on the first missionary tour described in Acts 13:1-13. When the going got tough he ran home to his widowed mother. Paul later said: "He went not with us to the work" (Acts 15:38) and refused him any further service. His uncle at great personal sacrifice took him under his wing and restored him to sacred service. Even Paul acknowledged his recovery (2 Tim 4:11) and welcomes his ministry.

Mark's runaway weakness teaches us two things. First, the best way to overcome trouble is to face it. Secondly, if we fail (as well we might) God will give us another chance to prove our selves. If we need it, we do well to take it.

"A fly in the ointment"

"Dead flies can make a whole bottle of perfume stink, and a little stupidity can cancel out the greatest wisdom" Eccles 10:11 (Good News Bible)

How easily may a good reputation be ruined! A moment of folly can cancel a lifetime of service, what men think about us does matter. An act of disgrace can sour our testimony, turning what should be the "sweet savour" of a godly life into a feted effluence of disgust.

Take David. One night of shame blighted his later life. "For David had done what was right in the eyes of the Lord ..... except in the case of Uriah the Hittite" *(1 Kings 15:5 NIV).*

This exception cost him a priceless reputation. Not only did he thus lose authority over his own family, he "gave great occasion to the enemies of the Lord to blaspheme" (2 Sam 12:14). Who can tell what influence this had on Israel's fortunes. Was it a remote cause of the division of God's people?

David was forgiven by God - but his defection was not forgotten by men. In my youth I once caught and handled a butterfly. The "powder" on its wings was disturbed, when freed it fluttered weakly away to die. I was sorry - but I had done something I could not undo. And there are consequences that not even divine forgiveness can stay.

The Christian's life is a noble way and well-worth commending to others, but "a dead fly", a little folly can turn people away from the very thing we wish to attract then to, turning our testimony into "a stinking savour". Live right: shine bright!

6 April

Skyway

"A highway shall be there" Isa 35:8-10

The way to Zion is described in terms that illustrate the way to Heaven.

It is the only way. There is no other road to Glory but by Jesus (John 14:6).
It is a straight way - a highway that leads up to God. Any other proposed way is but a by-path that leads to a moral and spiritual cul-de-sac.
It is a safe way. "No lion shall be there". On this holy track we are guaranteed a divine security. God who opened the way, guards the path of those who tread it.
It is a fool-proof way. "Wayfaring men, though fools, shall not err therein". If we trust in God we cannot go astray.
It is a holy way. Only, those dedicated to God may tread it. It is reserved for those who are "washed in the blood of the Lamb" (Rev 1:5, 7:14).
It is a way of companionship. A variation of verse 7 (according to A R Fawsett) reads: "for He (the Holy one) shall be with them". And with this agree the words of Jesus, "And lo, I am with you alway, even unto the end of the world" (Matt 28:20). We shall never walk alone on the way to the Holy City.
It is a way whose beginning is but a step away. Jacob saw this way years ago. It was to him a ladder whose top reached Heaven but the first rung was at his feet. So with us: the "skyway of God" is at hand. All we need do is believe and step out.

Lend your boat to Jesus

"He entered into one of the ships" Luke 5:1-11

Jesus was practical. As He preached on the Galilee beach the crowd tended to engulf Him in their eagerness to hear His remarkable sermon. Our Lord commandeered a nearby boat, pushed out a little and used the prow of this borrowed vessel as a pulpit. More people could then see Him, and the placid water served as a sounding board for His inspired oratory.

But God is no man's debtor. The talking ceased, Jesus told Peter to "launch out into the deep and let your nets down". The seasoned sailor objected. "It is useless, the fish are not just biting. We've tried all night - a fruitless task". One glance at Jesus changed his mind. "Nevertheless, since you say so, we'll do it". The result - nets bulging with fish. their "night-toil" was a waste: their "day-gift" a bounty. Peter had lent his boat to Jesus he was repaid a hundred-fold. Don't hesitate to lend your gifts to God - it pays.

Neither is contact with God an ordinary thing. Peter was smitten with holy fear at this miracle. He felt himself in the presence of "the Holy One". In the light of the divine presence his sinfulness seemed more sinful. His first impression was to flee this Person who had done such a wonder. Jesus calms Peter's fear, and said, "you're just the man I need. Follow Me!" The effect on the fisherman was terrific. Peter and Andrew, James and John, ceased catching fish to go catching men for God. When you lend your boat to Jesus you never know what may result.

Thermals

"They shall mount up with wings" Isa 40:30

I stood on the sea-front and watched the gulls gyrating and soaring like a merry-go-round of delight. A breeze homing in on a towering cliff had created thermals - rising currents of air. The birds used this atmospheric upthrust to perform aerodynamic wonders. The same natural principle is used by balloonists and hang-gliders to break the bands of gravity and rise into the clear blue sky.

Could there be such a thing as spiritual thermals. The natural ones are a combination of air and warmth. We have both in the Holy Spirit, who came at Pentecost as wind and flame. In the power of the Spirit there is a holy upthrust. By fitting ourselves to His operations we can free ourselves of earthly pull, and rise as on eagle's wings. One of the secrets of victorious living is so to discern the divine flow of activity, become by faith part of the Spirit's moving, and surge upwards joyously and effortlessly in "heavenly places in Christ Jesus". Paul learned this. After a vain struggle to conquer self in Romans chapter seven, he stopped striving and started trusting. In chapter eight we find Him led by the Spirit, and "more than conqueror through Him that loves us": Have you had a "thermal-lift" lately?

God is at work

"My Father worketh hitherto" John 5:17

When God "rested from all His work" on the Seventh Day, He did not abandon His creation. "He is still working", said Jesus, History is still His-story.

I came across a remarkable quotation the other day. It ran like this:-

> "God exercises His sway over the historical process in a continuous manner; His activity resides in the direction of events according to a plan formed in view of a determinate end ..... through the apparent confusions of earthly history it is His own work which He accomplishes"

But we cannot always trace His activities. We sometimes feel like the Psalmist: "Arise O Lord: let not man prevail" (Ps 9:19). In other words: "Please God, get involved; do something!" But God does not act according to our wishes or whims. He has His own purpose to perform. It took 4,000 years for God to provide the remedy for sin. What a distance between the crash of Adam's fall and the Cross of redeeming grace! But the atoning death of Jesus has provided "eternal redemption" (Heb 9:12) for all who believe.

Peter who at first found the idea of Messiah's crucifixion repulsive (Matt 16:22) lived to see that it was "the determinate counsel and foreknowledge of God" (Acts 2:23) to deliver up His Son to death for us. And God is ever at work for us to perfect our Christian lives and prepare us for everlasting bliss.

Assimilation

"Desire the sincere milk of the word" 1 Peter 2:2

Life is an assimilative process; we transmute into our own quality whatever we imbibe as food or drink. Walter de la Mare comically puts it this:-

> It's a very odd thing -
> As odd as can be -
> That whatever Miss T eats
> Turns into Miss T

And this applies to mental and spiritual ingestion - it is a law of life. The mind is nourished by literature, the soul by "the sincere milk of the word" - the Bible. As we ingest this heaven-born food it not only satisfies our spiritual hunger, it also transforms our spiritual life.

In milk there are all the essentials of physical sustenance - sugar, fat, carbohydrates, mineral, trace-elements and all in pre-digested form. So the Bible contains all the essentials to keep us in spiritual trim.

But it is not enough to ingest food, we must digest it. That is why the Bible says so little about "study", but much about "meditation". We are called upon to "taste" the word of God. That is so to contemplate its meaning, absorb its message and apply its monitions that we truly learn of God. This calls for set-apart intervals to personally read and reflect on the Bible story, not in time-scamped periods, but in thoughtful and concentrated systematic contemplation.

Prince-in-waiting

"And princes shall rule in judgement" Isa 32:1

Don't judge me for my present state and bearing; in actual fact I am a prince-in-waiting. When the King shall reign in righteousness, then I (and myriad's more) will rule with Him, sharing in His Millennial glory.

My earnest expection is valid for three reasons. First, I am of royal descent. Since I received Jesus I have become "a son of God" (John 1:12) and "partaker of the divine nature" (2 Peter 1:4). And because I am a child of God, I am an "heir of God, and joint-heir with Christ" (Rom 8:17). This is the more remarkable, seeing that Christ has been "appointed heir of all things" (Heb 1:2). In Him I am fabulously rich.

And all this is by divine decree. Those words, supremely fulfilled in Jesus, may apply also to me: "Thou art my son; this day have I begotten thee" (Psalm 2:7). One day in my boyhood I gave my heart to the Lord. He accepted me. I was born again made a subject of the Kingdom of God; nay more, constituted a member of the Royal Family.

"It doth not appear what we shall be" (1 John 3:2), but in the final denouement, when God makes all things new He will declare "I will be his God, and he shall be my son" (Rev 21:7). What a future! In the light and glory of this Saving hope I can live for Him through storm and calm, through sunshine and rain, for "the best is yet to be".

The man who was mugged

"A certain man ..... fell among thieves" Luke 10:30

Did Jesus relate an actual story? It is quite probable, for the Jericho road was wild and dangerous. Let us consider three things.

Violence. The age of Christ was an age of violence. The Pax Romana was only possible by military imposition. Where God does not rule Satan disturbs society. But all life has its dangers, hence the need for care, both personal and providential. Here a man is mugged; an ancient pastime of evil men, repeated with avid lust today.

Vacillation. Three men are involved in possible rescue. A priest, going home from Temple service ignored the victim - his religious duties were forgotten when he left the Holy City. A Levite does at least look; but vacillates. His own safety is paramount. But a Samaritan becomes a true "neighbour". His compassion was self-effacing, costly and kind. Indeed, a picture of Christ, who came along "the Jericho Road" to save us.

Virtue. No virtue is honourable if it is not practical. "By chance" - the sudden confrontation of necessity is a test of character. What we really are is demonstrated by our reaction to our brother's need.

Mugged by life, the toy of fate, the plaything of Satan? Fear not the "Good Samaritan" is near. He will tend your distressed condition, pour into your wounded life the wine of cleansing and the oil of comfort and lead you to rest and restoration.

The millennium

"They lived and reigned with Christ a thousand years"
Rev 20:1-10

After the Church Age is completed the earth will be "regenerated" (Matt 19:28) fulfilling the ancient promise of God that "the desert shall blossom as the rose" (Isa 35:1). The curse upon nature is going to be lifted by the power of the Cross of Christ. It is a period when:-

The Bible will be verified;
The devil will be nullified;
Messiah will be identified;
Earth will be pacified;
Light will be magnified
Nature will be fructified;
Life will be amplified
Martyrs will be vivified;
Israel will be occupied;
Nations will be multiplied;
Language will be unified;
The Church will be dignified;
Justice will be deified;
Grace will be satisfied;
GOD WILL BE GLORIFIED.

He who laid on nature a devouring curse will now lift it, for the atonement of Christ will not only bring pardon for sin but also freedom from the effects of sin. In glorious fact, wherever the tainting effect of sin is manifest throughout God's great universe, the precious blood of Jesus will cleanse, restore and revive. In our blessed Lord is universal and eternal victory over the sinful world, the flesh and the devil.

14 April

Prayer brings release

"Pour out your heart before Him" Ps 62:8

Modern psychology has re-discovered an ancient principle, that stress - the curse of our present-day hectic existence - can be banished by "pouring out our hearts", or in contemporary parlance, "talking out" the mind - obsessions that underlie much of our behaviour.

But why recline on the analyst's couch disburdening your inner self, when you can do this by prayer to God? Read Philippians 4:6,7, "Don't worry about anything, but in all your prayers ask God for what you need, always asking Him with a thankful heart. And God's peace, which is far beyond human understanding, will keep your hearts and minds safe in union with Christ Jesus" (Good News Bible).

What a promise! Our "hearts" (emotional disturbance) and our "minds" (mental doubts) preserved from attacks that would reduce us to moral and spiritual defeat. By prayer we are assured of a divine escort through life, and of an experience entrenched in divine protection; "kept as with a military guard, garrisoned by God" as the Greek term may be paraphrased. The city gates of our lives are guarded by angels, both ingress and egress are controlled. Thus our spiritual life is safe and secure.

15 April

Soft Pillow

"Let not the sun go down on your wrath" Eph 4:26

A Greek, philospher wrote:-

"Ne're suffer sleep thine eyes to close
Before thy mind hath run
O'er every act, and thought, and word
From dawn to set of sun;
For wrong take shame, but grateful feel
If just thy course hath been;
Such effort day by day renewed
Will ward thy soul from sin"

And such noble sentiments receive divine endorsement in our text quoted above. A goodnight exercise, it is spiritually safe, and psychologically sound. When we sleep not all of us is unconscious. This is confirmed by the dreams we have. Conscious thoughts occuping our fore-sleep minds, continue at deeper level. Feelings of anger retained as we become somnolent, will simmer through the night. Tomorrows advent may cause them to boil over. Our provocation may have been justified, but to retain such hurtful feelings only leads to bitterness and a tendency to recrimination.

In this state of mind Satan will seek to entangle us in vengeful fancies. Do not give him a platform to rocket you into wrathful, and unchristian, retaliation. Reflect and forgive. E'er that sinking sun goes down conquer the feelings of hurt, pardon the perpetrator of the things that upset you, and lay your head on the softest pillow. Jesus forgave you: you forgive them.

16 April

Fear God

"Fear God and keep His commandments: for this is the whole duty of man" Eccles 12:13

It took Solomon a lifetime to so conclude. But this should be our "beginning" not our end (Prov 1:7). All else leads to "vanity" - futility. But what is the fear of God?

First of all it is awareness of His presence. To feel that He is near us starts a train of effects. Secondly, to have a sense of awe of His Person. If God is so great, and I so small, at first it makes me feel so inferior. I am overawed. Thirdly, in spite of this holy dread, I am attracted to His Personality. My soul gravitates to Him as the source and sustainer of my being.

Fourthly, this longing to embrace Him leads to adoration of the perfection's of His character. This develops in me a disposition to avoid doing anything which might displease Him. To this end, fifthly, I joyfully accept His authority, confessing Him as Lord and master. Sixthly, I seek out His approval. And finally, accept His will, serving Him acceptably with reverence and godly fear" (Heb 12:28).

There are two important devotional activities that will help us to grow in the fear of God. The first is prayer. Earnest and effectual prayer will bring us into the presence of God. True prayer is more than words, it is a sacred tryst, a God-meeting experience. Then there is the Bible. In Psalm 19:9, it says, "the fear of the Lord is clean", where "fear of the Lord is a synonym for the Law of God as arousing in our hearts this holy feeling. So then, pray much, read God's word often, and so develop your spiritual life in the fear of God.

No second name

"There is none other name" Acts 4:12

Peter and John had just healed a hopeless paraplegic in the name of Jesus. When challenged by a pontifical hierarchy, the apostles replied, "There is no salvation by anyone else, nor even a second name under heaven appointed for us men and our salvation" (Moffatt) - that prime and powerful name is JESUS - God's salvation incarnate.

No alternative is given. Jesus is the exclusive Saviour of men. He Himself said: "No man cometh to the Father but by Me" (John 14:6). He is the only way to Heaven, He is the one Ark of Refuge, He is the unique deliverer from sin, from death, from hell.

No alternative is needed. He is the wholly sufficient Saviour. No one else, whether human or angelic, can provide the necessary remedy for a fallen race. "He is able to save to the uttermost them that come to God by Him" (Heb 7:25).

No alternative is possible. Man cannot save, for "None of them can by any means redeem his brother, nor give to God a ransom for him" (Psalm 49:7). Asking fellow-man to redeem us is like begging a bankrupt to pay our debts. We are all so indebted to the Almighty, we cannot be surety for any man. But Jesus can (Heb 7:22). He was sinless, and was able to lay down a perfect life for our redemption. As the spotless Lamb of God He was able to "take away the sin of the world" (John 1:29).

Mind set

"My heart is fixed, O God Ps 57:7

Words have their vogue-time. One modern term is "mind-set" - but the concept is not modern. David had it generations ago, but he called it a "heart-fix".

The idea is that of a mental attitude cemented into a mould, and fixed. Once set, it is hard to change.

This need not be a bad thing. Paul likens the doctrine he taught as "the mould into which you have let your nature be run" (Rom 6:17 - A S Way). A renewed mind will take the mould of God's will (Rom 12:2) and become heart-set after the spiritual pattern laid down in Scripture.

There are some basic issues that all Christians may take as abiding facts on which we need never change our minds. One, God is real. I may not be able to prove it logically, but I feel it, and believe it. Two, the Bible is true. As the infallible Word of God (2 Tim 3:16) it admits of no contradiction. It is authoritative, life-changing and behaviour correcting. I can trust it: it will never let me down. Three "Jesus lives and loves me still". The personality of our Lord shines clear to those who believe in Him. Thus, like the Psalmist, because my heart is fixed I can sing and praise the Lord through all life's circumstances.

Sound sleep

"I will both lay me down in peace, and sleep" Ps 4:8

The air was full of rumour, the day fraught with peril, furious assault imminent - but David slept. As soon as his head touched the pillow, he was away.

His darling, spoilt son, the handsome Absalom, had revolted and taken the kingdom. David's mind must have been in a turmoil, his emotions rampant - but he lay down and fell immediately into deep, restoring sleep.

Used to the softest bed, he now lies on a hard, military mattress, possibly under the open sky. He was weary with a forced march, with tired and aching limbs - but he laid himself down in peace and sank into a profound sleep.

His secret? Not some soporific drug, but the best of all tranquillisers, FAITH. It seemed that he had lost all, but he trusted God, and in that trust found true tranquillity. His retreat was not from fear, but from consideration of the safety of innocent people and the security of the Holy City. His spiritual resources were in the Lord who had called him and sustained Him: His will would be done.

Bishop Quail could not sleep. His mind was disturbed by His many tasks. He watched and prayed into the late hours. Then he felt God speak to him: "You go to sleep, Quail, I'll take over now". In faith he put his care in God's hands, retired to his bed - and fell asleep. God gives rest.

20 April

Facing life

"Life (cannot) separate us from the love of God" Rom 8:38

Life rushes on us with a battlion of woes, distress, demands and pressures. But in the love of God, revealed and extended to us through Jesus Christ our Lord and Saviour, we may find strength comfort, and spiritual sinew.

But what a battle it can become! Look at the relationships we are bound to sustain. Contact with fellow-man can be abrasive, domestic harmony elusive, civic demands obtrusive. Then list the responsibilities of life. The burden of toil as we maintain survival for us and ours "by the sweat of our brow", the dictates of humanity toward the needs of others, the demands of society in the struggles of civilised co-existence. And the risks. Disease and death lurk round every corner, dangers loom each passing day, time's ruthless pressures bear often heavily upon us, dangers oft beset us. Risk seems the essence of existence; we often feel ourselves the sport of fate with the dice heavily weighted against us.

Phew! What a baleful lot is ours! But wait. The Lord here says we can face life with all its pressures - and win. The love of God will refresh us so that we can overcome all that existence can throw against us. Nay more, we can be super-conquerors gaining from the conflict great rewards. Our spiritual life is enhanced by our tribulation, our enjoyment of God increased by our stand for righteousness, our heavenly hopes enriched by our distresses. We cannot help but win.

Facing death

"Nor death ... separate us from the Love of God" Rom 8:38

Death is our enemy: its remorseless hand ever stretched forth to grasp more and more hapless victims. The grave is never satisfied (Prov 30:16).

From the dawn of life the shadow of death can darken our days. "Death" is a non-word: we banish it from conversation in a desperate effort to exile it from our thoughts. But its inevitable finality fills us with dread. We struggle for survival, but we know that sooner or later it will overtake us. Death is stronger than time, no money can buy it off, no virtue enable us to escape it.

How then can we conquer this indomitable foe? We don't have to - Christ has conquered the monster for us. "It is Christ that died" ... He had bearded the lion in his den, He has driven out the very cause of death - sin - He has robbed the devil of his fearsome grip on mortal minds. Nay, more, "He is risen again". He has demonstrated that "the valley of the shadow of death" (Ps 23:4) is not a cul-de-sac, it is a through-way.

We who believe in Jesus can face death without fear. The resurrection of Christ has shown that personality persists beyond the grave; that complete man is forever body, soul and spirit; that the power of eternal life conquers death and the grave: "O death, where is thy string? O grave where is thy victory? ... Thanks be to God, which giveth us the victory through our Lord Jesus Christ" (1 Cor 15:55,56). In Him death is dead.

22 April

The paraclete

"Another Comforter" John 14:16

The Greek word parakletos is used of the Holy Spirit only in John's Gospel, and that four times (14:16, 26, 15:26, 16:7). It describes one who answers a call.

It has been variously translated by scholars and commentators. But no one term can absorb all that this word can mean.

The Holy Spirit is the Comforter - He fortifies with encouragement, boosts spiritual morale. He is Counsellor, giving advice on how to live and act, guiding into paths of truth and holiness. Our Companion - with us as a friend, and in us as a force. His presence cheers killing loneliness, His fellowship sustains. "Two are better than one" (Ecc 4:9).

The Holy Spirit is an Advocate presenting to us the claims of Christ (even as Christ our heavenly Advocate presents our claims before God 1 John 2:1). He speaks on His behalf to wean us from the world and woo us to Jesus. He is our Intercessor, helping in our prayer-life, inspiring us to present heart-felt petitions to God. Our joint suppli- cations, presented according to God's will and mind, find a response from Him who searches our hearts (Rom 8:27).

As we "call" on the Holy Spirit, He responds. He is there to enthuse us with His fire, impel us with His wind, secure us with His seal, inspire us with His foretaste of things to come and empower us with His dynamic. The same Spirit that "moved over the waters" (Gen 1:2) in creativity is ready to move in our lives to reproduce in us the likeness of God, give us holy dominance and strengthen us to do His will.

The baby sleeps

"The Babe lying in a manger" Luke 2:7,12,16

Luther's charming hymn for children unites simplicity with sublemity thus: "Away in a manger
No crib for a bed,
The little Lord Jesus
Laid down His sweet head;
The stars in the bright sky
Looked down where He lay,
The little Lord Jesus
Asleep on the hay"

Miracle. A virgin given birth to a man child. Impossible? It happened as the Bible said it would (Isa 7:14, Matt 1:23).

Manger. It is mentioned three times that the new-born baby was placed in the feeding - trough of the animals - he who was destined to feed the world with the Bread of Life. Is this a kind of parable?

Mystery. Shepherds may well wonder, wise men may well worship - here is "God manifest in the flesh" (1 Tim 3:16). What a mind boggling fact!

"Our God contracted to a span,
Incomprehensible made man."

So sang Charles Wesley, and so sing in unison all those who accept this Jesus as their Saviour. We wonder at the wisdom and grace of God; worship the risen and glorified Lord. He became part of the human race to redeem it. Bearing our sins on the Cross - extending pardon to guilty sinners. He died to save, he lives to keep. Blessed Babe: blessed Jesus: blessed Lord!

24 April

Wednesday's child

"Man is born unto trouble" Job 5:7

The nursery-rhyme says: "Wednesday's child is full of woe", but to link ill fortune with one's natal day is a fallacy. Trouble is neither attracted or averted by our birthday. Don't let horoscopes be "horrorscopes".

Eliphaz was nearer the mark when he proposed; "man is born unto trouble as the sparks fly upward". We may well ask, "But who lit the fire that made the sparks?"

The beginnings of history give us the answer. The first man, Adam, broke faith with His Maker, and plunged the human race into misery. His condemnation - "In the sweat of thy face shalt thou eat bread" (Gen 3:19). The legacy of our original parent is heavy, wearisome and irksome toil. Don't we know it!

But a merciful God did not leave things there. At that very same primeval judgement-seat He promised a deliverer from the curse. A "seed" would be born who would crush the serpent's power, though at the expense of being "bruised". This "seed" eventually came, "which is Christ" (Gal 3:16). After 4,000 years the Son of God came to save the world from its distress. He is called "the second man" in contrast to Adam "the first man" (1 Cor 15:47), for in Him God was to inaugurate a new race, "the people of God", born-again Christians. As "the last-Adam" he would undo all the evil the first Adam did. By Him sins are forgiven, by Him the curse is cancelled, by Him the universe will be totally purged of evil. Then will "trouble" banish for ever for those who love God.

Ball - boys

"There is a lad here" John 6:9

Where would tennis be without ball-boys (not forgetting ball-girls)? They return straying balls, for the service of the players, and make themselves generally useful.

The Bible gives us three examples of useful lads. When blind Samson groped for the supporting pillars of Dagon's temple, it was a lad that guided his hand. The supreme exertion of strength that brought the house down depended on the service of a boy (Judges 16:26).

Next we must note the lad who ran to collect Jonathan's arrow, thus innocently helping to warn David of the imminent danger of his life. Lads may perform meaningful service to great men - even when they don't know it. An obedient youth may perform a noble ministry (1 Sam 20:35)

And what of the time when Jesus would feed a multitude. The apostolic pantry was bare, but a lad offered his neatly packed lunch. Andrew felt this to be woefully insufficient. However, in the hands of Jesus the "five barley loaves and two small fishes" were multiplied to feed a multitude. The meagre snack of bread was as sufficient as a bakery, the few tiny fish provided as gigantic a dish as a whale (John 6:9).

The great need the small. An ocean liner is berthed by the nudge of tugs, so little things will always have a place in the work of spreading the Gospel. Nothing is small with God, He can even take "things which are not" (1 Cor 1:28), nameless nonentities, to fulfil His will. Small is useful when dedicated to Him.

26 April

One sweet maid

"A little maid ..... waited on Naaman's wife" 2 Kings 5:2

Naaman was "a mighty man of valour", but the military uniform covered bandaged limbs rotting with leprosy. His days were numbered, physicians were unable to cure him.

But a captive Israeli girl was maid to his wife. Note three things about her. First, in spite of her slave-condition, she held on to her childlike faith. She must have been well-taught by her parents to be so imbrued with a religious attitude. Slavery could not kill it.

Secondly, she was proud of her upbringing and people. The prophet Elisha was to her a national hero. Stories of his mighty deeds in God filled her young mind. To her, they were not just tales, they were realities.

Thirdly, she boldly testified of the great things God had done in Israel, and affirmed that - the desperate case of the stricken commander could be relieved by the prophet. Her faith was simple, but based on reality.

Desperation drives people to "grasp at a straw". The maids testimony was relayed to Naaman. The king bade him go. This "straw" of testimony was his raft of deliverance.

So do not hesitate to speak out your spiritual convictions. Jesus said, "Ye shall be witnesses unto Me" (Acts 1:8). True ministry is the expression of personal experiences of the power and presence of the Lord. Just a word from one sweet maid, proved a seed that bore a mighty harvest. Great Naaman, led to a great deliverance by a simple testimony of a young girl.

The devil doesn't like me

"Your adversary the devil" 1 Peter 5:8

They tell me the devil is dead, that he was slain at the Cross. It seems to me that, as Mark Twain (whose obituary was prematurely printed) said: "the report is greatly exaggerated". Satan certainly received a violent rebuff as a presage of his impending doom, and has had his claws clipped, but he still has evil ways, he still hurls forth his fiery darts, he still labours to impede the work of God, and harass the Lord's people.

Wrestling against him is not shadow-boxing, striving to overthrow his demonic doctrines is not an easy intellectual skirmish, opposing his evil sorties into social and spiritual spheres is no cake-walk - but in Christ we are sure to win as we act under the direction of the Captain of our salvation, "the Lord of Hosts", heaven's armies (Living Bible).

The Lord's strategy is wise, His tactics are wonderful. By Him we can wage a successful crusade against all evil. In Him we have powerful munitions ample supplies and complete weaponry, both offensive and defensive, to assure victory. He is not only our arsenal, He is also our morale booster. His Cross is our banner, His resurrection-life imparts stamina. His promised reward is our anticipation and ambition. We cannot but triumph over our formidable foe. "Salvation is of the Lord", victory is ours, "we are more than conquerors through Him that loved us" (Rom 8:37). Fight on! We are sure to win the day.

Ezra's watergate

"The street that was before the watergate" Neh 8:1

Ezra had his "watergate". But it had not the slanderous connotations of the White House "watergate" that caused the resignation of the U.S.A., President Nixon. Here was excitement, joy, and spiritual fervour.

It seemed that the whole population of Jerusalem were packed into that pedestrian precinct to listen to the reading the Scriptures, so long lost to their thirsty souls. They stood for hours - men, women and children - to imbibe what had long been denied them. God's word.

Ezra, with twelve other priests, stood on a specially erected platform, and read from God's law "distinctly", interpreting the sense in understandable terms. An atmosphere of reverence prevailed as Ezra prayed and unfolded the sacred scroll. As a nation in captivity they had long been denied the sacred Book, but now nationhood is restored the Scriptures take their rightful place.

But they do not merely listen, they obey; and the glorious "Festival of Booths" follows - this "watergate" became a watershed of blessing, the foundation of a new era of spiritual life. So the Bible can be to us a fountain of well being, a foundation of Christian living and a fund of rich blessings. The secret of personal and national happiness is in the scripture of truth.

Royal walkabout

"Jesus went ..... much people followed" *Mark 5:24*

Royal "walkabouts" are not new - Jesus engaged in them. Mind you, he mostly walked. When he wanted transport, He borrowed a donkey. But this brought him into close contact with the people. He was often within arms length of the folk that gathered around Him.

And that pleased Him, for He loved people. He often made a walk a kind of pedestrian pulpit, stopping occasionally to press a point, or sit to address a burgeoning throng, sometimes numbering thousands.

But other things could happen. In this case a distraught father sought help for his dying daughter. The crowd pressed in upon the apostolic group, impeding their progress. Even more, a timid afflicted woman, weakened with internal haemorrhage, pushed near enough to touch the fringe of His "Tallith" (the Jewish prayer-shawl). She was instantly healed as virtue flowed from Him to her. Faith had drawn power from the fountain of life. She believed that Jesus could heal her, she behaved with courage and hope, she received the divine boon of deliverance.

Our Lord went on to raise Jairus' daughter from death. Blessed walkabout! And He's just the same today. "Jesus is passing this way" reach out and touch Him, it can mean the greatest experience of your life.

Holy barbeque

"A fire of coals ..... Come and dine" John 21:9,12

A charcoal fire on the beach: what a sight for tired hungry men! But this is what happened on the shore of Galilee as the disciples landed their catch - their Miraculous catch.

What a vision of the risen Christ, and what lessons for us to learn! First, the risen Jesus was still concerned about the physical well-being of His servants. Tired men need food and rest. Jesus provides it - then proceeds to give them spiritual sustenance.

Then again, it was a miraculous provision. Where did Jesus get the fish from? And the charcoal? And the fire? One thing is clear the Christ exalted to immortal life is not above serving His servants.

And note that this "other-worldly" Christ is very down to earth. The boundary between the sacred and the secular does not exist with Him. Fried fish or fervent converse are both part of His ministry to His troubled disciples.

Should our concept of ministry be adjusted? Anything that enhances the lives of others is ministry. There may be varieties of service, there are planes of usefulness, there cannot but be varieties of contribution - but the God that can be served by "a cup of cold water" cannot but accept our kind of ministry, be it material or majestic - all are acceptable if presented with humility and sincerity.

Unloading bay

"Cast thy burden upon the Lord" Ps 55:22

Life is loaded with luggage. Some burdens are placed upon us by necessity others by choice. There is a load of 'musts' that often weighs us down, plus a load of 'maybes' that love accepts. We carry them lightly on our good days but sometimes we are 'in heaviness through manifold temptations' (1 Pet 1:6). There are times when weariness wins.

But God has provided an unloading base - 'Casting all your care on Him, for He careth for you'. The same Greek word is used when 'they cast their garments' on the ass to make a seat for Jesus at His triumphal entry into Jerusalem (Mark 11:7). May we from this suggest the thought 'saddle God with your troubles'?

How do we do this? By believing prayer. Take your carking cares, role them into a bundle, and cast them upon God. Commit all your anxieties to the Lord in 'prayer and supplications, with thanksgiving' (Phil 4:6-7). The result is peace. God's peace will garrison us from the invasion of morbid imaginations and destructive doubts. We will thus be sustained. God will either remove our burdens or strengthen us to bear them.

In any case the bane of crushing life - loads will be countered and cleared by the boon of divine grace. In prayer we find a place of unloading. We kneel in weakness, we rise 'like giants refreshed with new wine'.

2 May

Count your blessings

"Great fishes, a hundred and fifty and three" John 21:11

God's blessings, each a precious thought of the all-bountiful Creator, 'are more in number than the sand' (Ps 139:17-18). No computer can compass them, but it is well for us to count what benefits we receive and recognise. It teaches us how great and how good is God's loving care for us His children. They counted the fish; so we should:

'Count your blessings, name them one by one
Then it will surprise you what The Lord has done'.

Look at this catch: it was a miracle. A long dreary night of unsuccess ended with a net-breaking load at the word of the risen Lord. They were doing their job as fisherman - and God came in to bless their efforts. Have you ever thought of the miraculous in the common place? Our daily occupations can become enriched with divine blessing as we serve the Lord with gladness.

Again how foreseeing are the ways of providence! Jesus had asked His disciples to tarry for the Spirit - ten days without work with its essential benefits. But the 'great fishes', sold on the market, would go far toward providing their physical needs.

And in all this, Jesus proved that He was the same today as yesterday, with the implied assurance that He is the same forever (Heb 13:8). A miraculous supply of fish lead to Peter's conversion (Luke 5:4-11), now a further miraculous supply leads to his confirmation. Jesus is immutable.

Teddy-bear disturbs universe

"For none of us liveth to himself" Romans 14:7

A scientist once made a startling declaration: 'according to physicists, the most distant star is disturbed every time my son throws his teddy bear out of his pram'. Though we have no instruments capable of measuring such incalculable minutae, this is theoretically correct.

We used to tease a plump little bathing girl with the concept that when she plunged into the sea the water rose all over the world. Was it unkind? But she took it well: it was funny but factual. There is a deep sense in which our deeds and words though they may seem to fleet into thin air yet in fact are still exerting influence. This leads me to three perennial points.

First friend you matter. The universe cannot do without you. In greater or lesser degree your presence is felt. Secondly, you have influence. Your impact on society may be apparently minimal, but it is there, you exert influence.

Thirdly, you are part of God's creation and therefore needed. God did not make you to be a useless appendage. You are here by His will, therefore you are important.

As part of human society we can only fulfil ourselves if we seek God's ways and follow them. As the sun fulfils its destiny by shining, as the birds by singing, so we by walking with God in humility and reverence find that happiness that is inherent to our very being.

4 May

Moral poison

"The poison of asps" Romans 3:13

Many people infect themselves with moral poison that destroys their peace, undermines their health and vitiates their relationships. Sin bites like an adder, corrupting our ways. Let us consider 3 malignant mind-sets:-

1. <u>Worry</u> - The burden of anxiety can kill. God never intended us to carry tomorrow's load. His 'manna' of spiritual strength is a daily supply. We must slay our needless fears by faith,

> 'WORRY is an old man with bended head,
> carrying a load of feathers which he thinks are lead'.
> 'FAITH is a damsel bright and fair,
> who carries her load as if it were air'.
> To which moral generation do you belong?

2. <u>Resentment</u> - Daughter of jealousy, granddaughter of pride, this projeny of Satan is a drastic moral septic. It controls our attitudes, directs our actions and even discolours our words. Only love, like some divine pesticide, can kill it. But do so before it ruins your peace of mind, your physical well being and your relationships.

3. <u>Bad temper</u> - 'Love is not touchy' says one translation of 1 Cor.13:13, it is not readily provoked to heated response to injuries done or insults directed. We have enough trouble with our fickle, feeble and feckless existence to have to do with such venom. Let God-given grace inoculate us.

Fuel for the fire

"The wood offering...to burn upon the altar of the Lord" Nehemiah 10:34

In the newly organised Temple service certain sons of Israel were allotted the task of preparing wood for the altar fire. This holy ordinance of sacrifice depended upon two things - fire and fuel. We provide the wood; God supplies the fire. The simple fact is that the service of the sanctuary requires both.

Wood - the earthly part. God has ordained that His service must require the human element. The fuel of the altar is earthly, representing the endeavour of man. The dual aspect of worship calls for human consecration 'Here I am, send me'.

Fire - the heavenly part. No sacrifice can exist without fire, that is God's contribution. In all divine service human talent is not enough; cleverness, keenness, agility or ability can by no means make an acceptable sacrifice. No oblation is sufficient without immolation. At the altar, heaven and earth meet - that is the purpose. It is at this sacred spot that God and man unite. Calvary - summary of all sacrifice - is the trysting place where my soul makes rendezvous with my maker and redeemer.

But we must supply the wood the self-sacrifice, of willing service, of humble obedience, of living faith. Upon such an altar the fire of God falls,

'Let me not seek to be a clod,
make me thy fuel, flame of God' (Amy Carmichael).

6 May

Beware muggers

"A certain man went down" Luke 10:30-37

There is a sense in which we all tread the Jericho road. We have turned our back on the city of blessing, we lurch toward the city of curse.

Gravity - 'Down'. Human nature gravitates toward earthly sensual and devilish things. The pull is too great to resist. The result 'all have sinned, and come short of the glory of God' Rom 3:23. The downward trend is seen in all men.

Momentum - As life goes on this motion becomes more powerful, accelerating to the point of certain catastrophe, moral and spiritual ruin. Life is a perpetual hazard.

Rescue - A priest passes by but religion offers no help to the battered victim of the violent muggers. A Levite approaches - but the trained 'do gooder' does no good here. Works can not save. Then comes a Samaritan - an alien to this victim. Here are no racial or social obligations, but compassion leaps barriers of custom and culture.

This outsider considers not his own safety. He administers first aid, mounts the half dead victim on his own donkey and sees the wounded man to the safety of an inn. He does not inquire into his past, he treats the present need and guarantees his future care.

What a picture of a human being mugged by sin, mocked by religion, mistreated by unmerciful contemporaries but marvellously helped by a merciful Saviour. In the noblest way Jesus is the Good Samaritan to our souls.

Doorkeeper

"A doorkeeper in the house of my God" Ps 84:10

There is more pleasure in serving God in the smallest of situations, than major positions and privilege in unholy projects.

The fringe-benefits of working for God in the humblest capacity, give more soul-satisfaction than indulging to the full "in the tents of the wicked". To stand at Gods' doorstep is itself an enriching experience. The occasional glimpse of the glory within, the snatch of some celestial refrain, perhaps the distant view of the divine presence - all these are far better than to be wholly involved in the raucous, outrageous and lascivious orgies of carnal celebrations.

And the doorkeeper has the privilege of introducing the invited people to the holy conventions of the guests of the Almighty. What a joy to let others into the holy banqueting hall! Clad in the Master's uniform the sanctified janitor expresses a warm welcome thus:

> "Come sinners to the Gospel feast,
> For everyone be Jesus' guest;
> Ye need not one be left behind
> For God has bidden all mankind".

"Doorkeeper". If being a lowly servant of Jesus brings such blessed benefits, what will it be when the door opens wide to the janitor himself? "Come in, thou blessed of the Lord, wherefore standest thou without."

8 May

Power

"Anointed ..with the Holy Ghost and with power" Acts 10:38

There are many forms of power. There is physical power, whereby voluntary muscular contraction can promote activity; water-power, whereby a stream can turn a mill-wheel; chemical power that creates explosions; electrical power that involves effects of vision, music, working machines; steam power that combines fire and water to drive engines; the power of gravitation that attracts and accelerates falling bodies; wind-power that drives sailing ships; solar-energy that produces heat and light.

But beyond all these is the power of the Holy Spirit. This divine energy can produce miracles, inspire utterance, stir the conscience, open the mind to heavenly facts, strengthen failing morale, induce super-human endeavour, produce supernatural courage; in fact supply all the dynamics that makes Christian living and service successful.

And add to this the moral virtues that spring from the in filling of the Holy Spirit - love that conquers all, joy that bubbles up with exuberant delight, peace that tranquillises the soul, long-suffering that makes us patient and kind, gentleness that makes us tender and considerate, goodness that exudes beautiful charity, faithfulness that produces reliability, meekness that reflects the temperament of Jesus, self-control that conquers a reluctant ego.

And this power is ours, said Jesus, when the Holy Spirit dominates our lives (Acts 1:8).

Beyond the blue

"Received up into glory" 1 Tim 3:16

Have you ever wondered what is beyond the blue of our sky? Astronomers speak of the twinkling stars that embellish outer space as being billions upon billions of light-years away - almost incalculable distances: But the term "glory" implies that beyond the compass of the universe as we know it, is the dwelling of God where Jesus now is.

It is called "glory" because it is bright with God's presence; it is called "glory" because there is nothing better; it is called "glory" because there, is the throne of God. From here the vast expanses of infinity find there fulcrum point. Around this centre of ultimate density circles galaxies known and unknown. This is the control-tower of all creation. God is Sovereign; throughout all creation His will directs and prevails.

And He chose this earth - a speck of cosmic dust - as an arena to perfect His eternal purposes. On this minute planet Jesus lived and died to save sinful mankind. This power of His atoning blood penetrates all time and space. wherever sin has tainted, the precious blood can cleanse.

And Jesus dwells in that "glory" preparing a place for His saints who one day will join Him in happy splendour to perfectly share His love, His wisdom, His grace.

Has the past a future?

"God requireth that which is past" Eccles 3:15

Yes, for yesterday is the father of today. We cannot escape what has been, anymore than we can foretell what will be, and yet in the deepest sense, today is the vital issue! The past is not forgotten by God, but in Christ it can be forgiven. What is to be, is known to God, but mercifully hidden from us. We live today.

Yet God requires the past, that is why there will be a final judgement. For those who believe in Jesus, "There is therefore now no condemnation", but there must be an assessment of our works, "for we must all appear before the judgement-seat of Christ; that every one may receive the things done in his body, according to that he hath done whether it be good or bad" (2 Cor 5:10). And so:-

> "The deeds we do,
> The words we say
> Into still air they seem to fleet
> We count them past,
> But they shall last
> In the dread judgement they and
> we shall meet".

And so Christians though we are, it behoves us so to live, that in the day when we stand before our Lord we shall not be ashamed but receive His, "well done, thou good and faithful servant, ... enter thou into the joy of thy Lord" (Matt 25:21).

Just a cipher

"I am nothing ... " said Paul 1 Cor 13:2

"Until a man is nothing, God can make nothing out of him", wrote Martin Luther. And this is true. The other day I was reading a book by the great theologian Karl Barth. I turned to the end of the slender paper-back and saw a list of over 40 volumes, written about the work and the worth of this outstanding scholar. I burst into laughter. The thought entered my head, "No one has ever written a book about me, or is ever likely to. Outside a small circle of friends and acquaintances I am a nonentity". Then I remembered the words of Paul - "God hath chosen .... things which are not" (1 Cor 1:28), that is men of no account. The apostle said of his ministry, "As unknown, and yet well known" (2 Cor 6:9). He was a notorious nonentity: glorious paradox.

But this is so opposite to contemporary philosophy. "Realise yourself! release yourself" they cry. "You have divine potential, you are somebody, discover yourself". Paul's conception of himself was, that apart from the grace of God he was nothing. And all his endeavour was to be what God wanted him to be. He did not want to be a big man, but to be a little man with a big God.

12 May

The buck stops here

"Repentance toward God" Acts 20:21

It is an old game, "passing the buck". Adam started it. When charged with folly by God He replied, "the woman thou gavest me ..." Then Eve followed suit and blamed her defection on the devil (Gen 3:11-13). but you can't fool God. The only way to obtain His forgiveness and His favour is to repent. This calls for admission of our fault with the implication of regret and the desire to reform.

In reply, the Lord stripped them of their fig-leaf covering - their flimsy excuse and clothed them in the hides of slain animals, whose blood was shed in atoning sacrifice.

"The buck stops here!" exclaimed President Truman, implying that his own desk would be the final repository of all complaints submitted to him. He would not pass on or neglect to deal with such matters: they would be dealt with.

If you make a mistake, if you sin, the only way that God will overlook and forgive is "If we confess our sins, He is faithful and just to forgive us our sins, and to cleanse us from all unrighteousness" (1 John 1:9). The "buck" of sin cannot get past the cleansing blood.

No dogmatism please!

"Consider what I say" 2 Tim 2:7

Paul, except on vital occasions and on desperate issues, was never dogmatic. He would call on God to witness his words, he would appeal to sane judgement and sensitive conscience, but rarely was rigid in his statements, except when he has a word from the Lord.

A free thinker is a safe thinker. We are to be a voice not an echo; a solid and sober rationalist, not a mere reflection of other minds. Personal judgement, plus personal responsibility, are tokens of maturity.

As for me, I'll receive a "may", I'll even consider a "should" but God help me, I'll never submit to a "must". I'm open to be persuaded, but not brainwashed. I came into my Pentecostal experience free, I'll stay free. I refuse to be a rubber-stamp to others' decisions. Don't try to blinker me with claims of divine revelation, or baffle me with "visions of the night", or hype me up with stories of wonders past or present. The Bible tells me to be sober and diligent. I will accept its admonition. My decisions will be free personal and sincere.

So shall I be no man's mental slave, or padlocked to any school of thought. The Bible shall be my guide and mentor. It is the truth of God "and the truth shall make you free".

14 May

The "plus" element

Dr W Sangster, in one of his books, speaks of the experience of the Holy Spirit as a "plus" element. But should not this be the normal experience of every Christian? However, it is clear that the indwelling of the Holy Spirit can add to life energies and expressions that are supernormal - true "plus" elements. Let us note some definite divine "pluses".

"The Holy Ghost and wisdom" (Acts 6:3). Here is wisdom to guide us, a necessary element of service. When we don't know what to do, the Spirit comes to our aid.

"The Holy Ghost and power" (Acts 10:38). When dire occasion demands, the Holy Spirit can give us extra thrust like a "souped-up" engine. As wind comes in zephyrs or cyclones, so the Spirit of God is manifested in various degrees of energy.

"The Holy Ghost and joy" (Acts 13:52) A pioneer church robbed of its founders, finds overwhelming joy and victory in the Spirit's presence. The apostles are forced to depart, but the Holy Spirit remains to inspire and to bless.

"The Holy Ghost and of faith" (Acts 11:24) A Spirit-controlled believer can enjoy a faith, boosted by God, that can rise to extraordinary heights and add new dimensions to one's witness and worship.

Holy barbecue

Did you think that barbecues were a modern idea? You are wrong. This type of open-air grill is as ancient as the New Testament. In John 21 we see on the shore of Galilee's lake "a fire of coals ... and fish laid thereon, and bread" (verse 9). And the Host that had prepared this tasty snack of grilled trout and crusty rolls was none other than the risen Christ. What a charming revelation of our Saviour!

<u>God cares for our physical well-being</u>. We talk of "souls" as if a person were made of parts; the Lord looks upon us as an integral unity. He caters for the whole man (Ps 103:3).

<u>Jesus fed them before he taught them</u>. How wise! How considerate! A night's fishing had given them a ragging appetite. Jesus satisfies the pangs of hunger, so that, free from physical distraction they could listen without discomfort to His word.

<u>Food and fellowship may go together</u>. What a breakfast on the beach this was! There may be a place for fasting as a spiritual discipline, but there is also a place for feasting as a time of fellowship. When the Holy Spirit came, "they did eat their meat with gladness and singleness of heart" (Acts 2:46). Jesus showed that such impromptu "feasts of charity" may not only feed our bodies but enrich our souls - especially when He is the Host.

16 May

Donkey therapy

A County Health Authority is prescribing taking a donkey for a walk as a form of alternative medicine for heart disease, stress and depression. The psychological benefits of stroking pets are said to be proved by the experience of sufferers who find relief in close association with domestic animals.

But is this "donkey therapy" new. Balaam, the Old Testament prophet, was cured of obstinacy by a talking donkey. However we explain this hectic episode, it remains that donkey therapy, in this case, worked: "the dumb ass speaking with man's voice, forbade the madness of the prophet" (2 Peter 2:15, 16).

Three lessons may be learned from this. First, God can use "dumb" creatures to speak His will. What would your dog say to you if it could articulate its feelings? Secondly, greed can make us deaf to ethical and religious promptings. The glint of gold blinded Balaam to his prophetic integrity. Thirdly, if we try to side-step the direction of divine providence we take a lethal path (Numbers 2:2-25, 31:8). Balaam, frustrated by prophetic surge from gaining a colossal fee for cursing Israel, prompts Midian to vitiate Israel's morality by seduction. He died in the eventual judgement. Who was the biggest ass, the four-legged or the two-legged?

Up the garden path

Genesis 3:1-24

The first person to be "led up the garden path" was Eve; the garden was Eden, a veritable paradise; the leader was Satan.

First, he excited her curiosity - a talking animal; then he posed a disturbing question, "Hath God said?" She seemed unsure of the terms of divine reference. Then he cajoled her, implying that God didn't really mean it. Rather, the Lord was hiding the real feast. To eat the forbidden fruit would be enlightening. Greater still, "ye shall be as gods".

This is New Age Philosophy - the deification of man. It is simply the modern mask of devilish deceit. It is Satan leading feckless humans once more "up the garden path". The end is worse than mere disappointment it is moral delusion and eventual destruction.

Eve lost all she hoped to gain, and (together with her husband) passed on to the human race a legacy of woe. We still suffer from this primeval error.

God in His mercy, clothed their naked bodies with warm pelts. Were these provided from animals who died to give them covering? May we not here see a forecast of God's way of restoring lost-mankind to fellowship with Him - a blood - sacrifice, fulfilled in the Cross of Christ? Disbelief in god's word brought ruin, but faith in His promise of life brings restoration. Why not trust Him?

18 May

Taken for granted

"Forget not all His benefits" *Ps 103:2*

How bountiful has God been in His dealings with us! His benefits are loaded on us daily. And yet for all that, fickle human nature tends to forget. Does "familiarity breed contempt" even in spiritual things? Can God's goodness be forgotten? Sadly, it is so.

This is the import of the Book of Deuteronomy. Exodus gave us the law plainly and fully. Deuteronomy covers much of the same ground, but with additional touches that make the narrative both lively and more informative. One phrase occurs again and again - "Thou shalt remember". And such remembrance of God's blessing must always be with gratitude. Without His "benefits" we would never have been saved, without His "benefit" we would never survive. His providence is our preservation.

To remember God's goodness causes us to "Bless the Lord, O my soul" - a deep sense of thanksgiving to a God whose love "passes all understanding" and whose grace bestows you us "joy unspeakable and full of glory": Never take God for granted. Ever give Him praise and glory.

19 May

Middle C

The central point of music is Middle C. In a written score, below this central note is the bass clef, above it is the treble clef. Around this note all musical forms are arranged. One could call Middle C the master-key of staff notation, the decisive element of disciplined sound.

This reminds me of another middle C. When Jesus was crucified two others perished with Him - "on either side one and Jesus in the midst" - the middle cross. Here is the central point of the Christian faith: the focal scene of all its doctrine, the fulcrum of spiritual power, the hinge of salvation experience. On the hill of Golgotha, the Cross of Jesus proved a division of destinies between the malefactors who died with Him. On His right was the one who received Him as Saviour and Lord, on his left was the one who rejected Him; the one was blessed with "Paradise", the other endured the penalty of divine judgement and so with us today. "To them that received Him to them gave He the power to become sons of God" (John 1:12). The middle **C**ross is still the place to which we may look unto Him and be saved.

20 May

The third heaven

"Caught up to the third heaven" 2 Cor 12:2

So there are more heavens than one! A remarkable fact is hidden in the Hebrew word for "heaven" BERESHITH, a dual noun (Gen 1:1). There are two created heavens, the atmospheric heaven, where the birds fly, and the astronomic, where the stars shine. Beyond these is the uncreated heaven, the angelic heaven, the abode of those celestial beings that surround the throne of God. The superb place where the supreme being - GOD - dwells. "Our Father, which art in Heaven" (Matt 6:9).

What a place this must be! It is called Paradise, a region of beauty and delight. It is perfection where God's eternal plans are consummated and human hopes and aspirations fulfilled: happiness achieved, holiness realised. It was also pivotal. Just as the earth circulates around the sun, so the vast host of galaxies have their gravitational centre in this third heaven - the Throne of God, the pivot of the Universe.

And each of these had a means of contact. The first heaven is a place of natural vision - optics; the second a place of extended vision by optical instruments; the third by spiritual vision - faith. This inner vision, "the eyes of the heart" sees the invisible realities of this timeless abode.

Second-hand experience

"Sayest thou this thing of thyself" John 18:34

Pilate asked Jesus, "Art thou the King of the Jews?" It was a key question. On it could depend a verdict. Our Lord's response was pointed. It was a matter of <u>reputation</u> or <u>revelation</u>. The knowledge of the Procurator came from others, rumours remarkable filled the air. But rumours, however authenticated, are only second-hand experience. We can only know who Jesus is by revelation of God. So our Lord told Peter: "Flesh" and blood have not revealed it unto thee, but my Father which is in heaven" (Matt 16:17).

It is not enough to hear of spiritual things, we need to feel them, to believe them, to know them: Another's revelation is not sufficient, only a personal experience will suffice, a revelation that forces the confession, "Thou art the Christ". This living knowledge of the Son of God does something for us.

God spoke of Himself under the Old Covenant as, "the God of Abraham, and the God of Isaac, and the God of Jacob" (Ex 3:15) - a God of each individual, a personal God; each patriarch could say "My God". And truly that is the only God that matters, a first-hand God of my salvation.

Crumbling milestones

"He ..... hath forgotten that he was purged from his old sins" 2 Peter 1:9

Have you ever walked along on old highway and been attracted to the ancient milestones? Their directive terms are often scarcely legible, how many miles from here to there, hard to decipher. The years have taken their toll. Information so helpful to generations of travellers is now of little help.

Do moral milestones exist? Are those experiences and evidences of spiritual progress now a forgotten past? They once marked the pace of our progress. Certain red-letter days were counted as celebrations of holy advance.

But, according to Peter, our condition can so deteriorate that we only dimly observe the past and but weakly anticipate the future. Our range of faith and hope shrinks as we become morally myopic. All this is a symptom of spiritual decadence. A diagnosis of the divine doctor shows that we are sick.

The remedy? A daily dose of holy remembrance - in other terms a look at the milestone of life, that tells us where we have come from and informs us how far we have to go to complete our pilgrimage. We look back at the Cross, we look forward to the coming. The first Advent was the Epiphany of Grace the second Advent will be the Epiphany of Glory. Let not passing years erode the milestone message of salvation past and salvation to come.

23 May

Maranatha

"Maranatha, the Lord Cometh" 1 Cor 16:22

Under pressure from the Japanese invasion in December 1941, General Douglas MacArthur was ordered to leave the Philippines. "I shall return", he said, which phrase became a symbol of hope to the Filipinos. It was hailed as a rallying cry for millions. MacArthur kept his promise, landing on the beach at Leyle Island in the Philippines during October 1944 to drive out the invaders and free the nation:

The rallying-cry of the Early Church was "MARANATHA", Christ's promise to come back expressed in Aramaic, His mother-tongue.

The Second Advent is necessary to complete the First Advent. Jesus became part of the human race to redeem our souls from sin and its consequences, He is coming again to complete His work in redeeming our bodies. With souls cleansed and bodies glorified we shall then be fit to enjoy the eternal glory.

This climatic event is a source of comfort to the bereaved, a challenge to the believer, and a consecrating influence to the born-again believer. We know not the time, but we know the Saviour. He will keep His word: the Second Advent is as sure in time as the First Advent, so sure that we must be ready to meet Him at the moment He elects to return.

24 May

The tears of God

"Jesus wept" John 11:35

The word "wept" here means to shed tears. It was not the wailing of a hired mourner, it was the sympathetic expression of deep-felt love. These tears were the tears of God. We read three times that Jesus wept.

Weeping for individuals. Our text shows the link of Jesus with our personal sorrows. He came with comfort to bereft sisters, Martha and Mary. They thought He had forsaken them, but He proved the depth of His compassion by restoring to their fond embrace the brother so painfully taken from them.

Weeping for a nation (Luke 19:41). As Jesus looked over Jerusalem He burst into tears there were two reasons for His grief: one was that within a generation the city would be reduced to rubble. In prophetic vision He saw this - and wept. The other reason, was that God had visited them in His Son - and they did not know it, they were deaf to His pleas and blind to His person.

Weeping for a world. "With strong crying and tears" (Heb 5:7), sweating blood in anguish of soul, our Lord took upon Him the load of our sins. The agony was so intense He despaired of reaching the Cross, but an angel gave Him strength, and he endured to the end in His saving mission. His tears were not in vain; He was able to cry, "It is finished", hence forward to be "the Saviour of all men, specially of those that believe" (1 Tim 4:10). Have you ever wept over the salvation of others?

Spiritual Osmosis

Botanists tell us that some plants take in water and nutrients by a process called OSMOSIS. Surrounding moisture is absorbed through an extremely thin membrane into the metabolic system. The plant is nourished imperceptibly.

So with us. We cannot live spiritually without the Word of God as preserved for us in Holy Scripture; but there is more than one way of imbibing this essential water of life.

Ear culture. "Who hath believed our report", said Isaiah (ch 53:1). Paul takes this up and states that "faith cometh by hearing, and hearing by the Word of God" (Rom 10:17). Soul-food can enter by EAR-GATE (to follow John Bunyan).

Eye culture "Blessed is he that readeth .... the words of this prophecy" (Rev 1:3). This applies to the whole Bible. This Book of God is "milk" to the spiritual babe, and "meat" to the mature saint (1 Pet 2:2, Heb 5:12-14). But we must not only ingest it by reading, we must digest it by meditation.

Heart culture. This is where osmosis becomes a spiritual process. Paul exhorted Timothy not only to meditate on "these things, (that is Biblical instruction) but also to "give thyself wholly to them" (1 Tim 4:15) literally "be in ... them". Thus surrounded by "the water of the word" we may absorb it until it becomes part of our very being, a lasting source of soul-nurture, a permanent ministry of the culture of our inner man, the Word in us, part of us, our very life.

26 May

Does the past have a future?

(a brief dissertation on tradition)

"Our fathers have told us ....." Ps 44:1, 78:3

What a struggle there is between the old and the new, between the "trads" and the "rads". Jesus put traditionalism into words: "the old is better" (Luke 5:39); Luke reminds us that Athens was obsessed with "some new thing" (Acts 17:21). What part should the past play in our lives?

First of all, without a past there would be no future. Tradition passes on forms of words, style, of living, custom of attitude, ideas and ideals. Much of this is still good, but the ideological iconoclast comes to smash cherished ways with the hammer of neology. But what does he put in their place? Often a plastic monstrosity fills the site of a once stately and beautiful edifice.

Secondly, nevertheless, it is the present that counts, we may learn much from the antiquarians, we may anticipate much from the neologians, but NOW is NOW; a unique moment calls for unique treatment. Draw from the past, dream into the future, but definitely minister to present needs with present wisdom. "The present truth" (2 Pet 1:12) is the Gospel for now; its essence may be ancient, but its expression must be modern.

Thirdly, is not the best attitude and action to embrace and expound "things new and old" (Matt 13:52)? The best of the old and the best of the new can enrich the now situation with grace and growth.

Keep your hair on, Samson

"No razor shall come on his head" Judges 13:5

A Nazarite was a person specially devoted to God, either for a period or perpetually. Samson was so separated unto God from birth. What prospects lay before this remarkable child! He would "begin to deliver Israel".

One particular sign of Nazaritehood was that the hair was not to be cut. Samson eventually had "seven locks of his head" (Judges 16:13), long flowing hair. Were they curly or braided?

Two remarkable things developed. First, an idiosyncratic personality that made him both judge and joker. Secondly, an inspirational power that endowed him with supernatural physical strength.

His fore-ordained ministry was mapped by his inordinate love of women, his God-given ministry curtailed by his yielding to the love-pressure of a Philistine female - Delilah. Through fear of her overlords and force of bribery she wheedled the secret of Samson's strength out of him, and then lulled him to sleep and cut off his hair. The sign of the covenant so defamed, Samson became weak, was over-powered and enslaved.

He did recover to slay his enemies, but in the process destroyed himself. Far better to have exercised self-discipline and kept his vows. Who knows what might have happened if Samson had been true?

The boat-people

"Eight people were saved by water" 1 Peter 3:20

Thousands of Vietnamese people attempted to escape their vicious system and cruel rulers by leaving their country by boat. They were called "The Boat People" - a pitiful band of refugees whose distress forced them to dangerous expedients to obtain relief and a liveable life.

I am reminded of another band of "boat people", eight in all, ferried by a gigantic house-boat into a new world. But Noah and family were different from these Vietnamese.

First, they were directed by God to build a refuge - THE ARK. The world was putrid with evil, "the Judge of all the earth" decided to wipe it out. But Noah pleased God, who planned to begin and fill a new world with a new race built on this man of faith (Heb 11:7). He was enabled to create a majestic vessel, and supernaturally stock it with creature-life for a new world.

Secondly, they were protected by God in the waters of judgement - "saved by water" - the FLOOD. For one whole year this company of man and beast was preserved to emerge into a cleansed world.

Thirdly, they were settled by God on a new earth to replenish it and establish a family of God.

What a picture of our salvation Jesus is the Ark of Deliverance into which we enter and are saved from the judgement of sinners to emerge into "new heavens and a new earth" (2 Peter 3:11-13).

29 May

One thing lacking

We once took visiting friends to see London's sights. Crossing Horse Guards Parade we entered the Mall to find ourselves spectators of a massive parade - kerb-lined soldiers on both sides became the backdrop to an extensive march of mounted cavalry, military bands melodiously beat the rhythm of beclad infantry. Then the royal carriages. Had we inadvertently stumbled on Royal Birthday celebrations?

We soon found the answer. The royal coaches were empty. The Queen was missing. It was a full dress rehearsal of the real thing the following week. The one thing essential to make it an authentic parade was absent: it was only a show, a practice, a rehearsal.

Life is like that. It can be a glorious procession of joy and meaningful progress if Christ is there as king of our hearts, but without Him we are incomplete. Read Matthew 19:16-22 and consider.

Back-seat driver

"Thine ears shall hear a word behind thee saying, "This is the way, walk ye in it"." Isaiah 30:21

One of the greatest nuisances of the road is a backseat driver whose comments - sometimes acid - seek to direct, but only succeed to distract, the man (or woman) at the wheel. They are a pest. May their tribe perish! Is this a vain hope?

But in our text we have a voice from behind different and welcome. It is not the natural voice of a passenger, which is a menace, it is the spiritual voice of one who accompanies us through life as we trust and obey. This miracle-voice of God, speaking through conscience, Scripture, or inward urge of the Holy spirit will guide our onward way. "Walk before Me, and be thou perfect", said the Lord to Abram (Genesis 17:1). The complete life is one that issues from the God who watches our ways. When He says "Turn left", we are safe, when He says "Turn right", we do well, when He says "Pause", we do well to listen; when He says "Go on" we progress safely.

A surprise visit

"Behold I come quickly" *Rev 22:7,12,20*

Jesus, in the last chapter of the Bible states that His Second Advent will be a speedy event, a visit as startling and as sudden as a lightning-flash. It will be a surprise visit.

In these texts His coming is looked at from three aspects. First, READINESS. To be found keeping His word in sincere and humble obedience will be a rich blessing - the accolade of loyalty. Secondly REWARD. He will return with this hands laden with benefits, honours and praise for the devoted servant who fulfils his will. Thirdly, REACTION. When Jesus said, "surely, I come quickly", John's heart responds, "Amen, come as soon as you like". He longed for the Day and so should we "love His appearing", for therein is the realisation of our hope, the rewarding of our faith and the rapture of our love (2 Tim 4:7).

But our attitude? If you knew that the Lord would come tonight, how many adjustments to your life would you make? Let us so live in readiness for transit to Glory, with "our loins girt for action" and our lamps lit for motion (Luke 12:35) ready at all times for the upward call.

1 June

Thinking ahead

"O... that they would consider their latter end" Duet 32:29

Wisdom always looks ahead: ultimates direct their immediates. A pleasant path is no gain if it is going in the wrong direction. The "latter end," even if the road to it is rough, is best if it leads to life, to success, to prosperity. In many spheres of life, the one who looks and plans ahead comes off best, in chess, the skilful player anticipates his opponents moves and plots his own response. From opening gambit to closing checkmate he knows where he is going. And so in "the game of life". The sensible person denies a present ease to assure a future career. The provident saver will seek to bank a little week by week in order to acquire a secure shelter against "a rainy day". He does not rely on a fortuitous "nest-egg", he meets the uncertainties of life with the wise use of present opportunity and preparation.

Greater still, the person of understanding will consider the ultimate of being, this life will end: but there is the promise of a "life to come" in the scriptures, which are able to make us "wise unto salvation through faith which is in Christ Jesus" (2 Tim 3:15).

Integrity

The first principle of the kingdom of God is "righteousness" Rom 14:17

In practical terms, this implies integrity, that is moral rectitude. A good man is straight, nay, more, he cannot be bent. Integrity, moral worth, is the basis of "peace". Such peace, acquired by a living faith in the Lord, is threefold.

First, is embraces oneness with God, a result of that renewed relationship with the Almighty, we call JUSTIFICATION.

Secondly, that calm serenity of mind that issues from reconciliation with God and man.

Thirdly, that pacifying influence upon people and situations that makes a Christian an oasis of tranquillity in a desert of trouble.

And then comes "joy". Not the feeling induced by prosperity, success or sensual gratification, but a deep underlying sense that "all is well with my soul". It is both exhilarating and lasting, a joy that no earthly calamity can destroy. Read Habakkuk 3:17,18, and notice the "Although" and "yet".

All this becomes possible "by the Holy Spirit". His indwelling power can help us lead a life of integrity, tranquillity and holy hilarity.

Get with it Elijah!

"And I, even I only, am left" 1 Kings 19:10

What a pitiful plaint, where is the valiant prophet of Carmel, facing 400 idolatrous priests? But, "Elias was a man subject to like passions as we are" (James 5:17), given to changes of emotion, fire on the mount, fear under the Juniper.

Prophets, by their very nature, are often highly emotional. This gives fervour to their temperament, but can add bathos to their experience. But, whether prophet or plain Mr. Man, we must not depend entirely on how we feel. Our reliance on "the word of the Lord" must be our stay. Faith can be above feelings.

But was Elijah really with it? How could he have missed the 7,000 "all the knees which have not bowed down to Baal" (1 Kings 19:18)? He was a loner, and the trouble with loners is that when their self-confidence is undermined they have no support. "I am no better than my fathers," he cried. Did he think he was? We should never consider ourselves lone victors or victims, "knowing that the same afflictions are accomplished in your brethren that are in the world" (1 Peter 5:9). We need each other: we are never alone.

Preach what you practice

The Gospel according to Luke is a record, "Of all that Jesus began both to do and teach". (Acts 1:1).

How revealing these words, especially for preachers! First, they teach us that our sermons must be tested: in the laboratory of experience before we impose them on a congregation. We should say it because we live it. And yet how often our utterances fly far beyond our achievements.

Secondly, Jesus "BOTH" did and taught. Doctrine and deeds should match: we need, as heralds of God, to display both. The word of God we believe should be incarnated into living example. A preacher should witness both by life and lip of the grace and mercy of God. Experience is great - "O taste and see that the Lord is good" (Psalm 34:8), but the scriptures are greater - "a more sure word" (2 Peter 1:19), that reveals and regulates our lives. Experience needs the word to explain it, excite it and endue it with endurance.

Thirdly, both our doings and our sayings will be enabled and enhanced by faith. "I believed, and therefore have I spoken" (2 Cor 4:13). We must not only believe, we must also behave as we present the word of God to men.

Isaac

Exodus 3:15

This patriarch had the misfortune to be placed between two outstanding men - his pioneer father, Abraham, and his colourful son, Jacob.

He was pampered as an only son; he was passive in temperament; pacific in nature; pliable in conduct; placid almost to the point of indifference. He became prosperous, and seemed to settle down to a premature senility. Purblind and pleasure-bent on roasted venison, he almost committed the grave error of bestowing the covenant blessing on the wrong son, the profane Esau, a man who had not a spark of spirituality in him.

His alert wife, Rebecca, took matters into her own hands, and saw that (unfortunately by deceit) her beloved Jacob received what God had originally intended he should have.

Does the Lord approve of such unethical methods? No, but in His infinite wisdom He superimposed His will on the situation.

But to give Isaac his due, he did pass on the torch of witness, in spite of his weakness, to Jacob, the son that God had elected to inherit the birthright of the Covenant.

This mad, mad world

Man is called "homosapiens"- I can accept the "homo", but I'm not sure about the "Sapiens." Solomon is nearer the mark when he says of mankind, "madness is in their heart while they live" (Eccles 9:3).

The same Hebrew word is used of "chariots (that) rage in the streets" (Nahum 2:3) - literally, "the chariots are mad." So mankind, left to itself, rushes through life at runagate speed, hurtling down the "broad-way that leadeth to destruction". (Matt 7:13).

Civilisation has only served to accelerate the gravitation to hell. Faster transport, more immediate information, get-rich-quick ideas - all proliferate in a world that is driving furiously to its own demise.

Will man never learn! Some seek to steady the mad stampede, but in vain. With the frenzy of the Gadarine maniac we plunge on regardless. But Jesus entered this man's pathetic situation, cast out the devils of lunacy and restored the unfortunate man. He was found "sitting, and clothed, and in his right mind." Jesus alone can resolve the madness of sin to the sanity of grace.

Debunking

An Americanism denoting the exposure of false claims to goodness or moral character. It is a counter to that sentimental exaggeration of the lives of acclaimed people of honour or fame. Rose-coloured spectacles are exchanged for probing x-rays, skeletons-in-the-cupboard are ruthlessly dragged out, past peccadilloes exhumed - to the (often intentional) destruction of reputations.

Such character-assassination has often behind it personal vindictiveness or political strategy. The troubles that most people have, are incidental failures they'd like to forget. To dig them up can become a shameful exercise.

And what of the debunkers? Are they acting from sincere desire for truth, or merely seeking to gain some pecuniary or political advantage? It may inflate some people's ego to deflate another's good name.

"If Thou, Lord, shouldest mark iniquities, O Lord, who shall stand?" (Ps 130:3,4). But he who knows us best is willing to bury our past in "the depths of the sea" (Micah 7:19), sunk without trace. "There is forgiveness with Thee" - should not there be forgiveness with us. Keep the dustbin lid on.

Immortality

The question came like a bolt form the blue: "Uncle, what is immortality?" She was only three years old. How can you explain such a concept to a tiny-tot! I did my best. But, to come to the nub, what really is immortality.

Etymologically it means no death, eternal life. But there is more to it than that, both philosophically and spiritually.

It speaks of the incursion of eternity into time. Man is not a transient being, God intended him to live forever. Although a time-fraught creature, he has auguries of greater things to come, for God "has also set eternity in the hearts of men" (Eccles 3:11). It is when this innate instinct is stopped by sin that human life loses its value in the minds of depraved mortals. Hence the low regard for life evidenced in the brutal murders, senseless time-killing pleasures and drug-degrading addictions.

But it also distinguishes between life and mere existence. God created man "a living soul", but the quintessence of his life was in its fellowship with his Maker. Left to himself man merely vegetates, linked with the Lord of life he is vitalised into "life more abundant". And this is possible by faith in Jesus, who died and rose to save us.

9 June

Steady up Jehu!

As a charioteer, Jehu was noted for his "furious" driving. He was an early version of "motorway madness" (2 Kings 9:20), full of the fury of speed. His impetuosity seemed to permeate his whole being. He was a fanatic charioteer.

The trouble with a fanatic is that he often goes too far. He rightly despatched vicious Jezebel, but need he have assassinated a whole royal household? He plotted to obliterate Baalism, but need he have been so bloodthirsty? God did not approve, and later visited judgement on the house of Jehu (Hosea 1:4).

A fanatic is often carried by passion beyond the bounds of principle. Jehu, who sought to purge Israel of irreligion, used irreligious means. And when his zeal for this necessary cleansing had subsided, he pursued with the same speed to political expedience, and "departed not from the sins of Jeroboam". His greatness was flawed. Had he moderated and directed his zeal into channels of wisdom and the knowledge of God, he could have established a dynasty of spiritual force and equity.

Watch him, Eve, he's a devil

The first lady in the new world was naive. How was she to know the serpent was a devil incarnate? But she had a native wisdom, and should have considered the tempter's character.

Don't kid yourself, Eve, that you can deal independently with Satan. He's been at it longer than you, he's as subtle as a serpent, he wants to catch you on your own. You should have stuck by Adam's side, You became vulnerable.

Look how the devil manoeuvred. First, he cast doubt on God's word, playing on your inexperience. Then he leads you, with satanic logic, from one point to another. A past-master in psychology, he questions not only the wisdom of God, but also his integrity. He then appeals to human "self-hood." "Step up to egoistic greatness," he insinuates, "you will be your own deity".

Eve swallowed it down "hook, line and sinker," truly hooked by a wise tactician. The Fall was imminent.

The devil comes to us seeking to destroy our faith. "Look out for him," said Peter, "resist him steadfastly." "He will flee" from us. God will give us grace to ground him, faith to frustrate him.

11 June

Traffic jam

Nahum's words are intriguing. "The chariots shall be with flaming torches.... shall rage in the streets. They shall jostle one against another in the broad-ways. They shall seem like torches, they shall run like lightning's" 2:3,4.

Some see in this a sign of the approaching Second Advent. It certainly seems a picture (though not really a prophecy) of modern life: traffic-jammed streets, speed-packed motorways, glaring headlights. We know it too well. But let us comment on the up-to-date principle.

<u>The age of mechanism</u>. From the wheel to the whirlpool of modern technology, the inventive capacity of man has led us into an era of mechanism. More and more mechanical wonders have edged out the manual tasks to be taken over by patented automatons. Is man therefore free? No, he is now slave of his own creation.

<u>The era of speed</u>. Faster and faster man must go. Will he ever exceed the speed of light and disappear? Everything must be "instant". Time is saved, but not savoured. In the daily rush most people leave behind the basic realities of peace and contentment.

<u>The extension of self</u>. The hurry to get there is an attempt to pack more into the day than it can take. We seek to extend our capability, yet only succeed in reducing our capacity for real living. "Be still and know" (Ps 46:10).

12 June

"What happened next ....?"

In a Television feature, "A Question of Sport", a clip of an event is cut off short, and the panel is challenged to guess what followed.

The words of Jesus, "After that ...." (Acts 1:8 AV - the translation I prefer) seems to take up the same concept - "what happened next?" When the epic scene is unfolded we see surprising activities swamping Jerusalem with miracle power and mighty preaching.

"Ignorant and unlearned men" (Acts 4:13), that is illiterate laymen, disclose a theology and a transforming energy unknown to this city since the departure of the prophet of Nazareth or was in fact a continuation of His ministry, He "began to do and teach" (Acts 1:1), His disciples continued. "What happened next" was implied in what had happened before - a wonderful surprise.

And all this was implicit in that word, "ye shall receive power", or to give the Greek original DYNAMIS. This divine dynamic, this holy potential, was released on that wonderful Day of Pentecost, and has been the pattern and longing of the Church ever since. But we can know it for ourselves. When the Holy Spirit comes, "what happens next" is revival.

Shock tactics

The method of massive attack with terrific momentum - blitzkrieg so successfully used by Hitler, is not as original as historians may suggest. The devil used it long ago.

Look at Job, some 3,000+ years ago. Satan came in like a raging torrent, a tornado of terror. In one fell swoop he deprived this godly man of his cattle, then his flocks, then his herd of camels. In a single day he was reduced from prosperity to penury. Worst of all, a hurricane sweeps away his whole family, seven sons and three daughters (Job 1:1-22).

What does he do? He worships God, and voices his indomitable faith in words that have been the stay of battered saints ever since: "the Lord gave, and the Lord hath taken away; blessed be the name of the Lord!"

Trust in God accepts His denials as well as His donations. Faith is victory: "Amidst the wildest storms he stands undaunted, nor quails before the loudest thunder shock."

The secret: "When the enemy shall come in like a flood; the Spirit of the Lord shall lift up a standard against him" (Isa 59:19). The Lord who permits temptation also empowers us to resist it.

14 June

Overflow

Jesus spoke of eternal life as a fountain springing up within the heart of the believer (John 4:14), giving satisfaction for soul-thirst. He later spoke about "rivers of living water" flowing out of that same inner self in service to others (John 7:32,33).

The difference is that the "well" can be self-contained but the river is an overflow. Regeneration is a wonderfully thirst quenching event, but the Renewing of the Holy Spirit (Titus 3:5,6), begins an outflow that is inexhaustible - "rivers" flowing with refreshing energy from US to OTHERS.

But what an amazing thing Jesus stated. What starts as a "drink" becomes "rivers" - many channels .... outreach a saving mission. In Ezekiel 47 healing waters issue from the throne of God, widening and deepening as they flow. But there are not tributaries, the supply all-sufficient. As we advance in his ways the water of the Spirit deepens we are swept off our feet - "Waters to swim in."

15 June

A bit missing

"One thing thou lackest," said Jesus to the rich young ruler (Mark 10:21). But it was vital. He felt it - or he would not have asked, he failed to provide it, for it seemed too drastic. But what value is wealth if it cannot purchase life!

What did he lack? Love - for how could he be rich while his neighbours languished in wretched poverty? Faith for he did not believe he could exist if he obeyed Jesus. He valued his soul in cash.

I was once an enthusiastic photographer - amateur, but avid. I remember dashing out to snap a tidal sunset: it was beautiful. Other scenes of people and places followed. But I became dubious. The 36-exposure film seemed to have no end. I opened my camera up in the dark. My groping hands could find no film. It was a rank and foolish oversight. All the science that produced by SLR camera was wasted, all my expensive equipment futile, all my enthusiasm vain. My machine lacked one thing - the sensitive roll of celluloid - the FILM.

And so our lives. Moral living is not enough, civilised behaviour will avail little, good works, pious thoughts fall short: the essential is Faith in Jesus.

Dumb does

Dogs were meant to bark. Their vocal cords, their protective instinct, their added training all fits them for their place in life as guardians of their owner's interests and safety. If they fail to bark in danger's hour, they are more than a loss, they are a menace.

Isaiah thus describes the leaders of Israel. "They eat, they slumber, but they don't bark" (Isa 56:9-11). They fail in their protective duty.

Is not the Church of today guilty of "barkless" ministry? Cowered by fear, cosseted by favour, covetous of status, chary of criticism, her leaders (most, but not all) are dumb. When did they last speak out on the grave moral issues of our time? They fear to speak of sexual deviation, of contemporaneous lust for money, of vital national issues lest they be called "political," or offend the humanist lobby.

There was a time when nonconformity was dubbed, "the conscience of the nation." Biblical principles were not merely tacitly accepted, they were boldly advocated. The Sabbath commended, alcoholic excesses frowned on, adultery condemned, penal remedies advocated. God give us back our barking prelates, our "watch-dog" preachers, our hounds of safety.

17 June

Underinflated?

The RAC remarks that millions of motorists are risking accidents because of underinflated tyres, such tyres are strained by an increase in the flexing of the side wall, thus generating heat. This may push tyres to breaking point, and produce blow outs, especially at speed. So the experts!

It is interesting to note that the term "pneumatic" (used of air-filled tyres) is derived form the Greek word <u>pneuma</u>, the very word used for "Spirit?" So a Spirit-filled believer is not only charismatic, he is also pneumatic-filled with the wind of God.

And what applies to the natural may also point to the spiritual. We need to be continually "filled with the Spirit" (Eph 5:18) if we are to safely and successfully negotiate the highway to Heaven.

Are you underinflated? Then, by seeking God in prayer and supplication, humbly seek a renewed spiritual inflatus that will refit us for our journey homewards. Check your pressure: bring it up to the needful standard - and travel safely.

18 June

"God be in my head...."

"God be in my head, and in my understanding," opens an anonymous chant from a Sacrum Primer: old but full of meaning.

Some votaries of "science, falsely so called" (1 Tim 6:20) consider faith in God as irrational, an emotional flight from reality. But the Christian religion is far from that. It has to do with a God who calls us to "reason together" (Isa 1:18), demands us to "love the Lord thy God ..... with all thy mind" (Mark 12:30), and calls upon our total surrender to Him as "our reasonable service" (Rom 12:1).

The fact is that faith in God is not irrational (cf Acts 26:8) but itself is the very foundation of understanding "by faith we understand....," asserts (Heb. 11:3). Surprisingly, the Greek word for "understand" is <u>noeõ</u>, used of "rational reflection or inner contemplation" and is akin to our modern <u>nous</u>, equalling "common sense, gumption" (Concise Oxford English Dictionary). Faith and reason do not cancel out each other, they are complementary.

God gave us brains to use. Our rational powers, devoted to God, are loaded with good. May our prayer ever be, "Take my intellect and use every power as Thou shalt choose."

19 June

The generation gap

The coming of the Holy Spirit was intended (among other things) to bridge "the generation gap." In the blessing of Pentecost "young men see visions, old men dream dreams" (Acts 2:17). Each section of society receives divine inspiration, yet retains its characteristic temperament. "Vision" and "dream" are forms of ministry, complementary and cohesive.

In the spirit - controlled church there is no "generation gap", children, young men and fathers coalesce to form "one body" (1 John 2:12 - 14).

YESTERDAY'S MEN, "fathers", are sometimes derided as "old fogies", but their experience is valuable as both guide and spur. The heroes of faith in (Heb 11) are yesterday's men whose lives "yet speaketh" (Heb 11:4). We need them all.

TODAY'S MEN, strong physically, virile spiritually, alert mentally - "you young men". How we should value them! Upon them falls the main burden of active service. Consecrated youth is a vital asset to the church: "Daniel's Band" (Daniel 1:8) of consecrated purpose can, achieve great things.

TOMORROW'S MEN - "Little children". How we need to cherish our younger end. One generation hence, they will be valiant youth; two generations hence, the solid maturity of experience. We need all ages: When God is in charge we all (young and not so young) grow together in God.

Is beauty only skin deep?

It all depends on what you regard as beautiful. There is pleasure in physical perfection - in a woman attractive, in a man admirable. But the Bible speaks of a moral beauty called "the beauty of holiness" (Ps 96:9), that makes our worship acceptable to God.

The exhortation of Peter (a married apostle - 1 Cor 9:5), is not to major on "outward adorning" - elaborate coiffure, expensive jewellery, fashionable dress - but rather on "the <u>hidden</u> man of the heart, the ornament of a weak and quiet spirit". (1 Peter 3:3,4). As Paul expressed it, modesty and restraint become "women professing godliness" (1 Tim 2:9,10). Neatness - yes! Tidiness - yes! Attractiveness - yes! But eye-catching sex-traps - no!

<u>Character is more than clothing</u>, yet our attire says much about our attitude to life, to others, to God. Clothing was originally intended as <u>protection,</u> but it actually becomes a <u>projection</u> of our personality. What do people see when they regard our attire? A trumped - up society - seeking person, a fashion - bound slave, or a believer who, without losing taste or trimness, displays a pleasing aspect. Our inner poise can be reflected in our outward appearance.

21 June

Hiding from God

The first reaction of a guilty conscience was to hide oneself from God (Gen 3:10). After a pitiful "cover-up" of leaves, Adam and Eve hid behind bushes. But the voice of God searched them out.

The fact that you cannot hide from God is emphasised in (Ps 139). David flinches from the all-knowingness of the Lord, but finds he cannot escape the omniscience of the Almighty. He flees-up to heaven, down to hell, beyond the horizon, behind the pall of dark night, but God is there. Happily, on fuller deliberation of the majestic yet merciful greatness of God, he yields and welcomes the all - searching gaze that reveals his sin, but also leads him "on the way everlasting".

But why do we still weave our pitiful aprons of fig - leaves? Good works, pious thoughts, religious rites - none of these of themselves cover our guilt and shame. God himself has shown as the way of atonement. A blood - sacrifice provides "coats of skins" - durable, protective, but also symbolic of the truth of redeeming grace that provides a covering through our Lord Jesus Christ, whose death made it possible for our sin to be covered and for us to be "accepted in the Beloved".

22 June

The big bang

One scientific theory of creation is that a sudden spasmodic release of intense explosive force sent out electro-magnetic energies that, throughout countless aeons of time, evolved the universe as we now know it, with its vast ever-expanding space-time continuum of limitless duration and depth.

Genesis chapter one, verse one, puts it simpler: "In the beginning God created the heavens and the earth". Here we see power and phenomena proceeding from a PERSON, God. Science may not approve, but faith apprehends (Heb 11:3). Whether by explosive clatter or express command, "He spake, and it was done" (Ps 33:6-9). The universe still "stand fast", upheld "by the word of His power" (Heb 1:3).

Whether the universe began with a "bang" or not, we know that it will end with a bang, when "the heavens shall pass away with a great noise, and the elements shall melt with fervent heat" (2 Peter 3:10).

Those whose interests and activities are fixed on material things will lose all in "the Day of God," but to us who believe in Jesus as our Saviour and "look for new heavens and a new earth" this epochal event will be a matter of eternal life and felicity.

23 June

All roads lead to Rome

The Romans were superb engineers. Their vast empire was intersected by a network of highways with Rome city as the centre. The body politic and geographic was linked together like a great arterial system with "the Eternal City" as the heart. Even the distances were measured by so many stadia from Rome. All roads led to this central point. From this focal point law and authority extended to the uttermost reaches, to this central point came the resources and riches of the Empire. Rome was the hub of civilisation.

It was said of Jesus, "and they came to Him from every quarter" (Mark 1:45). It still applies. Christ Jesus is the very heart of Christianity, the life-bond, the focal point, the service-hub of His Kingdom. All vital blessings emerge from Him, all true worship flows to Him. Together with His Father and the Holy Spirit, they form the very epicentre of spiritual life and power. "In Him dwelleth all the fullness of the Godhead bodily" (Col 2:9).

And as all roads lead to Rome, so from any point in this habitable world may a seeking soul come to Christ. All ages, all classes, all tribes and nations, rich and poor, literate and illiterate, nobles and nonentities may find in Him their way to life. And the wonder of it all is, that He will receive us when we come to Him, for "whosoever shall call on the name of the Lord shall be saved" (Rom 10:13).

24 June

Man of many friends

The appendage to the Epistle to the Romans (chapter 16) is a catalogue of saints, a vivid compendium of friends of Paul who had settled in that hub of civilisation: As the centre of the Gentile world, Paul was drawn to Rome like a magnet. Had things gone his way it would have become a centre from which he would have reached and influenced many people. Paul's own plans became lost in a wider and bigger divine scheme.

While imprisoned there he received a fresh and fuller vision of Christ which he embalmed in his writings from there - the Prison Epistles, Ephesians, Philippians, Colossians and Philemon. These became a legacy of Christology from which the Church has benefited ever since.

What a revealing list of Christian workers and friends! Let us note three remarkable things.

First, out of some thirty names, ten are women. Paul was not the misogynist he is sometimes reputed to be. He recognised women's ministry and appreciated the important role that female believers played in the work of God.

Secondly, Paul was a man of courtesy and grace, ever ready to acknowledge the blessings he had received via other servants of Christ. He never forgot a favour.

Thirdly, with all his powerful and almost forbidding intellect, he showed himself a man of deep sympathies and emotional maturity. "He that hath friends must show himself friendly" (Prov 18:24). Paul did this and built up an army of joyful fellowship, a man of many friends.

25 June

Thanks a million

I don't know who coined this pregnant phrase, but it aptly expresses the kind of thanks we should give to God, "who giveth us richly all things to enjoy" (1 Tim 6:17). "Thanks a million," because there are a million things to bless God for. We do this for many usual and obvious benefits, but how often do we thank Him for the unusual, yet important and essential gifts?

Think of the gift of "life and breath" (Acts 17:25) the essential conditions of existence. What of the law of gravity that keeps our feet on the ground, the fact of friction, without which we would slide along without interruption; atomic structure and molecular arrangements that give form, shape and consistency to matter?

Isn't it a good thing that some substances are harder than others? What would we cut the butter with if all things were equally sharp? Then look at capillary attraction that makes the rising of sap possible, plus other effects; of transpiration that enables trees to give off their cooling and vivifying vapours!

We could go on od infinitum, but beyond the realm of nature is the realm of supernature. And here our thanks are more than figures can tell. God's "unspeakable gifts" (2 Cor 9:15) call for uncountable thanks. We owe everything to God. To acknowledge this in word and worship is not merely our duty, to those who love the Lord, it is our endless delight.

26 June

This world of books

John the Apostle closed his Gospel with a remarkable statement. He writes "many others things which Jesus did, the which, if they should be written every one, I suppose not even the world itself could not contain the books" (John 21:25).

This may seem like hyperbole, but the author of the fourth Gospel was writing under a divine anointing. Who dare question the integrity of the Spirit of God?

It is evident that the life of Jesus was so intense. Though restricted to thirty-three years of time, the ministry of our Lord was instinct with eternity.

Again, the words of Jesus were pregnant with inspiration, keys to fuller meanings, capable of infinite expansion, the essence of truth, of wisdom, of beauty.

Grammar cannot contain God, nor literature the limitless attributes and activities of the Almighty. When Paul went to Paradise he heard things beyond the power of rhetoric to describe or lexicon to explain. So with Jesus: He is bigger than words. Etymology cannot embrace Him, or characters contain Him. No human vocabulary can define Him or ultimately express all that He is and does. He is infinite.

To bind Him in a book is hopeless. No computer can contain Him or library imprison Him in words. The Lord is Great. He will forever meet our expanding needs and satisfy the desires of His vast and varied people.

27 June

"If I were you"

Job chided his visiting "friends" with caustic sarcasm. "If your soul were in my souls stead, I could heap up words against you" (Job 16:4), words that reflect the oft-quoted sentiment, "if I were you". Let us note:-

First, as we differ so much from each other, no one can fully understand his neighbour. This should moderate our judgements and temper our criticisms. The answer is! "You are not me. If you were, you would feel as I do".

Secondly, it is so easy to develop a mind - set that reduces all issues to the limits of our prejudices. Many have their own moral tape-measure which is hardly long enough to stretch to some cases. We should know our own defective slide-rule of conduct sufficiently to appreciate that some cases are beyond our ken, but not beyond our kindness.

Thirdly, at least we should seek to "love our neighbour as thyself" (Lev 19:18), and extend to others the care, concern and consideration that we bestow on ourselves, and mitigate our judgements of others as we often do for our own behaviour.

Alas, we often set standards for neighbours that we fail to observe ourselves. But if we excuse our own behaviour on principle, we should extend moderation to allies in practice.

"If I love you" - should not become a shooting of arrows of judgement, but an extension of moral first-aid to wounded spirits. "Miserable friends" can thus become mollifying fellows".

Individuality

"I called him alone," said God of Abraham (Isa 51:2), thus emphasising a basic dealing of God with man. He made us unique individuals, we are alone in our creation, He calls us to Himself as individuals, we are alone in our vocation; He judges us as individuals, we are alone in responsibility.

Ezekiel is the great exponent of personal onus for behaviour. "The soul that sinneth, it shall die" (Ezek 18:4). God repudiated the idea that the father ate bitter grapes that set the children's teeth on edge. Although we are influenced by many pressures and forces, yet final decision is ours.

This should be obvious. The power to choose is mine. In the basic sense I have a free will. I may not always be able to exercise it, but it is there. And freewill implies responsibility, which also implies moral judgement. My innate sense of right and wrong - conscience - is not only my mentor, it is my judge and my executioner (Rom 2:15).

Man is not a mindless automaton, he is free to choose, made in the image of God. This is where salvation comes in. Sin is voluntary transgression of God's law. If we are in bondage, it is our own fault. But God's free salvation, too, is a personal matter, "If any man thirst, let him come unto me and drink", said Jesus (John 7:37). I must drink for myself, no one can do it for me.

29 June

I am unique

"I'm glad there's only one of me", said a man to his friend, "I couldn't stand the competition", "I'm glad there's only one of you", riposted his friend, "I couldn't stand the strain". But for all that it is both a fact and a wonder that each individual is unique.

This is scientifically established. We all have distinct finger - prints. The whirls, arcs and ridges that characterise the area of skin that covers our finger-ends are unique to us. I can be convicted of crime by the presence of my dabs on the scene or instrument of wrong.

Then comes our voice - print. Our particular way of enunciation is ours alone. We can recognise our friends in the dark from their peculiar intonation and sound - quality.

And now it has been established that each person has a genetic - print. The arrangement, quality and variety of our genes is the code (DNA) of our gifts, character and qualities:- We are "wonderfully made" (Ps 139:14).

Our uniqueness means that we each have something that others haven't got. It also implies that we each have something we can minister to others. It sets a rarity of each one of us. We are valuable because we are rare. But it also means that it is not easy to understand another person. This should moderate our judgements and regulate our approaches.

30 June

Mobile vulgus

Have I got my Latin right? Anyway, what I intended to say was "The Fickle Crowd". When crowds gather they can so easily become the prey of rabble-rousers. The herd instinct is strong. Human psychology is such that a decent individual can deteriorate into a less than rational being when part of a crowd. Mob violence can match the stampede-syndrome of scared animals. On the plus side, a skilful orator can so manipulate a crowd that their minds are directed into making mass decisions almost beyond their normal sapient state. Rumpus and revival have similar psychological roots.

Jesus, who loved humankind as individuals, did not trust himself to crowds, for "He knew what was in man" (John 2:24). When an excited army of miracle-fed people rushed to make Him King, He escaped to His prayer-haven after dismissing His close followers. He wished His kingdom to be based on something more solid than mass hysteria.

And look what happened the last few days of His life. One week the crowd hailed Him with "Hosannas", the next week they yelled "Crucify Him".

Like our Lord we must beware the plaudits of men, at the same time as we despise their insults. But also like Him, we must love our fellow-humans even to giving ourselves for them.

Beauty contest

It may be natural to pretty females to display their charms. It is part of the divine mating-syndrome. But to expose oneself for vanity or vaunt ones attractions for lucrative advantages takes the shine off beauty. The wealth of moral character is, in the eyes of God, "of great price" (1 Pet 3:4).

And yet the Lord once used a beauty contest to save His people Israel from extermination. The devil, through the instrumentality of Haman, a vile aristocrat, sought the destruction of Israel; but God was several moves ahead of Satan, whose plans were not only frustrated, but also his agent was hung on gallows he himself had erected.

Read about it in the Book of Esther. This lovely maiden, as sweet of temperament, as fair of face, was catapulted into queenship of the Persian Empire through her physical charms enhanced by cosmetic attention. Ahazuerus, the wife-deposed emperor, found in this Jewess a beauty that enraptured him.

In this royal position, Esther, on the advice and guidance of her shrewd guardian Mordecai, was able to counter the plots of wicked Haman, and save her people who had been condemned to "ethnic cleansing".

God uses many means to fulfil His divine purpose: a woman's beauty, a man's bravery - Greatest of all, to save a world condemned to a destiny of woe, He sent His only begotten son to deliver it.

This is love

Song of Sol 8:7

This remarkable book expounds the qualities of love between a man and woman, "the way of a man with a maid" (Prov 30:19), at the same time as it reflects by poignant illustration the exquisite perfection of God's love to us, and our responsive love to Him. (1 John 4:19), "we love Him because He first loved us".

Such love is shown to be QUENCHLESS; So intense is its flame that all the hose pipes of hell cannot put it out. It is white-hot. No criticism can chill it, no dire circumstances can dampen it. In spite of test, temptation, trouble or tempest, it burns on: it is unquenchable!

This love, which has its source in God, is also PRICELESS - "if a man should give all the substance of his house for love, it would be utterly contemned". Love cannot be bought; but it is always given. The real values of life are always beyond price, and love excels them all in its incalculable worth. He is rich who possesses the sincere guileless love of a devoted wife: and vice-versa. He is forever rich who possesses God's "unspeakable gift" (2 Cor 9:15), the gift of "the Son of His love".

Then again, this love is TIMELESS. "Love never faileth" (1 Cor 13:8), or, as A S Way translates, "love's flower-petals never fall". The vicissitudes of life may quench enthusiasm, the changing seasons of experience may cause passions to fade, but love, like an evergreen tree, is fresh and firm through all the periods of time, and extends into the ages of eternity. It lasts - for God is love.

Ten steps of effective prayer

The Lord's prayer (Matt 6:9-13) is a precise yet poignant compendium of prayer-power. "When ye pray..." states the practice of prayer: "say" implies the intimacy of prayer - a talk with God. The words that follow fill up the pattern of prayer. Let us note ten steps intimated in this precious direction:

1 Affiliation - "Our Father". In the same breath that we enunciate the divine paternity, we also express the holy fraternity. If God is "our" father then all we are brothers and sisters - family.

2 Adoration. All true prayer is an act of worship. We acknowledge God in praise, we approach Him in faith.

3 Anticipation. "Thy Kingdom come". We enjoy present grace by faith; we anticipate future glory by hope - a buoyant emotion.

4 Activation. "Thy will be done". Prayer not only discovers what we should do, it releases the incentive and inspiration to do it.

5 Application. "Give us this day our daily bread" - the only petition for material benefits. A daily need calls for a daily application.

6 Association - "Forgive us our debts", Our relationship with God depends on our relationship with our brethren. Forgiveness is God's example of how to mend broken links.

7 Apprehension "Lead us not unto temptation" - for we cannot trust our own resources.

8 Aggression - "Deliver us from evil", or "the evil one", in the warfare of good against evil we are armed and defended by prayer. When God is brought into the situation we are sure to win.

9 Acclamation - "Thine is ....the glory". True prayer always finishes with praise and thanks given to the God of grace and glory.

10 Affirmation - "Amen". May this ever be so.

Beyond measure

Of the ninefold fruit of the Spirit (Gal 5:22) it says, "Against such there is no law". This puts these spiritual graces into a class all of their own. SCIENCE is confined to observation and measurement - Bunsen-burner, test-tube, microscope, telescope, and so on, all instruments to assess change or state. But the values that enrich life are more concerned with meaning, where quality is more important than quantity.

In this bracket may be listed these spiritual "fruit" of our text. NO laws restrict their use, their growth, their depth; they are above computation. Take the first three manifestations of divine life.

Love - "the love of Christ, which passeth knowledge" (Eph 3:19). It has "breadth, length, depth and height", but these extend to infinity.

Joy - to believers is "joy unspeakable and full of glory" (1 Pet 1:8), an ineffable rapture that brings Heaven into our experience.

Peace - "passeth all understanding" (Phil 4:7). We may not grasp its exquisite tranquillity with our minds, but we can feel its intense presence in our hearts, banishing worry and fear.

And so, although we value rationality, there are forces that are beyond (though not against) it. There are the things that matter most.

5 July

Genealogy

Our genetic descent from ancestral lines is both factual and fortune-fraught. We may inherit more than a legacy of property or name from our progenitors. Our genetic code, built up from a concentration of innate chemico-physiological substances, decides and directs the whole course and character of our lives.

But, more mundanely, our list of descent called genealogy has its importance and interest for us all. In point of fact, could we trace our descent to its source, we would all go back to Adam, "for God hath made of one blood all nations of men" (Acts 17:26).

With most of us our genealogy is limited. Lack of records "binds us to few generations"; but our Lord could trace his natural descent back to the first man - Son of God to "son of God" (Luke 3:38), thus linking Jesus to humanity, not only in essence but also in evidence. He was truly "the Son of Man" - real man, ideal man, representative man.

Yes, genealogy is important with regard to inheritance, inherent qualities and general interest, but it is more important to know where we are going to than where we came from; destiny is not decided by ancestry, but, as the Bible makes clear, by God's plan of salvation that brings to those who believe a genealogy "without beginning and without end" as we become "Sons of God" (John 1:12, 1 John 3:2).

What a question!

Romans 9:20

There are many kinds of questions. There is the why? of science, the how? of technology, the when? of chronology, the where? of locality, the who? of personality, the what? of allocation, the whence? of origin, the whither? of destiny.

But most poignant in use is the question in our text: "Why hast thou made me thus?" It certainly is an acknowledgement of fact that God has made us, that each person is a unique individual. But it contains what might almost be called an accusation, an indictment of the Almighty. "You've made a mess of me?" or "I can't help being what I am. My failings are genetic, so I am not to be blamed for my faults". It is almost a denial of morality, blaming God for my sins.

There is also a suggestion of acceptation. The context stresses blame, but the contrast intimates blessing. If God has "made me thus", it is for a purpose, and the greatest thing in my life is to discover that purpose and exploit it to the perimeter of possibility.

This is the way of release, bringing me into the liberty of the Sons of God. It is also a realisation of the potential latent in my God-formed being. To be conformed to the image of Christ is to achieve Christian perfection.

7 July

The shadow of death

I once attended a sale of household goods. Among them was a striking picture, not so much from its art as from its aspect. Close to, it depicted a boy and girl seated under an archway, but looked at from a few yards away the arch appeared to be a skull, symbol of death. Its message was clear. Death overshadows us and ours. No age, or sex, or situation is free from its menace. As the Book of Common Prayer states: "IN THE MIDST OF LIFE WE ARE IN DEATH".

But there is hope in God, for, "though I walk through the valley of the shadow of death, I will fear no evil, for Thou art with me" (Ps 23:4).

Here are three precious things, <u>first</u>, shadows are caused by light. Death might seem a fearful passage, but there is light at the end of the tunnel. <u>Secondly</u>, we may enter, but there is an exit, we pass through. Death is not a cul-de-sac, it is a thorough-fare. <u>Thirdly</u>, the Lord is with us. In our direst experience His presence is there to strengthen and sustain. Nay, more, in our Lord Jesus Christ we see victory over death. He has blazed a trail through this region of distress - "the path of life" - and risen from the dead to live forever. We, too, in Him, shall triumph over sins darkest penalty and live with Him.

Surprise! surprise!

"Wondrous things ....." Psalm 119:18

George Herbert (1593-1633) has an intriguing line in one of his poems: "Bibles laid open, millions of surprises". This may appear to be hyperbole, but the experience of multitudes of Bible lovers prove this to be true.

The bible is a book of wonders. As we read it in humble appreciation, truth leaps out at us with all the surprise of a spiritual ambush. Oft-read words often flash with new revelation. Time does not dim this ancient book, its message is ever-fresh with the dew of Heaven.

The bible is a book of wideness. It gives a wide-angle view of life, embracing comprehensively the acts of men, the aspects of God and the attitudes of existence and circumstance. There is no part of life that is not reflected, directly or tacitly, in discerning scrutiny.

The bible is a book of worth. We cannot afford to be without it. It is the official guide to holiness, to happiness, to Heaven. It gives in prophecy, in promise and in pragmatic reality the life and ministry of the most wonderful person ever to tread this earth - our Lord Jesus Christ. To know Him is to love Him, to trust Him, is to honour Him, to commit our welfare to Him is salvation.

Gone with the wind

"The ungodly... are like the chaff which the wind driveth away" Ps 1:4

In ancient times the harvested corn was threshed, usually, on an elevated place. Then it as winnowed by tossing the grain and chaff into the air with a wooden fork or shovel that the wind might blow away the chaff.

The Psalmist likens people who have no room for God in their lives as chaff for two reasons.

Weight. Chaff is light. While the grain falls back on the threshing-floor, the chaff is blown away. It is unstable. So are those who do not know the Lord. They are prey to "every wind of doctrine" (Eph 4:14), subject to the ever-changing philosophy of men. Whereas believers are controlled by the gravity of truth, these "men of chaff" believe anything, are sure of nothing.

Worth. The chaff is of little value, it is "burnt up ..... with unquenchable fire" (Matt 3:12), its worthless existence consumed in flames of judgement. So the wicked meet a deserved end of their useless lives. Maybe rich, powerful or great in the eyes of the world, but before the Judgement-Seat of God their supposed benefits are gone with the wind. But the "corn", the servants of God, are gathered by Him to everlasting joy and gladness.

10 July

Ticket to nowhere

Jonah, patriotic prophet, tried to frustrate God's judgement on Ninevah by running away (Jonah 1:3). But you can't escape God.

He paid his fare to Tarshish, an expensive gesture, for this city was at the opposite end of the Great Sea. It turned out to be a ticket to nowhere: God cancelled the trip, by a furious storm, and brought Jonah back to his place by "a great fish".

Three days of submarine transport brought the prophet into a state of penitence and preparedness to serve the Lord on His terms - as it should be.

In this brief Book of Jonah we see land and sea obeying God, storm and calm fulfilling His will, the animal and vegetable world subject to their Creator. But a disgruntled prophet seeks to deflect God's merciful grace to a sinful but penitent city.

We know that Ninevah was a political menace to Israel, but men matter more than patriotism, a lesson Jonah found hard to accept.

And we, too, must not be prejudiced against different colour, culture or creed, but look upon all men as salvable souls - the "whosoever" that God wants to reach with His love.

11 July

The integrity of God

God "cannot deny Himself", wrote Paul (2 Tim 2:13). How different from fickle human nature! The Lord will, indeed must, retain His integrity whatever else may happen or ensue. And this fact expresses three glorious truths.

<u>God is immutable</u>. He is not subject to the mutations of nature, where change is essential to continuance. He cannot change, for He is perfect: He can never be less than He is; it is impossible for Him to be more. His word is reliable, His mercy is dependable. He is a faithful God.

<u>God is interminable</u>. "Thy years shall not fail" (Heb 1:12). God will never grow old. He is "the Ancient of Days" (Dan 7:9); He is "the eternal God" (Duet 33:27). He is before, beyond and through time, living in everlasting "nowness".

<u>God is infinite</u>. There is no way that we can measure Him. He is beyond our comprehension, except as He reveals Himself; He is beyond our reach, except as He condescends to draw near to us.

But to us sinners, it is His infinite mercy that is our salvation. Sin must be penalised, for God is just; but He Himself bore our penalty in Christ (2 Cor 5:19) and thus retains His integrity as righteous and merciful.

The pen of God

The written word is permanent. Whereas the spoken word is but temporary (save in the memory of those who hear it) the penned word may last for ages. The written word is ubiquitous. My addresses are confined to an auditorium (except when recorded on tape) but my articles may go where I have never been. The spoken word depends on memory, sometimes unreliable, for its impact, but the written word, unless tampered with, continues intact, an immutable record. So God's written word.

The Father wrote. From His "moving finger" came Ten holy precepts (Ex 31:18). God's blue-print for effectual living. From the same hand came penalties upon godless defiers of His law. (Dan 5:5).

The Son wrote His judgements in the sand (John 8:6) then wiped them out. The message convicted the accusers of an adulterous woman. Did the wiping out indicate possible forgiveness?

The Spirit wrote, and still writes. Not now on stone or sand, but on the human heart. Not etched in marble or fingered in shifting sand, but "in fleshy tables of the heart", that is, deeply engraved in human nature. So does the Lord implant within us His saving and sanctifying Word.

13 July

Microscopic might

The greatest force in punctuation is the period. Other "points" say, "Steady up", or "Pause", but this says "Stop!" A tiny dot at the end of a sentence indicates finality, absolute authority, a literary barrier beyond which the sentence must not proceed.

And it is just a macroscopic, pin-head-size, spot of ink. Once used, the sentence is complete. We must start again. It is like a policeman's raised hand holding up a double-decker bus, intrinsically weak, but authoritatively strong.

Little things are often big in importance, influence or impact. A released atom can create havoc, a minute cotter-pin secure a massive wheel, a tiny tug nuzzle an ocean liner into its berth.

And so to higher things. An insignificant band of "nonentities" changed the face of civilisation (cf 1 Cor 1:26-28); one dissatisfied monk led Europe from "the dark ages" to a reformation that re-directed its destiny; an undistinguished "Bible-class", seeking God, became the launching-pad of pentecostalism with its profound impact on twentieth - century life. To "despise the day of small things" (Zech 4:10) is neither wise nor witty. If God is in it, a "dot" becomes dynamic.

Invisible allies

Rarely seen, but always there, are God's angelic armies. He is truly "Jehovah Tsebaoth" (Lord of Hosts). Their main ministry is to succour the children of God. Legion upon legion await the divine commission to sally forth to war with evil. Nay, more, each saint has his own guardian angel to watch over his welfare (Heb 1:14).

But they are "spirits" not only above the laws of our four-dimensional world, but also mostly invisible to our natural vision. They are there whether we sense it or not.

You don't believe it? Let the Bible speak for itself. Elisha, prophet of God, is invested by a Syrian army sent to arrest him. His young assistant is appalled to see the host of chariots and horses surrounding the city where they lodged. Not so the prophet: "they that be with us are more than they that be with them", he assured his servant. And when the Lord opened the young man's eyes at the request of the prophet, "behold, the mountain was full of horses and chariots round about Elisha" (2 Kings 6:13-17).

Is God the same today? (Ps 34:7) says so, "The angel of the Lord encampeth round about them that fear Him, and delivereth them!" Our defence is sure.

15 July

"I thirst"
John 19:28

These words not only fulfil scripture, being a quotation from Psalm 69:21, they also present a problem. Why did our Lord decline the medicated drink offered to Him (Mark 15:23), yet here request a drink? Two reasons.

First, the "wine mingled with myrrh" was a pain-killer. Our Lord refused this analgesic lest anyone should complain that Christ Jesus had not touched the depths of human suffering, and so not met the needs of the greatest sufferer. He drank the cup of pain to its dregs for our sakes: no one suffered more than He.

Secondly, the loss of blood, the long exposure to sun, the exhausting lack of moisture had so parched His tongue that He found it difficult to speak. "My tongue cleaveth to my jaws", it was said prophetically (Ps 22:15). With a desperate effort He articulated "I thirst!" He was given a spongeful of sour wine. Relieved, he cried with a loud voice, "It is finished" - a voice of triumph. Jesus fulfilled on the Cross all that was necessary for our forgiveness. "By His stripes we are healed".

Deo volente (God willing)

This Latin phase, often reduced to DV, expresses a profound and essential concept. But the expression, "Thy will be done", may be understood in different ways. Let us consider three of them.

First, acceptance of the inevitable (Acts 21:14). The friends of Paul could not change his mind, so they said (with a shrug of the shoulders?), "The will of the Lord be done". A well-known motto says: "God grant me the serenity to accept the things I cannot change". It is a way of peace: why bash our head against a brick wall?

Second, anticipation of the incalculable (James 4:15). Life is uncertain, but we can pre-empt disappointment and dismay by committing our way unto the Lord in simple faith (Ps 37:5), trusting Him to direct our path. "If the Lord will" can banish uncertainty and fear.

Third, adoption of the invincible. In the Garden of Gethsemane our Lord prayed, "Not as I will, but as thou wilt" (Matt 26:39). It was hard, it cost sweat and blood and tears and torture, but once Jesus accepted the will of His Father, victory was assured. "He that doeth the will of God abideth forever" (1 John 2:17). We are impregnable when we are in the centre of God's will. Accept the will of God, and be "more than conqueror".

"Warts and all"

The artist called to celebrate in oils the Lord Protector of the Commonwealth, Oliver Cromwell, hesitated to portray the somewhat pock-marked features. "Paint me as I am, warts and all", enjoined this great man. That is true humility, a mark of moral greatness.

Many biographies fail their best because they record highlights and not shadows. But it is often the very failings of successful people that magnify their real humanity. I may be blinded and baffled by the scintillating of stars of society, but a glimpse of the sometime gloom is light to my seeking mind. Hudson Taylor once despaired to contemplate suicide, General Booth had a fiery temper, C H Spurgeon smoked cigars - so what! Their weakness enhanced their greatness, and showed them to be, as Elijah was, "a man of like passions as we are" (James 5:17). Does this lower them? No, but it lifts me. God can use us in spite of what we are, "warts and all".

All this serves to enhance the Biblical portrait of our Lord. No warts are portrayed, because there are no warts. Though truly human, though brought under pressure, He never failed, He was "yet without sin" (Heb 4:15). But only a sinless Christ could save us (2 Cor 5:21).

18 July

The cutting edge

"If the axe is dull and he does not sharpen the edge, then he must exert more strength" (Eccles 10:10, N.A.S.V.)

In Christian service, as in manual labour, we need tools. But we must keep the cutting edge sharp in order to be most effective. There are three ways to do this.

First, education. As in 1 Sam 13:20, where "all the Israelites went down to the Philistines to sharpen.... his axe", so we must needs often go to the seminaries of the world to hone our mental faculties.

Second, discussion. But happier is he who is privileged to whet his abilities in Christian fellowship. "Iron sharpeneth iron: so a man sharpeneth the countenance of his friend" (Prov 27:17). Compatibility of nature (iron upon iron) plus closeness of contact will not only be exhilarating, it will also sharpen spiritual efficiency. On the whetstone of communion we will refine our cutting edge.

Thirdly, discipline under devotion to Christ. The word for "disciple" could also be translated "apprentice". It is as the apprentice imitates his master that he achieves "perfection". So we who are in the service of Jesus will learn from Him, and with diligence and devotion, "follow His steps", and graduate in the school of Christian experience and ministry.

19 July

The equation of life

On my desk is permanently fixed, the text: "As thy days, so shall thy strength be" (Deut 33:25). It was the closing section of Moses' parting word to the tribe of Asher. This gains greater meaning when we realise that Asher's "lot" was in the far north-west of the Promised land: what miles of weary transport with his large family and impedimenta! But he was promised iron-clad boots and oil for tired feet. Most of all, each days demands would be met by each day's supplies.

When I learned algebra I was faced with "equations": a kind of hieroglyphics, where letters took the place of numbers, and a mysterious "x" called for a solution, exercised my mental powers. But there was always that equals sign (=), that assured me of a balanced situation.

So with life. The problems we meet are not easy to understand, and it is often difficult to interpret that illusive "x" of meaning. But the promise of God assures us that our sustenance would always equal our needs: days of distress would be met by "grace to help in time of need"; God's help would be always "present" (Ps 46:1). And the answer is ever in that mystery element, the powerful, all-resolving "x" - the providence of a mighty Maker whose directive will balance all our equations.

Dilemma

Matt 1:18-25

Joseph, the betrothed of Mary, faced a dilemma. His covenanted bride was with child under strange circumstances. What should he do? He was "righteous" and could not overlook this dire situation. But he was also merciful, not wishing on his beloved the full rigour of the law. He contemplated an out-of-court settlement wherein a cloak of privacy could hide the shame. It was a moral and emotional dilemma of vast proportions to this kindly man.

But an angel came to his aid. This event was epochal: the expected babe was the promised Messiah: here was the entry of God into history, the Incarnation, "God with us".

The incarnation still presents problems to natural minds. How can God and genetics mix? How can a person be absolute deity and complete humanity at the same time? This problem is solved by faith. When we accept the divine record our understanding is quickened to embrace "the mystery of godliness". In Jesus, God is indeed, "God manifest in the flesh" (1 Tim 3:16).

And so with all our dilemmas, especially those about our life in God. The answer is in the Lord Himself; earth's queries may be resolved by Heaven's responses. It is a matter of trust.

The God of the Bible

Gen 1:1

The Bible introduces God without argument or question. But what a God He is! Before all things, beyond all things, behind all things, He is the CAUSE, He decides the COURSE, He determines the CONSEQUENCES of life.

He is a living God, the Great I AM, underived, self-existent, eternal, immutable - the God who imparts life in creation and new life in conversion, "the Saviour of all men, specially of them that believe" (1 Tim 4:10). He is a lasting God, "the Ancient of Days" (Dan 7:9), "the King eternal" (1 Tim 1:17). He is a luminous God, His glory is "above the brightness of the sun" (Acts 26:13) - brighter than bright. Clouds of unknowing veil His Presence, but He is eternal light. He is a loving God, for love is His very essence (1 John 4:8,10). His bountiful munificence preserves us in life; His saving grace redeems us from death. He is a liberating God. He sets us free from the bondage of sin, granting us deliverance from evil, distress and fear. He is a loyal God, faithful to Himself, retaining His own integrity in that He cannot deny Himself, break a promise or deny a penitent sinner the salvation for which Christ died. He is a listening God, He hears and answers prayer. Sometimes we may feel like crying out, "Is there anybody there?" But though He may sometimes put a screen up, He is always behind it.

And this God calls us to worship Him, for our greatest duty and privilege is to honour Him that made us. "He that cometh to God must believe that He is, and that He is a rewarder of them that diligently seek Him" (Heb 11:6). Try it - and see!

Sanctuary of the heart

When evil conspires against us, we may retreat in "the Sanctuary of the Heart", so inferred Peter, when he wrote: "Sanctify the Lord God in your hearts" (1 Pet 3:15).

Opposition can produce fear, but we have a haven of peace within, it is "Christ in you, the hope of glory" (Col 1:27), where our fears may be quieted and our disturbed situations calmed.

The Tabernacle of old was a remarkable structure. It was a portable temple, a prefabricated sanctuary set up in the midst of a camp of some two million people. Can you imagine the noise of such a vast encampment, barking dogs, braying donkeys, lowing oxen, cries of children at play, and all the raucous sounds of a nomadic settlement? However could the priests minister surrounded by this cacophony of gypsy life?

The wooden structure of the Tabernacle was covered with four layers of heavy draping that in effectively kept out the noise. These servants of God ministered in an atmosphere of calm; an oasis of quietness in a wilderness of hectic toil and labour.

And so with us. Our hidden "sanctuary of the heart", enfolded with love and grace, with faith and hope, provides us with a "peace that passeth all understanding". The noise and strife of a mad, mad world are shut out. With holy quietness our fears are allayed, our worship of God made sure.

23 July

Afterglow

After 40 days on the mount with God, the face of Moses shone. His skin had absorbed the glory of God's presence, and is now reflected in a holy afterglow.

There were two effects. First, Moses himself was unaware of it; secondly, it filled his compatriots with fear.

Innocence. True spirituality is always accompanied by humility. Had he gazed in a mirror, Moses would have known why people were so affected at his presence: but great people are often mirror-shy.

Impact. The effect of his unassumed brightness, a facial-glow of holy light, scared his beholders. He had brought back a bit of Heaven; they could not bear this reflection of God.

And it was a reflection. This glory was not innate, it was imparted. We, too, may reflect God's glory, but we must first experience it for ourselves.

During the blackout of War I, a young man came to our house, exposed a luminous button to the gaslight, then turned out the light. It glowed in the dark - a protection in the darkened streets. And so as we expose ourselves to the presence of God, our glowing lives may reflect His glory - an afterglow of grace.

24 July

God-fearers

In conclusion the Preacher, after exploring the vicious and vain vicissitudes of life, is that the only sane and solid ideal is to fear God (Eccles 12:13). It is not only the essence of true living (Prov 1:7) it is the ultimate source of happiness.

But what is the fear of God? It is:-

First, awareness of His presence. When God draws near our attitudes change.

Secondly, awe of His person. His greatness overpowers thought, His holiness makes us feel our worthlessness, His love revives our spirits.

Thirdly, attraction to His personality. At first we dread, then we delight. The beautific vision both stuns and stimulates.

Fourthly, adoration of His Being. We worship Him in the beauty of holiness, waiting upon Him in humility and trust.

Fifthly, acceptance of His authority. We recognise His Lordship and yield Him sovereign control of our lives.

Sixthly, activation of His purpose. We seek His will and delight to do it, the whole meaning of life unfolds to us, as our belief resolves into behaviour.

Seventhly, abasement at His footstool. In realisation of His deity and acknowledgement of His condescension to bless us in spite of our failings, we lie at His feet, ever ready for His word, yet ever mindful of His love. All this, and more, is implied in the term "Fear of God".

25 July

Oh, help!

An hotel in Coleford, in the heart of the Forest of Dean, is entitled "HELP ME THROUGH THE WORLD". Alas, it is now vacated, and fast becoming derelict.

But did the help it asked for come through what it represented - "wine, women and song"? And all to be paid for!

Yet so many people need help. In spite of advanced scientific and technological advances, many human needs are still uncatered for. Poverty abounds, disease proliferates, distress mounts. And why? Debased human nature, with its lust for gratification and selfish passions, has corrupted moral standards. Civilisation is no longer a cloak for evil, it is a chariot on which it blatantly careers through society. A recent Daily Mail leader stated, "There is something rotten in the fabric of modern society. To pretend otherwise is not only to delude ourselves but to betray generations unborn".

There is help. It is from the Lord, "a very present help in trouble"(Ps 46:1). But we must call upon Him. The help that will see us through the world is He that made the world. In His Son, Jesus Christ our Lord, He has provided a sufficient Saviour.

The two epiphanies

In a remarkable passage, Paul speaks of two "appearings", or, as the Greek word has it epiphanies (Titus 2:11-14).

The epiphany of grace. When Jesus came into the world a light appeared in the darkness. His life, His ministry, His death and resurrection made life liveable for all who trust Him. He is able to "redeem us from all iniquity, and purify unto Himself a peculiar (in the sense of "special") people zealous of good works".

The ephany of glory. The Second Advent of Jesus is our "blessed hope". Not only so, it is our sanctifying influence. Looking for His return enables us to "deny ungodliness and worldly lusts" and "live soberly, righteously and godly in this present world".

Grace and glory - what a combination. God's free grace not only extends to us salvation, but also guarantees sustenance through our earthly days. Glory will crown our service with eternal joy in Heaven. The grace of God is glory begun: the glory of God is grace perfected.

27 July

The original calculator

Why did God limit His basic moral law to "Ten Commandments"? (Ex 34:28). The reason is simple. Man has ten fingers, five on each hand. By these he learned to count. The beginning of mensuration was indeed "hand-made". Here is the primitive abacus, the original source of calculation.

With this natural aid to memory, each Israelite would learn to appreciate the Decalogue; the "ten words" could ever be at his finger-tips.

Two hands equal two fives, the division of God's life-plan into its two essential parts. The first five commandments are summed up in the term PIETY, our obligation to God (of which parent-honour is a part). (1 Tim 5:4); the second five denote PROBITY, our obligation to our fellow-man.

And they are in their right order. God must come first, but this does not rule out our duty to men. In fact, the latter can only be fulfilled by the inspiration of the former. Complete well-being involves both - with God a priority.

These words were written in stone to emphasise their permanence; but they can only be truly embraced by being written in our hearts by the Holy Spirit, (2 Cor 3:3).

28 July

Who is my neighbour?

Was the lawyer's question a legal side-step or a genuine desire to know the truth? (Luke 10:25-37). He acknowledged the authority of the law, "Thou shalt love thy neighbour as thyself" (Lev 19:18), but was he trying by a legal quibble to evade the moral issue?

The word "neighbour" means one who is nearby - but how near? Was the despised Samaritan or the hated Roman included in this injunction. How could Jesus answer this loaded question?

There are different forms of definition. One is by etymology or by comparison of terms. This is often insufficient, giving but, in many cases, a superficial and unsatisfactory explanation.

Our Lord adopted a better way. He told a story. A man is mugged on a lonely highway, and left for dead. A priest, official minister of the Temple, passes by without helping the victim of terror - So does a Levite, a lay-minister. It seems that their religion was confined to temple-courts, it had nothing to offer this needy traveller. Then came a Samaritan (representative of a mongrel-race). He rescued and cared for the hapless human, who could have been a Jew.

Jesus let the moral sense of the lawyer dictate the answer. The real neighbour was the man who helped his fellow-human. Now comes the rub: "Go, and do thou likewise". Being a neighbour is to help those in need, irrespective of colour, class or creed.

29 July

God's condescension

"Thy condescension hath made me great" (Ps 18:35) (Revised Version margin). What a statement!

God's goodness In Christ Jesus God stooped into the human race, the infinite God embraced in finite flesh. The eternal one entered into time, the originator of all things became subject to His own laws of creation. This is a startling wonder, but it is true. In order to rescue the human race from its depravity and ultimate destruction, He joined it. As Augustine stated: "He condescends to us in order that we might ascend to Him".

Our consequent greatness We, through Christ, became great in privilege, called "sons of God" (1 John 3:2); "great in promises" (2 Pet 1:4), precious intimation of still better things to come, great in precepts, the "royal law" of love laid upon us that exceeds all that the Law of Moses ever envisaged. Great in possibilities, with a divine potential that when released invests us with great propensities for good.

Why God should be mindful of such a minute creature as "man" (Ps 8:4), especially insubordinate and unruly "man", is beyond human apprehension. The only adequate answer is that He loves us, because He is love. He lowered himself to lift us: His undergirding arms sustain us. Glory to God!

Money talks

"Money answereth all things", said the shrewd (and somewhat cynical) writer of Ecclesiastes (10:19). How right was he?

The world attends when money talks. Listen to what it says (at least to me):

"I am more than matter, I am might;
I provide munitions, I can fight;
I buy prosperity, I luxury bring;
I purchase goods - most anything;
I bribe my way to honours great,
I pave the path to high estate;
But honest be - I must confess -
I cannot purchase happiness."

But God is deaf to current coin. In fact money, the source of so much concern and covetousness among men, is an abomination to God (Luke 16:15). Men praise it; God detests it. He may use it to perform His own purposes, as when Peter caught a fish with a coin in its mouth (Matt 17:27) but when men love it, He hates it.

The Christian church started out a penniless society. "Silver and gold have I none", said Peter (Acts 3:6). But he had "something more than gold". When the church values cash more than charisma it is in deep trouble. Money talks, but its accents are often carnal and corrupting.

Leitmotif

The idea of a recurring musical theme in dramatic compositions was developed by Richard Wagner. And how effective it became! The recognition of persons and places by a repeated sonic phrase made his creations more colourful and interpretative.

But this is not a novel concept confined to music. Long ago it was manifest in the Holy Scriptures. When evangelist Philip witnessed to the Ethiopian dignitary in the Gaza strip (Acts 8:32-35), as he read the words of Isaiah, it says, "Philip opened his mouth and began at the same scripture, and preached unto him Jesus". That magic name, in its interpretation, if not in to verbal repetition, is the leitmotif of the Bible, the key to its understanding. Without this key-note of destiny the Bible is just another book, but with this dominating theme, the Scriptures become "the living word of God" (cf Heb 4:12).

In his book, "Christ in all the Scriptures", A M Hodgkin shows how the whole Bible is redolent with the fragrance of "The Rose of Sharon", our wonderful Lord. But he only does what Jesus Himself did earlier, "And beginning at Moses and all the prophets, He expounded unto them in all the Scriptures the things concerning Himself" (Luke 24:27). The written word and the Living Word are eternally linked.

1 August

God's voice - print

Science has shown that the human voice not only is coloured by our personality, but is also unique to each person. We can be recognised by our voice-print as surely as by our finger-print.

Has God a voice-print? Elijah found it so, he lived by "the word of the Lord" (cf 1 Kings 17:2,5,8,16, 18:1, 19:9, 21:17). Out of touch for a time, he was directed to Horeb. He hid in a cave, symbol of his retreat into his morbid, mortal self. God passed by. Neither tornado, earthquake or blistering heat could draw him out. Then the Lord spoke softly, hardly above a whisper. The prophet recognised those well-known accents. He hides his face and comes into the open. The "voice" comes again. It is God. Recommissioned, Elijah comes back in God-directed service. How could he mistake that voice!

So Mary Magdalene by the garden-tomb. Jesus appeared. She did not recognise Him, His resurrection form was so different. Then He spoke: "Mary". No one could whisper her name like that but the One she loved. She burst out "Rabboni" (My dear Master) and in her ecstasy embraced Him (John 20:11-18).

> "There is no voice like the voice of Jesus,
> Tender and sweet its chime,
> Like musical ring of a flowing spring
> In the bright summer time."

"The sheep follow Him, for they know His voice" (John 10:4).

2 August

A matter of taste

"O taste and see that the Lord is good" cried the Psalmist (34:8), and in doing so presented a three-fold fact.

First, taste is very personal. Hearing, seeing, smelling may all be group-experiences, but not tasting. We can only taste for ourselves. And taste is so intimate. We can see afar off, we can hear from a distance, we can smell something on the wind, but taste involves contact. It is a personal experience. So with the knowledge of God. Books cannot do it, teachers cannot do it, rites cannot do it - only personal trust can bring to our hearts a living, loving experience of God.

Secondly, taste is peculiar in its essence. It is almost impossible to describe a taste. Sweet, sour, salt, savoury - how limited these terms when we wish to describe the delicacy of a flavoured drink. "Taste and see" is the only sure method of telling others. And so with salvation. "God is good", we say, but these words convey so little until the person himself tastes God. A personal experience explains itself.

Thirdly, taste can be memorable. To call to mind some gustatory delight "makes the mouth water". Even so, an experience of God is not only enjoyable with exquisite thrill, it is also unforgettable.

"O taste and see". Tasting is a deliberate act. So is calling on God for salvation.

3 August

Travelling light

In the race of life we are exhorted to "lay aside every weight" (Heb 12:1). No impedimenta should be allowed to slacken our speed or reduce our momentum in this vital progress to glory.

But what "weights" are we to cast off? Let us look at three.

The "weight of worry". To run the Christian race with success we must rid ourselves of the clinging doubts that often beset us. Faith wins the days, as the whole "cloud of witnesses" declare.

The "weight" of wrongdoing. We sin when we take our eyes off the mark set before us. To look around is to invite disaster. We trip up when we avert our gaze from the rewarding winning-post. Anything that saps our energy or weakens our morale must go. Whatever impedes our Christian endeavour, to us that is sin.

The "weight" of worthless ideas or habits. The contradiction of sinners must never deter us. No false view or vicious behaviour must hold us back. We cannot stop to grieve on some less-than-worthwhile ideas, we cannot waste efforts in debilitatory behaviour. Time and talent, temper and thought must all concentrate on our going. Neither gold nor grief, luxury or loss, pain or pleasure must hold us back. We run to win: the prize is "the joy set before us".

4 August

Red alert

The "Bewares" of Jesus were not meant to scare us, but to save us, to be a "red signal" of awareness of evil. Let us pinpoint some of these warnings.

Leaven. "Beware of the leaven of the Pharisees and of the Sadducees" (Matt 16:6,12). Leaven is a good thing gone bad, sour dough. Some doctrines have a modicum of truth destroyed by over-or-under-statement, or even distorted emphasis. With the Pharisees it was religion marred by show for effect, a "political correctness" that destroyed God's truth by a literality that was superficial, but morally flawed.

Lucre. "Beware of covetousness", said Jesus (Luke 12:15). Lucre (that is financial gain) only becomes "filthy" when it is obtained by wrong means or motives (cf Titus 1:11). The love of money is a source of multitudinous woes. As Christians we should use it, not abuse it.

Lie-mongers. "False prophets" (Matt 7:15) are those who speak lies in the name of God. But their lives deny their words, and their smooth words cover their ravenous lust for power and pelf.

The end-time era will spawn many prophets of evil. They are as subtle as Satan. Watch the red light of Bible direction and steer clear of them.

Bedrock

The superstructure of life-building can only be safe as its infrastructure is sound. So intimated our Lord when He advised us to "dig deep" and "lay the foundation on the rock" (Luke 6:48). Safety can only be secured as we discover rock-bottom reality in the precepts and the Person of Jesus Christ. "That rock was Christ", said Paul (1 Cor 10:4) as he describes the issuing waters from a stricken desert rock.

Not only does Christ as the Rock supply us with a firm foundation, He also provides a reliable refuge. As "feeble" conies shelter in rockybound holes, so we by faith may secure safety in the "Rock of Ages" (Prov 30:26). It was from "a cleft of the rock" that Moses saw the glory of God (Ex 33:22), and we, hidden in Christ, may also find refuge as our life is "hid with Christ in God" (Col 3:3).

The rock is not only deep in its setting, it is often also high in its soaring. In the torrid eastern sun its shadow would come as a restful relief to heat-fraught travellers. So when the blazing rays of temptation oppress us, we may find relief under the shadow of His protective presence.

The odd sparrow

Comparing scripture with scripture we learn that "two sparrows (are) sold for one farthing" (Matt 10:29); while "five sparrows (are) sold for two farthings" (Luke 12:6).

Sparrows, the poor man's "roast chicken", were retailed on skewers of ten. If you wanted two, they were broken off the stick, but if you could afford five, an extra one was thrown in. When our Lord used this illustration of the care of God for His creatures, He emphasised the fact that our Heavenly Father does not overlook any of us - even "the odd sparrow", the social make-weight.

What men value little, God often values much. We may not be marked out as members of <u>the intelligentsia</u> of this world, but our knowledge of God may baffle the egg-heads; our <u>influence</u> may seem weak, but our impact on life-changing can be great; we may not be <u>aristocratic</u>, but we can be noble in character and behaviour. In fact, we may be looked down upon as nonentities, ciphers in the scale of social importance, but God takes up such "nothings" and cancels out the know-alls of this world. If you don't believe me read (1 Cor 1:26-31) - and rejoice.

7 August

Nostalgia

Paul had a remarkable experience on his first missionary journey. At Lystra he was stoned, and dragged out as dead beyond the city boundary. As the disciples stood round his emaciated body, he suddenly stood up perfectly recovered. A miracle - and more so.

Fourteen years later (2 Cor 12:2-4) he describes this out-of-the-world event as a visit to “the third Heaven, Paradise”. He didn’t know whether he was alive or dead, but his persecutors did - they considered him to be dead, hauling his corpse over the cobbles to rid themselves of his presence.

He never got over this taste of bliss. He had paid an impromptu call on his heavenly home, and was ever after plagued with a holy nostalgia.

Its effect upon Him was profound - First, it increased his passion for God. He could not explain all that Paradise taught him, but it made him long for more. Secondly, he ever after saw the things of earth from a heavenly standpoint. Nothing could now hold him back. Even death was “far better” in this light. Thirdly, his longing for “Home” drove him to make the best of his period of probation on earth.

Longing for home is a mark of a Christian Pilgrim (Heb 11:14, 2 Cor 4:18).

8 August

Neologians

"Meddle not with them that are given to change" said the wise man (Prov 24:21). In every society there are those who want to change things, from idealists who are never satisfied with the statusquo, to iconoclasts who seek to smash altars of devotion established by antiquity. But whether in vision or by violence, these neologians worship novelty.

They cover a whole spectrum. There is the disgruntled group, whom you can never please, the disfunctional group, who blame their inadequacies on the current system, and the dangerous group whose concepts are dominated by anarchism, "angry young men" of disillusioned society.

There is also a super-class, the "new thing" group (Acts 17:21) who assume to be deep, but in reality are but shallow seekers of novelty.

Not that all that is old is therefore good, or that change is not sometimes essential: but mental and moral balance must be maintained. Evolution accomplishes more than revolution, and is less costly.

And so: "God grant me the serenity to accept the things I cannot change, courage to change the things that can and should be changed, and wisdom to know the difference". A sensible motto.

Antiquarians

While it is true that if there had been no past there would be no present, yet we cannot live in the past, though we may benefit from it.

"Trads versus mods" is a current issue. Many traditions enrich us, but much-trodden paths may also become ruts that lead us nowhere.

Antiquarians beware. "Say not thou, 'what is the cause that the former days were better than these?' For thou dost not inquire wisely concerning this" (Eccles 7:10). History may not be "bunk", as Henry Ford affirmed, but neither is it repeatable, except in principle.

Futurists behave. Your visions are yet unproved, your avant-garde concepts yet undeveloped. To paraphrase Rudyard Kipling: "Dream on but do not make dreams your master".

Realists balance. History is a rich storehouse for us, "upon whom the ends of the world are come" (1 Cor 10:11). The future may brace us to prepare for and enjoy those things. God has shown us how he works: as He was so He will be. The future may beckon us to reach out for greater things, but the past assures us that God is ever the same.

10 August

God and time

"In the beginning God...." Gen 1:1

Thus opens the Bible. There was a point of existence when the eternal God entered into time: He was before time, but when He acted, time began.

Reflecting His own triune being, time embraces PAST, PRESENT, AND FUTURE, each element essential to the rest.

TIME IS MOTION. When we say "Time stood still", we mean that some moments seem like millennium - but time itself goes on, inexorable in its progress, unstoppable in its movement, irreversible in its essence. We may turn the clock back, but we cannot reverse the cosmic process of existence.

<u>Time is measurable</u>. It is difficult to define time, but we can put its passing into measured portions. With regard to our planet it is set by the sun and moon into time and seasons (Gen 1:14). With regard to the cosmos in light-years, reducing baffling distances to a yard-stick approaching infinity.

<u>Time is motive</u>, the arena in which God perfects His purposes. He uses time to work out His saving project - the Eternal God is man's Redeemer.

God and space

"God created the Heavens and the earth" Gen 1:1

This links the Deity to space. The concept of created emptiness is difficult to grasp, but (Rom 8:39) makes it clear that "height and depth" is a creation of God.

God is bigger than space. Solomon said: "The heaven (that is the Universe as one whole) and heaven of heavens (that is the combined island universes we know as galaxies) cannot contain Thee" (1 Kings 8:27). He fills all things; in fact, He made space to fill it with matter within the dimensions of length, breadth and depth - a tri-unity reflecting His own nature.

God has bound space, though He himself is boundless. Three great facts link the vast elements of the Universe- gravity, radiation and electro-magnetic force. Does the last embrace the rest? And may not this dynamic energy be but an expression of the all-pervading and all-powerful Spirit of God? An atom, the building - brick of matter, is a swirling microscopic form of energy, a kind of microcosm bearing the same characteristics as the macrocosm.

The Universe is finite, but is an eternal expression of the infinite Creator who uses space to perform His will.

12 August

God and matter

"God created...." Gen 1:1

"Things which are seen were not made of things which do appear" (Heb 11:3), that is, phenomena is an effect of an ultimate cause - that first cause of all is GOD.

Matter inanimate comprises energy, motion and phenomena - another tri-unity. In fact the whole physical universe may be summed up in SPACE, TIME and MATTER; God's works bear the stamp of His own triune nature. The doctrine of the Holy Trinity is not an irrational concept, every aspect of nature bears this "trade-mark" of Deity.

Matter animate. Earth and air do not contain all that God can do. To mineral He had added vegetable and animal, imposing on inanimate substance the gift of life with its qualities of reproduction "after its kind", accumulation and adaptation to environment. The modern science of biology has discovered DNA - the peculiar life - programme of all animate objects. Intricate and complex, this pattern of life is the basis of all that we are. As far as humans are concerned, the Psalmist (139:14-16) ascribes it all to God. May not it be wise of us to ask of our Creator: "Why hast Thou made me thus"? (Rom 9:20).

The breath of life

There is a paradox of Christian experience in the terms "Spirit in you" (cf Rom 8:9) and "you in Spirit" (Rev 1:10). But this is resolved by analogy of the atmosphere that surrounds us.

<u>The breath of life outside</u>. The air we live in is ubiquitous, it surrounds our whole environment. It carries the essential of life, oxygen; it receives our output of carbon dioxide: thus completing the cycle of life. It exerts pressure, it produces climate, it absorbs meteoric attacks, it shields us from harmful rays from outer space. So we "live, and move, and have our being" (Acts 17:28), surrounded by the Spirit's omnipresence His nearness ministers the essentials of spiritual life, protects us from alien forces, presses our spirits with awareness of His holy presence. Christians live and walk "in the Spirit" (Gal 5:25).

<u>The breath of life within</u>. Physically, we have the ability and the capacity to breathe in the life-sustaining air. So with the Holy Spirit: He surrounds us, but He can also fill us. But we must breathe in the holy air. Our spiritual life depends on this inspiration. In fact the double-action of respiration, the inbreathing and the outbreathing of God is life indeed. We take of Him; we tell of Him; this breath of life creates and preserves in us our spirituality.

14 August

Mountain-top experience

At the Transfiguration of our Lord (Matt 17:1-8), Peter, James and John (the favoured three) "beheld His glory" (John 1:14). They were thrilled: they never forgot it. Peter refers to it over 30 years later (2 Peter 1:17,18). His words, "Lord, it is good for us to be here", reflect the common feeling of the select trio.

We no doubt feel the same when "Heaven comes down our souls to greet". It is good to experience these exalted times, but the whole episode tells us three things.

<u>You can't be on top all the time</u>. The "black-letter" days far out-number the "red-letter" periods, but we thank God for those "glory" times that lighten our path and excite us to do more for God.

<u>You don't need to be on top all the time</u>. Canaan was "a land of hills and valleys" (Deut 11:11), so different from Egypt where the flat delta was fed by annual inundation of the Nile; here was seasonal "rain from Heaven". To make progress in the Promised Land involved "ups and downs". So with us: the "ups" of inspiration is followed by the "downs" of service. Hill and vale balance our lives.

<u>You should not need to be always on top</u>. If we truly absorb the "glory" we may fully enjoy the "grace" that enables us to move on in God.

15 August

Potato-gun

One of the toys of my childhood was a "potato-gun". It comprised of a small metal tube with a plunger. The tube was dug into the soft flesh of the potato to collect an air-tight plug. In went the plunger, air pressure built up, and the plug was ejected with a "pop". It was fun: but the soft missiles had little power.

So with criticism of the Bible. To those of us who believe that, "All scripture is given by inspiration of God" (2 Tim 3:16), the attacks made upon its authenticity and reliability are like the pitiful shots from my "potato-gun".

We welcome, and are indebted to, those textual critics whose labours have assured us a reliable text. And some higher criticism has enabled us to understand the Sacred Word. But there are those who, vaunting "a science falsely so called" approach the Scriptures with carnal half-baked philosophy. They join the "serpent" in casting doubt on God's clear word.

The real source of their attack is anti-Godism, but their rationalistic armoury is impotent against the truth of God, which will ever prevail.

16 August

Hair-care

"The very hairs of your head are all numbered", said Jesus (Matt 10:30). The infinite God cares for the infinitesimal part of our being. Each hair is His concern.

God's artistry. Each fine strand is a filament of perfection: each has its nerve, its muscle, its follicle, its lubricating oil and its colour-gland. What divine thought is packed into so small a space! The finest of dimensions is called "a hair's breadth". The three divisions of mankind can be traced from a cross-section of hair. Round-section, with a pithy centre - the Semitic races; flat-section frizzy hair, the Hamitic race; ovate-section, the Japhitic races (cf Gen 9:18). Bible history stamped on each human hair.

God's arithmetic. God knows more about me than I do about myself. I can only guess my number of hairs, but the Lord marks each one, singly and numerically.

God's attention. Mere mensuration is nothing to God, His counting is dynamic. He numbers because He cares, His knowledge is dynamic knowledge, not mere awareness, but deep concern - we are precious to Him, every hair of us.

But God's attention to my affairs is not just "hairs", it is also "heart". The external and the internal facets of my life are the subject of His loving care. To Him I am not a bundle of parts, I am a whole person whom He loves.

Borrowed tools

The incident of the lost axe-head recorded in 2 Kings 6:5, where the unfortunate "son of the prophets" cries out, "Alas, master. For it was borrowed", teaches us three things.

First, the principle of dependence. Only God is self sufficient. We mortals depend on Him for being and becoming. But our emptiness attracts His fullness, for "Blessed are the destitute in spirit; for theirs is the Kingdom of Heaven" (Matt 5:3).

Secondly, the principle of stewardship. If all our gifts are from God - time, talent, strength and ability - we are under stern obligation to use them wisely as faithful stewards. We owe all to our Creator; we should not only recognise this, but also respond by devoting ourselves to Him.

Thirdly, the principle of accountability. God's gifts imply responsibility, and for this we must all eventually "stand before the Judgement Seat of Christ" to give an account. The righteous Judge will praise or punish, to our eternal gain or loss.

But what if we fail? The young enthusiast felt his loss and cried out, "Alas, Master". And "whosoever shall call on the name of the Lord shall be saved". The Master was at hand, and on the confession of the loser, introduced a new element into the hopeless situation. As Elisha cast a branch into the turgid stream, so Christ in His cross. A miracle ensues; "the iron did swim".

Highway to heaven

"An highway shall be there, and a way" Isa 35:8

An eighteenth-century military leader turned the rough track of a highland glen into a firm highway. What was impassable in winter became an all-weather road. This beneficial act was commemorated in verse thus:-

"Had you seen these roads
Afore they were made,
You'd go down on your knees
And bless General Wade".

Isaiah's highway is fulfilled in the life and ministry of Him who said of Himself, "I am the WAY" (John 14:6), not to an earthly Zion, but to "the city of the living God, the heavenly Jerusalem" (Heb 12:22).

It is a sure way. The simplest of believers cannot miss it. "Way-faring man, though fools, shall not err therein".

It is a safe way. The ravenous beasts of evil, including the devil himself "as a roaring lion" will not impede our progress. When we walk with God we walk in safety.

It is a sacred way. "The way of holiness". Only the redeemed "the ransomed of the Lord" can tread it. It leads to Glory - and we enjoy glory as we sing our way along.

19 August

Statistics

Statistics play a great part in modern life. Censuses, analyses, polls, graphs, charts fill an important role. But how much should such things play a part in church life, in the spiritual realm?

There is a place for statistics, as Acts 1:15 suggests: "the number of the names together were about 120". Without this membership list we would not realise how greatly God did work with so few disciples. This evidence of organisation emphasises the need of "belongingness". Free-lance Christianity is a misnomer. It is essential for a believer to be part of a fellowship.

But statistics must be kept in their place. In the Authorised Version, this statement re numbers is in a parenthesis, that is, grammatically it is a verbal by-path. We love to count, but arithmetic is not the best criterion of God's work.

Statistics do not say enough. They may appear scientific, but they do not reach beyond the countable, tangible elements. As Paul Tournier says in His, "A Doctor's Casebook", "The sphere of science is that of quantitative. Meaning pertains to the realm of quality".

God does not depend on numbers. As in Gideons case, where his army was reduced from 32,000 to 10,000 to 300, (Judges 7:2-7). One tenth of one percent - men with real faith - was enough to scatter the enemy.

20 August

D I Y morality

Modern philosophy spurns the idea of absolutes and makes each man a judge of his own attitudes and actions. In what is called "Situation Ethics", the circumstance becomes the criterion of what is right or wrong.

But this "DO IT YOURSELF" concept is no new idea. They had it over 3,000 years ago, when "every man did that which was right in his own eyes" (Judges 19:1, 21:25). What social chaos resulted! What moral corruption! What God-forsaken people!

God had, years before, given them an order to live by. The decalogue was a ten-word guide to ethical and spiritual stability. In their decline, the newly-established tribes of Jacob, neglected (almost rejected) these divine guide-lines to holiness and happiness. The outcome was almost national disintegration.

And upon this generation in our once Christian land will come decay - moral and social - as we become our own judges. We need the standards of the Bible to spur and sustain us. The principles made so clear by our Lord are the only way to personal and national stability and happiness.

Pebble in a pool

I tossed a stone into a pond, and watched the ever-widening circles of ripples. Though weakened at every repeat reaction, they eventually reached the shore on all sides.

So with life. Who can tell the influence of "a good deed in a naughty world" (to use Shakespeare's words)?

It cost a lot for Stephen to "earnestly contend for the faith" (Acts 6:3-14), but the word cast into the pool of Saul's mind set up an ever-expanding series of events. Saul resisted at first the "wider Gospel" of salvation for all men, but the character and message of martyred Stephen would not let him rest. The revelation of Jesus "whom thou persecutest" (Acts 9:5) brought to an end those prickings of conscience in Saul's total surrender to the Saviour.

But the message of Stephen persisted as Saul (now Paul) preached the same soul-saving message to Jew and Gentile alike.

The stone of truth cast into the life of Saul of Tarsus spread until Rome itself became the centre of his teaching. Cast in the stone; the pool will do the rest.

22 August

Is your heart in it?

Jesus accused the Pharisees of "lip-service", and hurled at them Isaiah's caustic accusation: "This people.... honoureth Me with their lips; but their heart is far from me" (Matt 15:7-9).

It is not enough to "speak" religion, we must live it. Our whole heart must be in everything we do for God.

Mark Twain once told a preacher that he had got his sermon in a book at home. He later sent the indignant proclaimer a dictionary with the caption: "Words, words, nothing but words". Our testimony to Christ must be sincere to be effective. Our words must convey our heart-thoughts and our depth-feelings. Not only our minds, but our hearts must be in them.

John puts it well. "Let us not love in word, neither in tongue; but in deed and in truth" (1 John 3:18). He advocates a holy pragmatism - the incarnation of doctrine into deeds.

And practical James links "faith" with "works" (James 2:14-17). It is not enough to say to the destitute and hungry, "Be warmed and filled", we must do something about it. And if our hearts are right we will not be content with mere diction, we will fulfil our word with action.

Vain worship puts litany before concern for others. He is nearest God's heart who expresses love in activity and care.

Holy habits

Jesus followed the religious customs of His day (Luke 2:41,42), making Himself subject to God - established tradition.

He also exercised the holy habits of attendance at the House of God (Luke 2:16) and of prayer (Luke 22:39). The beloved Luke, whose Gospel reveals Jesus as THE SON OF MAN shows how our Lord, while subject to the limitations of humanity, yet maintained His spirituality by the scriptures, by prayer and by fellowship - three vital elements of true Christianity.

We need the daily intake of "the sincere milk of the Word" (1 Peter 2:2) to sustain us; the daily exercise of prayer to strengthen us; the regular meeting with God's people to encourage and enlarge us.

The persistent act will soon become a habit, and such holy habits are not mere "religious ruts", they are "means of grace" that minister to us and by which we minister to others.

To know the Bible is to know more of God; to "pray without ceasing" is to draw closer to God; "not to forsake the assembling of ourselves together" (Heb 10:25) is to enjoy fellowship with those who love God as we do. Let us develop holy habits: they are good for us.

24 August

Don't kid yourself

This is my "modern" version of (Gal 6:7). "Be not deceived; God is not mocked" - that is you can't fool God, even if you fool yourself.

Paul could be severe. Sometimes he had to. It was not that he did not love his people, it was because he did love them enough to rebuke them.

The Galatians were "bewitched", hypnotised by specious arguments of self-important "prophets". The apostle had vividly set forth the Cross of Christ as the only way of salvation. Now they were retreating to a "lesser" Gospel of works, which could lead them into bondage.

And would-be prophets are alive (and kicking) today. They seek to impose philosophies of human concoction upon susceptible believers. The appeal is to material advantage, to "rational" assessment of situations, to other-than-biblical resources. But the ultimate is spiritual sterility.

The answer? Don't kid yourself that you know more than God, don't be taken in by suspicious teaching. Be sound in holy doctrine, making the Scriptures the litmus-paper of truth or error. As Jesus found, the Word of God as truly understood is a defence against Satan.

Who runs the church?

"The church is subject unto Christ" Eph 5:24

Who runs the church?
"I", said the Pastor,
"I am the master.
I run the church".
Who runs the Church?
"I", said the deacon,
"Don't think I'll weaken.
I run the church".
Who runs the church?
Said the man in the pew,
"Let me tell you,
I run the church".
Who runs the church?
All these are wrong.
This is the right:
When Pastor and deacon
And men in the pew
Are simply just channels
For God to flow through -
GOD RUNS THE CHURCH.

The Church of Jesus Christ must ever be subject to the guidance of His Spirit and His Word. And this subjection will show itself in "a meek and quiet spirit" that is ever available to needy service, yet never seeking to be dominant

Our Lord became servant of all: we reflect His nature when we too are ready to minister to others - saint or sinner - in order to do them good and lead them closer to God. Let Him run our lives - and the church.

26 August

The missing virtue

The Seven Cardinal Virtues of Christian theology cover the essential points of effective living. Possess them, practice them - and we draw near the perfection Jesus spoke of (Matt 5:48).

Think of them: Faith, Hope, Love, Justice, Prudence, Temperance, Fortitude. Best of all, do them. They will become soul-anchors in the turbulent seas of trial and temptation, as well as a banner of truth and light in a world of falsehood and darkness.

But as I went over them again in my mind, I felt something was missing - the missing virtue; HUMOUR.

Is this the “salt” of (Col 4:6) that seasons our behaviour? Job illustrates this concept thus - “Is there any taste in the white of an egg”? The albumen may be nourishing, but it is insipid. But he had already given the answer: “Can that which is unsavoury be eaten without salt” (Job 6:6). And so with life. A touch of humour (especially holy glee) can make the tasteless repetitions of ordinary living to have an acceptable and enjoyable aspect. A pinch of humour adds piquancy to living.

The deadliest sin

Theologians mark out the Seven Deadly Sins as Pride, Covetousness, Lust, Envy, Gluttony, Anger, Sloth. To banish these by their destruction, or by the domination of virtuous living is the whole object of sanctification.

These are indeed lethal, but there is a sin that exceeds them all in vicious intent or vapid ignorance. It is refusal to believe the Gospel of Jesus Christ.

The issue is clear. There are no grey areas, no neutral ground. So Jesus declared it: "He that believeth and is baptised shall be saved, but he that believeth not shall be damned" (Mark 16:16). To reject the Son of God as the only way to Heaven is to be lost forever.

The depth of this "deadly sin" is seen in that "he that believeth not God hath made Him a liar; because he believeth not the record that God gave of His Son" (1 John 5:10). Strong language! Not too strong; for if we cannot accept God's word, we cannot know His saving grace. Make God a liar, and truth is destroyed. It is the deadliest sin.

Harvest home

One of the surest things in nature is the link between "seedtime and Harvest" (Gen 8:22). Given the right conditions, what we sow we shall reap.

And this is true in the spiritual realm. This divine law is operative in grace as well as nature; "for whatsoever a man soweth, that shall he also reap" (Gal 6:7-9). Three principles are seen in harvest laws.

First, <u>you reap IF you sow</u>. The law of harvest calls for activity. The sluggard who neglects to sow will not gather any grain (Prov 20:4).

Secondly, <u>you reap WHAT you sow</u>. "Sow to the flesh - reap corruption, sow to the spirit - reap life everlasting". "Well-doing" augurs a harvest of well-being: but evil spawns evil.

Thirdly, <u>you reap MORE than you sow</u>. Scatter wheat on prepared ground and it will reproduce itself up to a hundred-fold. What benefits are heaped on those who benefit others, but what sorrow springs from those who sow hatred. Sow well: reap well.

And so, "Let us not be weary in well doing; for in due season we shall reap, if we faint not". Harvest-home is blessed when we sow good.

29 August

A prodigal reflects

In the incomparable story of "The Prodigal Son" (Luke 15:11-32), the turning point of the wastrel's restoration occurred when "he came to himself". Up to then he had been "beside himself", for sin is a form of moral madness. Mind you, it took a dreadful toll of shame and loss to bring him there; but now, hungry and lonely, sitting by the pig-troughs, he reflects on his condition.

The man I was. The once despised home is looked back on as now desirable. He had had his fling; it had flung him into depression and despair. Far from the home he had fled, he was now homesick, longing for lost benefits.

The man I am. He was not only spent up, he was also ashamed. He had gambled - and lost. Now wretched, despised, abandoned, far away from the father who loved him. He had messed up his life, missed its purpose: he was a sinner.

The man I might have been. "If only" is a sad complaint. A little more patience, and concern for others would have saved him from loss, and given him space to mature.

The man I still can be. He went home - blessed turning point. His gracious father restored to him the full status of sonship. Prodigals may still return and find in God a loving Father.

30 August

"The Compleat Angler"

This English classic by Isaac Walton is not only a literary wonder, it is also a guide to the skills and joys of angling.

But the words of Jesus to Peter put fishing into a higher order: "Follow Me, and I will make you fishers of men" (Matt 4:19). Three aspects of this piscatorial art are here emphasised.

First, fishing is the transportation of a creature from one environment to another. In the natural sphere it is death to the fish, in the spiritual sphere it is life on a higher plane.

Secondly, fishing is the art of persuading fish to accept the luring bait. Excepting trawling, fish are caught individually. Spiritual angling is making the Gospel so attractive that sinful men "take the hook" and are netted into the Church.

Thirdly, as in the case of Isaac Walton, so in the spiritual realm fishing is learned by imitating the expert. "Follow Me", said Jesus. His masterly way of winning souls is an example to us all. With one or with many our Lord's approach with compassion and wisdom teaches us much about this great ministry. Lovers of Jesus and lovers of men will likewise endeavour to take people alive for God.

31 August

Storm - proof

Life is full of trouble. Storms of passion, tempests of temptation, tornadoes of misfortune molest us all. Eliphas was right: "Man is born unto trouble as the sparks fly upward" (Job 5:7). You've said it, brother!

Our Lord confirms this at the close of His "Sermon on the Mount" (Matt 7:24-27). Where all, both "wise" and "foolish" are beset with storms. The trials were from three elements. RAIN, equals trials from above. God tests us to prove us (cf Gen 22:1): FLOODS, trials from below - the enemy often "comes in like a flood" (Isa 59:19) the devil is prime tempter of men: WINDS, from all quarters of the human situation that surrounds us - peer-pressure, persecution, deception, theft, neglect. What a weight of woes hurled against the sons and daughters of men!

But we can withstand them all if we take the essential safeguard. Jesus said, "Build on my words and you will be secure", for if the infra-structure is sound, the superstructure will be safe.

The only life worth living is that which is built on divine standards. The elements of evil cannot overthrow the one who by faith relies on God's word.

Lazy man's lion

"The slothful man saith..... a lion is in the streets" (Prov 26:13), then turns over in bed for a little more sleep.

How the Book of Proverbs lampoons the sluggard: to the sage a lazy lout is but a caricature of a man who drowns his propensities in slumber.

"A lion in the street"? Then why not rouse a few neighbours and drive it out. Children and old people are at risk. But no! Cowardice and comfort become twin vices to restrain him.

"The slothful man saith". He is all "say" and little "do". He can invent a thousand fanciful situations that forbid his leaving his bed; his imagination takes over from his intellect; his excuses are reason gone.

Who does he think he's kidding? Those that know him despise him, but fail to argue him out of his conceit. He is wise in his own eyes. But his self-deceit is his own loss. He lacks life's essentials, for he toils not; he loses the respect of his fellows, for he becomes a burden to them; worst of all, he forfeits his manhood to become a drivelling sycophant.

Honest toil is rewarding. It earns a living, it merits appreciation, above all, it pleases God.

The bed of Procrustes

This man was a legendary robber who fitted his victims to a bed by stretching them or cutting them to size by lopping off their feet.

We have their mental and moral counterparts today. From a mind-set fixed to rigid ideas, they cut every notion to their static concepts. There is no elasticity, no give, no bend in their philosophy. All must fit their "bed", or else be trimmed to size.

But this is no new attitude. Peter spoke of those who "wrested...scripture to their own destruction" (2 Peter 3:16). They twist and distort God's word to fit their own prejudices or whims. What is to an honest reader plain truth, to them is mystic meaning. By subtle (though often obvious) distortion they reduce divine directions to esoteric mysteries, holy writ becomes to them cryptic hieroglyphics.

God meant His word to be understood, a ministrant of grace and help to simple faith. But some use what was intended to expound truth and torture it by squeezing into set philosophical moulds. Peter says that such are "unlearned" that is mentally incompetent, and "unstable", that is morally weak and unbalanced. Avoid them!

3 September

Cause and effect

When Jesus quieted the tempest in Mark 4:37-41, a "great storm" became a "great calm". More than that, His words dealt with both cause and effect - "He rebuked the wind and said unto the sea, "Peace, be still"." The waves could not subside until the winds were subdued. It is good to know that our Lord can not only deal with results, but also banish the reasons for those results.

Have you ever noticed in John's First Epistle how he deals with "sin" and "sins"? That inbuilt principle dominant in human nature is "sin"; the effects of yielding to this "law in my member's" (Rom 7:23) is "sins".

These single acts of failure to do God's will must be confessed to be forgiven. But the sin-principle itself can be purged by "the blood of Jesus Christ". Entire sanctification is therefore possible as we "walk in the light of God".

So in both realms of nature and grace our Lord can deal with both effect and cause. He not only can wipe away the cobwebs of evil, He can kill the spider that spins them.

What a waste

When Mary of Bethany poured a flask of expensive ointment on the feet of Jesus, His disciples were shocked. "To what purpose is this waste"? they said (Matt 26:8). But John gives us another angle to this event. He points out that Judas Iscariot, who led the protest, had himself embezzled the apostolic funds. Critics should beware lest their own defects crush their criticisms.

"Waste"? Much depends on your system of values. There are times where money doesn't matter. Woe to those whose only reckoning is in terms of cash. What did it matter that the equivalent of a year's wages was expended; this was an act of adoration, and who can measure worship by wealth!

"Waste"? It happened that Mary saw more deeply than the rest: she knew that crucifixion was near, and anointed her Lord beforehand for His burial. Nicodemus loaded expensive spices on the dead body of Jesus, she gave Him her best while He was still alive. It was a memorable act.

"Waste"? Even today the world cannot understand the life-style of lovers of the Lord Jesus. Dr Albert Schweitzer achieved greatness as theologian, philosopher, musician and doctor. When he went to Lamberene in darkest Africa the world of science bemoaned his loss, his talents buried in an outlandish place. But he chose to minister to neglected nobodies. The world could not understand, but Jesus did, and this noble missionary stands high in the list of those who loved the Lord more than wealth, fame or success.

5 September

To let!

Our Lord spoke of an unclean spirit leaving a man to wander. It returns, finds the "house empty, swept and garnished", and reoccupies its former abode with "seven other spirits more wicked than himself" (Matt 12:43-45). The first lesson is that mere reformation is not enough, only regeneration, whereby the Holy Spirit enters the life, can secure the soul.

Another lesson. The devil rushes into every vacated area of human life unless it is occupied by spiritual good.

Beware those who talk of "emptying the mind of all thought or emotion". This is the basic element of transcendental meditation. The result? Evil powers take over, the vacuum is filled. But Christian Meditation is filling the mind. "My meditation of Him shall be sweet" (Ps 104:34) and the mind, being inspired with adoration for Jesus will resolve itself to worship. The door is thus bolted against evil. "Looking unto Jesus" (Heb 12:2) is a safely-lock the combination of which Satan will never know. Our hearts are safe from evil.

And a vital aid to this is to "meditate in God's law day and night" (Ps 1:2). Thus "the counsel of the ungodly can have no place, for the mind and heart are filled with thoughts of God. Any stray thought are brought under captivity to Christ" (2 Cor 10:5). Our mind is "Not to let".

6 September

Under new management

Paul speaks of "the life which I now live in the flesh I live by the faith of the Son of God" (Gal 2:20). Hitherto he had lived his own life, now he was under new management, a "slave of Jesus Christ" (Rom 1:1), for so "servant" means.

A new principle possessed him. The love of Christ "who gave Himself or me" had driven out self-love. Now he was a captive of this all-pervasive emotion. The love of Jesus was in charge.

A new power propelled him. Christ lived in Him, a propulsive energy that impelled him to prodigious crusades in spreading the Gospel into all the world.

A new purpose pervaded him. "Crucified" to the world and all its wasteful ways and woeful wants, he nevertheless gave himself to the world in such service as led many to accept the same Saviour and the same sacred servitude that had taken over his own life. His friends thought him mad, his enemies concluded him bad, but in this new employment in the service of Christ he was supremely glad: life to the full was his. His faith in Christ linked him to a love that was a source of endless joy and a life that was eternal in its exquisite essence and its everlasting enjoyment!

7 September

Golden wedge

"A wedge is a tapering piece of wood or metal with a sharp edge that is driven between two objects or parts of an object to secure or separate them". So the Concise Oxford Dictionary. The power of a wedge can be great. A stone-mason takes a lump of rock, tamps a small hole in it, sets his steel wedge and hammers it: the mighty rock is split.

There are moral as well as material wedges. So found Achan, whose "wedge of gold" eventually severed him from the life of Israel (Joshua 7:21-24).

And gold is still a wedge. Its force can sever a man from morality, cut him off from eternal life, damn his soul to perpetuity. It is not the yellow metal itself, it is the love of what is can do - the power, the prestige, the pleasure - that is lethal. "For the love of money is a root of all kinds of evil" (1 Tim 6:10 NIV). How many a man has sold his soul for gold!

A wedge has a sharp narrow end - "the thin end of the wedge". A seemingly simple desire or deed can begin a process, which, hammered by increasing lust, can split the user from all that is good. Money, meant "to go round doing good", can become a menace to moral integrity, and produce an increasing momentum to an overweening covetousness where GOLD becomes our GOD. Watch it, Brother, love of money can result in moral murder.

The maze of life

Hampton Court maze is a well-known labyrinth of hedge-bound paths in which it is easy to get lost. So many avenues lead to nowhere, so many openings prove abortive - the would-be pursuer of conquest can feel utterly frustrated. Such is life!

We chase down cul-de-sacs, we take the wrong turnings, we become baffled by the very complexity and vicissitudes of our experiences. Life is indeed a puzzle, often painful, sometimes even pitiful.

But Hampton's maze has a guide on an elevated spot who is able to direct anyone in perplexing difficulties. So with us who trust the Lord. "I will guide thee with mine eye", He says (Ps 32:8) - His watchful providence is ever toward us, "I will instruct thee and teach thee in the way thou shalt go". His word is a pointer to the way out of our predicaments.

But, He continues, we must be like a well-trained horse that responds to a touch of the bridle or a simple word of command. We need not be lost in the maze of life, for as the Psalmist confided: "Thou shalt guide me with thy counsel, and afterward receive me to glory" (Ps 73:24). Following His direction we will reach glory at last.

9 September

She let her hair down

So it is said of Mary of Bethany (John 12:3). But it was not in abandonment, it was in embarrassment. At the feast where Jesus was honoured quest, she had a sudden surge of emotion. Why should not Jesus have her treasured ointment? He was worth it: what does expense matter? You cannot weigh all things in terms of gold.

She could not reach His head as He reclined at table, but His feet were stretched out behind Him. She poured the precious perfume on them. But suddenly realising that she attracted attention from the crowded room, she looked for a napkin to wipe up the excessive lotion. She had none - she let her hair down (a shameful exhibition!) and tenderly wiped Jesus' feet.

In doing so she gave herself a holy shampoo. The fragrance she lavished on her Lord was now part of her own cosmetic condition. She exuded the same perfume as Jesus did. Nay, more so, that fragrance permeated the whole festal chamber, and has since filled the ages of time and the realms of grace.

So those exuberance's of holy love not only glorify the Saviour on whom they are expended in worship, those who so adore their Lord become fragrant with His fragrance and sound out far and wide the fragrance of His name.

Give me a kiss

A kiss is an ancient mode of caress, and is associated with many forms of human behaviour. This osculatory contact varies in intensity and meaning.

Prevailing custom. A kiss of greeting (Luke 7:45) or farewell (Acts 20:37) was, and still is a form of welcome or parting. It can speak more than words. A holy salute (Rom 16:16).

Personal affection. When David and Jonathan parted, their deep friendship was expressed in a fond embrace (1 Sam 20:41).

Passionate emotion. The kiss of a lover expresses the intoxicating power of "the way of a man with a maid" (Prov 30:19, Song of Songs 1:2).

Pious homage. "Kiss the Son" (Ps 2:12). God's appointed King - Jesus - commands our worship and submission. It is interesting to learn that the Greek word for "worship" means "to kiss the hand towards". As Charles Wesley puts it:

> "O let me kiss thy pierced feet,
> And bathe and wash them with my tears".

Pardoning grace. The kiss of a loving father spoke volumes to the Prodigal Son (Luke 15:20). The sinner's confession was smothered in paternal affection. And so with us all, who turn to God from sin.

The old man of Mow

Mow Cop is a rocky eminence north of the Potteries, overlooking the Plain of Cheshire. From a hollow near the summit rises a stony pillar which in profile (plus a little imagination) looks like an old man at prayer - hence the sobriquet - “OLD MAN”.

But more interesting is the cross etched into one of the rock faces. It is a surveyor’s sign, but remarkably it represents the boundary between two neighbouring parishes, it also is the dividing point between the See of Lichfield and the See of Chester, further still it marks the division of the Province of York and the Province of Canterbury. It is the ecclesiastical centre of England.

And the Cross of Calvary is the centre of the divine scheme of salvation, the hinge of all Christian experience, the focal point of all Biblical theology. May we go further? The vast Cosmos centres for its life and existence on the Cross of Christ. Around it circle all God’s purposes for the created universe.

It was there that “righteousness and peace” embraced (Ps 85:10), where God’s grace “kissed a guilty world in love”, where penitent sinners still find pardon.

All Christians are eccentric

Unbelievers think we are odd, cynics say we are mad, but the truth is we are not off centre, but twin-centred. Our life revolves around two focal points - Calgary and the Upper Room of Pentecost.

They call us eccentric: but eccentricity is power. In mechanics an eccentric crank-shaft can convert backward-and-forward motion into rotary motion. This is the element that turns piston-power into wheel-power - the basis of motor transport.

And so our seemingly strange behaviour is really the source of our power, the driving force of our Christian testimony. We are not really odd, we are just different.

But this difference - the saving power of the Cross, and the potential energy of the Holy Spirit - propels us into a realm of holy service and gives us spiritual drive. Some may call it "madness" (Acts 26:24) but it is the sanest of experiences, "wise unto salvation" (2 Tim 3:15).

Tepid is torpid

Rev 3:16

"You make me sick", said the Lord to the Church of Laodicea. They were well off in material benefits, but lacking in holy fervour. Their complacency induced a baleful torpidity so hateful to God.

The Lord even preferred frigidity to this lukewarmness - so He said. Look at it like this: hot water is a tonic, cold water is refreshing, but lukewarm water is an emetic.

But this church was blind to its condition - "wretched, miserable, poor, blind and naked" - and that was the Lord's assessment. Worst of all, He was outside. What a parody! Christianity without Christ?

But the Lord loved them, so he rebuked them. Did His words fire them up? We don't know. But one thing we do know, that if Christ is not central to our lives, all other apparent benefits may prove but bane's. It is not liberal finances that make a live Christian, or fine clothing, or ample goods - it is a heart burning with love to Christ, fired with fervent zeal, a hot-gospeller in the truest sense of the word.

14 September

God's traffic lights

Someone has said that in seeking the will of God we should think of traffic lights: RED for stop, AMBER for caution, GREEN for go. And do not drive on until the green light shows, otherwise a crash may occur.

Let me nominate three examples.

Stop - "cease to do evil" said Isaiah to his people (Isa 1:16). The word "evil" means to be tumultuous or raging and speaks of the gathering speed of undisciplined behaviour - "keep a hold on yourself, put the brake on your passions, don't jump the lights".

Caution "Ponder the path of thy feet", said the wise man (Prov 4:20). There are times when we should pause and consider our ways. Yet, while we ponder, let us prepare to move when the light shows green.

Go Jesus said, "Go....." (Mark 16:15). When He gives the signal we should drive on. Christianity is a "go" life. Though we observe the red and honour the amber, they are but part of the Gospel-traffic scene. The Holy Spirit sometimes says "No"! (Acts 16:6,7), sometimes "wait" (Luke 24:29), but more often "Go" (Acts 8:26). We do well to follow His lights.

15 September

The mirage of life

“The parched ground” of Isaiah 35:7 could, according to Gesenius, the Hebrew lexicographer, be translated by “mirage....a phenomenon frequent in the desert”. Such, often, is life. We vision happiness, it turns out to be an optical (or rather, a pragmatic) disappointment.

Even Solomon, with all his ability and opportunity, found it vanity, a term used by him in Ecclesiastes many times. And he tried hard enough to find happiness. It was not in wealth, he was rich, but miserable; it was not in women, he had 1,000 in his harem, yet not a real “woman” among them (Eccles 7:28); it defied his work, plans and products gave him no inner content; even his wisdom, let him down, no human philosophy could satisfy his restless spirit. He was a wretched man. Life was a sham, a disappointment, a mirage.

But he eventually found reality, it was in God’s word - the law, and more so in the great Lawgiver Himself. Worship, the fear of God, was the key to the best life. The remedy for earth’s ailments is in Jehovah, who turns the deceptive mirage of life into a delightful “pool” of satisfaction.

16 September

God's plimsoll line

All sea-going vessels have a mark on their hull that fixes the point that should never be underwater. It is the "Plimsoll line" - a legalised bond of safety that ensures (and demands) that no merchant-ship should sail over-burdened, and so in danger of capsizing or otherwise destroyed in stormy weather.

God has His "Plimsoll - line" for His children. As David puts it: "For He knoweth our frame; He remembereth that we are dust" (Ps 103:14). He knows how much we can take, and so "He will not suffer you to be tempted above that ye are able (to bear)" (1 Cor 10:13). Nay more, when the test comes He "also makes a way to escape". With every trial there is an escape - hatch.

More than this, our God, knowing the pressures of life we often bow under, asks us to cast all our care (our anxieties and fears) upon Him, "for He careth for you" (1 Peter 5:7). Our Lord is truly concerned about us. He allows testings and trials, for moral strength is produced by resistance to evil, but He is "the God of all grace" whose strength makes us steadfast and unmoveable in all our afflictions, perfected thro' suffering.

17 September

Dirty windows

A woman looked out of her wash-house at her neighbours laundry on the line outside. "She should wash her whites cleaner that that"! she ejaculated. Her near-by friend called out, "When did you last clean your windows"?

And so with us. How often our criticisms of others are just a projection of our own defective judgement? Jesus put it vividly thus. "Why worry about a speck in the eye of a brother when you have a plank in your own"? (Matt 7:3 Living Bible). Reverse this: a speck of dust on our spectacles is magnified into a boulder in our vision. Don't charge your neighbours with a fault that only exists in your own defective vision.

The colour of our lens can distort reality. "And Saul eyed David from that day and forward" (1 Sam 18:9). The green eye of envy coloured all he saw. However David acted, it was all distorted by this jealous spirit. While it is true that "rose-coloured spectacles" can lead us to fatuous optimism, it is also true that a discoloured outlook can turn innocent statements into threats and kind words into curses. Keep your windows clean, for "to the pure all things are pure" (Titus 1:15).

18 September

It happened on the Gaza strip

It was a long journey from Samaria to the Gaza highway, still longer from revival city to desert sand - but this event was epochal - a Gentile was to be ushered into the Kingdom of God.

The story is told in (Acts 8:26-40). What a tale of miracle - timing.

An important Ethiopian diplomat beguiles a long journey reading a precious manuscript. Was it newly purchased from Jerusalem? It was the Book of the prophet Isaiah. This educated and opulent courtier was reading aloud.

Many miles away in Samaria an angel instructed Philip to go to this desert road. A chariot appears on the dusty highway. The Holy Spirit tells the evangelist to join it. As he runs alongside he hears the important official reading. "Do you know what it means"? asks Philip. "Come up and explain", responded the amiable traveller.

The passage was Isaiah Chapter 53 - the "Suffering Servant" narrative. Philip recounts the story of the Cross of Jesus. The Ethiopian eagerly absorbs the message and spying a wayside pool, asks to be baptised.

Who can tell the influence of this divinely - arranged meeting? Did Ethiopia respond to their Chancellor's testimony? We shall know one day.

God knows your address

Have you ever thought that your friends have forgotten where you live, that your telephone number has been expunged from the directory? Be of good cheer, the Lord knows where you live.

So He said to the Church at Pergamos, "I know where thou dwellest, even where Satan's seat is" (Rev 2:13). The fact that their neighbour was the devil himself did not put off the Almighty from a friendly visit. Men may forsake us: God never will.

The Lord knew Peter's address - "he lodgeth with Simon the Tanner" (Acts 10:6), and initiated a move that led to SALVATION. Coincidental vision led Peter to the household of Cornelius to become to this military officer and his compatriots the key to open the door of the Kingdom of God to Gentiles (Acts 11:18).

The Lord knew Saul's address - "the street which is called Straight" (Acts 9:11), and sent a little-known disciple to declare to him a call to SERVICE. Thus the Apostle Paul was launched into his soul-saving career.

God knows where you live, and will see to it that you are visited by Himself or His servants. So cheer up!

The man next door

Forced out of the synagogue by obstinate Jews, Paul moved in with Justus, "Whose house joined hard to the synagogue" (Acts 18:7). What irony! Hope they had thick walls. Paul must have held a house-church there - and Pentecostals have never been noted for muted worship.

We read next that Crispus, chief ruler of the synagogue, believed. Was it a result of "the man next door" giving vocal testimony to a fuller and better life? In any case, it was but a small step to the neighbourly church, though a large step religiously for Crispus. He strode from Judiasm to Christianity - a leap of faith, a step to eternal life in Jesus.

His successor, Sosthenes, did not fare so well. An abortive court-case against Paul brought down the wrath of the Greek populace on the Jewish accusers. They beat up the new synagogue-chief. "And Gallio (the recently appointed proconsul) cared for none of those things". He treated the incident with indifference and the Jews with contempt. Is this the "Sosthemes" of 1 Cor 1:1? Possibly so. What a difference between his experience and that of his predecessor. It only took "a still small voice" to convert him, with Sosthemes it called for a storm of wrath, fire of persecution and earthquake of mob-violence. How mysterious are the ways of Providence.

And it all came because "the man next door" stuck to his Gospel-guns. What effect do you have on your neighbours?

21 September

Persona non grata

"Get thee hence, Satan"! said Jesus to the devil as He rebuked him for his profanity. The prince of darkness is persona non grata to all who follow Jesus. We cannot stop him coming to trouble us, but we can hasten his going by a steadfast refusal to listen to his lies or submit to his insidious suggestions.

"He is a voracious lion", said Peter (1 Peter 5:8,9). He tries to scare us with his arrogant "roar". But we must "resist, steadfast in the faith". If we hold tenaciously to the faith of the Gospel we may flout all the subtle or shocking untruths of the devil. Satan can't stand opposition. "Resist the devil, and he will flee from you", said (James 4:7). Never bow down to Satan.

But Satan has more ways than a frontal attack. Jesus used similar terms to Peter, his close friend, as He did to the arch-enemy himself - "Get thee behind Me, Satan, was his rebuke" (Matt 16:23). Why did our Lord come on so strong. "Flesh and blood", that is, human nature, often fails to grasp spiritual truth, and can become an impediment to the purpose of God. The sin of Ananias was that his pride, evidenced by his hypocritical desire for a good reputation at the expense of false claims, let the devil in. "Neither give place to the devil" (Eph 4:27). Give him an inch and he will take a kilometre.

"If I were you"

Job's appeal. "If your soul were in my soul's stead, I could heap up words against you" (Job 16:4) is often repeated in the well-meant advice, "If I were you". To this we may answer:

First You are not me. No two persons are alike. We are often diverse in features, in temperament, in outlook, in ideas.

Secondly, if you were me, you'd do the same. It is difficult, in some cases impossible, to know how another person feels. If I held his views, possessed his weaknesses and strength, was put into his situation, I, very likely, would act like he is doing.

Thirdly, I cannot make myself the arbiter of another's actions'. We need an external standard by which we all are measured. Just as Israel's fiscal system was based on "the shekel of the Sanctuary" (Num 3:50), so our ethical standards must be according to the divine absolutes of Him who said: "Be ye holy, for I am holy" (1 Peter 1:16).

But, for all that, our approach to others can be smoothed by the oil of sincere sympathy, or, to put it better, Christian love. I may not fully understand my brother, but I can feel with him and for him, and so "bear his burden" (Gal 6:2).

23 September

A hole in my pocket

There is a spiritual side to money. Used well - it multiplies. So said Jesus (Luke 6:38): not used well - it mysteriously disappears through a hole in the pocket (Hag 1:6 - "a bag with holes").

While it is true that "a good man...will guide his affairs with discretion" (Ps 112:5), yet it is also true that plenitude or poverty may issue from our bounty or our stinginess.

But there is more than one kind of riches. Money cannot buy happiness for oneself, but use it to relieve those in need, and O, the joy it can bring! "The liberal soul shall be made fat" (Prov 11:25). Money is like corn-seeds, scatter it, and it will multiply, keep it in the barn and it will be destroyed by mildew or eaten by rats.

Poverty comes to him "that withholdeth more than is meet" (Prov 11:27). The hole in your pocket will grow bigger if you fail to give to God's cause and to men's needs. But it will be sewn up if from your pocket it goes to there's. The essence of a good life is giving and receiving, and of these two the former finds most blessing (Acts 20:35).

Divine alchemy

The alchemists of the Middle Ages sought "the philosophers stone" that would turn base metal into gold. It was a fatuous quest, for if gold became so common it would lose its value.

But what these ancient philosophers failed to do, God has done, and will do. He can turn base evil into blessed good. So Joseph said "Ye thought evil against me", he reminded his brothers, "but God meant it unto good", he triumphantly added (Gen 50:20).

There are things that seem to harm us which, by divine providence turn into everlasting joy. In fact, "All things work together for good to them that love God" (Rom 8:28) in whose lives a holy purpose discloses itself.

Look at Paul's imprisonment at the end of his days. Is this the reward for a life of obedient and sacrificial service! It seemed hard. But Paul in prison led many to Christ, wrote letters that have blessed and edified the church for centuries and left an example of enduring faith. Your life seems but "lead" - heavy and base? The Lord can transmute it to gold. Trust Him.

25 September

"I die daily"
1 Cor 15:31

There are more deaths than one. there is physical death, the separation of the soul from the body; spiritual death, separation of the soul from God; worst of all, "the second death", separation of the whole personality from the presence of the Almighty (see Revelation 20:14).

But there are minor deaths, indifference or ignorance to the worlds around us. A tone-deaf person is dead to the world of music; a bigoted sot to the world of decency; an ignoramus to the world of fame; an illiterate to the world of literature; a stick-in-the-mud to the world of adventure.

A consecrated Christian is "dead to the world and all its toys"; a sanctified believer is dead to the old life; a fervent servant of Christ is dead to self. With Paul, to "die daily" meant three things. First the constant danger of opposition; secondly, his consecration to the point of complete surrender to God, "taking up his cross daily", (Luke 9:23), thirdly, his ever-readiness to give all to the service of Christ.

So may we learn to daily give ourselves to Christ that we may daily live to Him.

26 September

Last in the queue

"When all the people were baptised, ... Jesus also, (was) baptised". So wrote Luke (3:21). With sweet diffidence our Lord took his place at the end of a long line of candidates waiting for John to immerse them in Jordan.

The Baptist must have been tired with the long queue of penitents - but an amazing sense of something unusual now gripped him. He felt himself in the presence of someone greater than himself, and the baptiser craved to be baptised of Him. Did he recognise Messiah in this peasants outfit!

But Jesus came last. He was not only willing to take His turn but also reticent to attract attention. He exhibited in His modesty the humility of God.

And is not that the whole story of the life of Jesus? He never willingly sought publicity. When He "lifted up His voice" it was an epic occasion.

Is this not an example for us! If we seek to "follow His steps" we will not hug the limelight, but ever be willing to be nothing that God may be everything.

"Haste ye back"

I found Scotland one of the most hospitable places. At the end of one visit, "a canny Scot" gripped my hand and said those never-to-be-forgotten words, "Haste ye back"! Thus my departure was linked with hope of a future meeting.

When Jesus left this earth for Heaven's glory, "two men" in dazzling white assured them of His return. "This same Jesus .... shall so come in like manner", that is, personally (Acts 1:11).

And throughout those earliest years of the infant Church the hope of Christ's return was looked forward to with eager expectation. This "blessed hope" (Titus 2:13) became the SPUR to their endeavours, the SUNSHINE that brightened the dark days of persecution, and a SANCTIFYING reality that urged them to be ever ready to meet him without shame on that glorious day, the day of His return.

This expectation was very much alive to the end of New Testament times. "Behold I come quickly", said Jesus twice (Rev 22:7,12), winding up with His last word of assuring promise, "Surely, I come quickly" (vs 20). "Amen, even so come, Lord Jesus" responded John. In other words, "Haste ye back"! Are you ready?

28 September

Shut that door

So exhorted Jesus. "When thou prayest, ... 'shut thy door'," (Matt 6:6). Joint intercession should hold a permanent and prominent place in Church life (Matt 18:19,20, Acts 2:42), yet nothing can do for our spiritual life and health what personal private devotions can accomplish.

There are two sides to a door. Closing it can <u>shut in</u> or <u>shut out</u>.

When we thus draw nigh to God in secret we <u>shut out the</u> world. How blessed to turn our backs for a brief period on the turbulence that surrounds us. To spend time alone with God is like discovering an oasis of calm in a desert of tumult. Try it. It works beautifully.

When we thus enter the "secret place" of personal devotion we are <u>shut in with God</u>. "Draw nigh to God", said James, "and He will draw nigh to you" (James 4:8). At such times of holy tryst "Heaven comes down our soul to greet": In such holy silence we can hear "the still, small voice of God", by such blessed contact we are strengthened to meet life's demands, in such spiritual worship our roots go deeper and deeper into the life of God. In His light we see light. Our problems are seen from God's standpoint. We leave radiant with joy, with hope, with love. Don't forget to shut that door.

29 September

A puff of wind

Gen 4:1,2

Adam and Eve entered a dismal world when they were expelled from Eden. But the darkness was lit by a candle of hope - "The seed of the woman shall bruise the serpent's head". When Cain was born they felt this deliverer had arrived - his name meant "an acquisition", in other words, "We've got him (that is, the promised seed). He's arrived".

Then came Abel, whose name means "a puff of wind, a vapour" or an intrusive nobody. There could only be one Messiah, and Cain was he, Abel was superfluous.

But, as it happened so often in the subsequent history, the "despised and rejected" becomes the useful and honoured. Cain followed his father in agricultural pursuits - the important source of maintenance, for animal flesh was not used until after the flood. Abel kept sheep, which were kept mostly for sacrificial purposes.

But when Cain brought his own works to God, they were rejected. Abel, seeing the spiritual significance, brought a lamb, and was accepted. He may have been rejected by his family, but God took him to heart. And that's what matters most.

30 September

Adam's rib

The first ever surgical operation on a human body was performed by God. With Adam under divine anaesthesia, the Lord extracted "a rib", and expertly sutured the wound. But the amazing sequel to this act was that of that piece of "bone and flesh" the Lord God made a woman, a "help meet" for the first man. It was the origin of marriage, "they shall become one flesh" (Gen 2:18, 21-24).

Our Lord laid this down as the divine pattern and purpose of marriage, for all time "from the beginning" (Matt 19:3-9). The life-long union of one woman to one man is God's standard. To depart from it leads to personal, domestic and social disaster - a message for our times.

Marriage, as decreed by God, embraces three basic principles:

First, <u>companionship</u>, for man was not meant to be alone: he needs a mate.

Secondly, <u>co-habitation</u>, for the intended issue of "male and female" is the procreation of children. Family is the "building-block" of society.

Thirdly, <u>co-operation</u>, marriage is a joint-venture. It is as husband and wife work together that domestic harmony and service prevails.

Adam was never complete without Eve. Only she could fill up the vacancy.

1 October

The challenge of change

"The old is better" quoted Jesus (Luke 5:39); and in many cases this is true. The peaks of perfection in Ancient Greece in sculpture, philosophy and politics are still held in admiration. And what modern sounds can equal the music of Beethoven, or art the paintings of the medieval masters?

But change must come, for life can never be static. But how to keep balance between old and new is a challenge to all of us. The older generation usually resists change; the younger generally insist on change - but who is right?

A well-known saying offers help. It is an appeal to God, who alone can solve this dilemma: "God grant me the serenity to accept the things I cannot change, courage to change the things I can, and wisdom to know the difference", is the usual form. But item two is a misquotation. It should read, "courage to change the things that can and should be changed".

This makes all the difference. Not all things call for change. Tradition and custom are not all bad. The angry young man would abolish well-tried ways. He often ends up with Elijah's complaint: "I am no better than my fathers". Let us maintain what is best of old and new. Why should we squander our treasured culture or refuse newer ideals?

The body of Christ

We must draw a distinction between "the days of His flesh" (Heb 5:7) when Christ lived on earth, and the days of His heavenly session. In His earthly body He travelled far, laboured much and suffered intensely - and all for us.

Now He has a spiritual body, the Church (Eph 1:23) into which and through which He pours His fullness. What He "began both to do and teach" (Acts 1:1) He continues, and will continue through His people to the end of time.

St. Teresa of Avila (AD 1515-82) puts it well thus: "Christ has no body now on earth but yours, no hands but yours, no feet but yours; yours are the eyes through which is to look out Christ's compassion to the world, yours are the feet with which He is to go about doing good, and yours are the hands with which He is to bless us now."

Is this what Paul had in mind when he exhorts us to "present your bodies a living sacrifice . . . unto God"? (Rom 12:1) Why present our bodies and not our souls? The body is the active agent by which God's will may be done, the living vehicle by which He may fulfil His wishes toward men, the vessel of clay that may bear the water of life to the world.

Acid rain

Air pollutants from factory chimneys and car exhausts are deposited (often very far from their source) by what is termed “acid rain”. It is destructive of tree-life, and forests in Norway and Sweden are being devastated by this poisonous deposit originating in Britain.

In moral circles there is a more sinister deposit that destroys reputation, mars relationships and discolours fellowship. It is gossip, particularly that gossip that carries mischievous innuendoes, questionable rumours or denigrating spite. The Lord said to Israel: “Thou shalt not go up and down as a talebearer among Thy people” (Lev 19:16). A scandal-monger, a peddler of confidences (Prov 20:19), a petty detractor can do much harm. Like “acid rain”, it can pollute minds, spoil good repute and poison friendships.

But gossip may be redeemed by making it a vehicle of God’s message to needy humans. We can, in the words of a late missionary, “gossip the Gospel”. If we feel it necessary to criticise, let it be open, fair and constructive. But we are all human, and sometimes slip on the banana-skin of gossip.

4 October

Vision that counts

"Where there is no vision, the people perish" (or "go to pieces") Prov 29:18

But there are various aspects of vision. First, there is preceptive vision enshrined in God's Word for all of us, for all time. Our text implies this, "but he that keepeth the law, happy is he".

There is also perceptive vision, where with eyes open to truth we adjust our lives. With regard to the past, we learn from history; with regard to the present, we discriminate good from evil, embracing the former and eschewing the latter; with regard to the future, we anticipate what is to come by regulating our lives by the will of God.

There is certainly personal vision by which we seek to embrace God's plan for our lives. Destiny often hangs on our choice to look ahead, and be directed by ultimates rather than immediates.

And this applies to nations as well as individuals. The words inscribed on the monument to mark the completion of the Zuider Zee dam profoundly illustrate this: "A nation that lives, builds for its future". To have a worthwhile aim in view is a spur to present activity. Vision can make the difference between sterility and progress.

"One step at a time"

Isaiah said a remarkable thing: "They that wait upon the Lord . . . shall walk and not faint" (Isa 40:31). After the "flying" and the "running" it seems like an anticlimax to "walk".

But is it? May it not be that a consistent progress in the Christian life is the most impressive testimony to the strength and reality of godly living?

William Carey, father of modern missions, was once asked how he had achieved so much. "I can plod," he replied, "I can persevere in any definite pursuit. To this I owe everything." He is the patron-saint of holy plodders. Grace be with them.

"To walk humbly with thy God" (Micah 6:8) is a great experience. A walk requires BALANCE, spiritual equilibrium; PACE, not lagging behind or running before, but "keep in step with the Spirit" (Gal 5:25 NIV); DIRECTION, going God's way to the destiny prepared by Him; and a firm DETERMINATION to press on the Pilgrim Way. Walking calls for effort, but only thus can we make progress in the Christian life.

What is worldliness?

John describes it as anti-Christian (1 John 2:15-17) a lethal mixture of materialism, egotism, ambition and lust - all mingled together in a moral death-potion. James describes it as an enemy of godliness (James 4:4). We cannot be "other-worldly" and "this-worldly" at the same time. We have to live "in" the world, but we need not be "of" it (John 17:14-16).

But how may I define "worldliness"? A W Tozer gives us a guide. He writes: "Whatever promotes self, cheapens life, starves the soul, hopes without Bible grounds for hope, adopts current moral standards, follows the way of the majority, indulges in the pleasures of the flesh to make bearable the secret thoughts of death and judgement - that is the world."

Thoreau speaks of those who "march to the sound of another drum" - the Christian often seems out of step with the world around him, and is talked of as eccentric. But it is the beat of God's drum to which he conforms his step. And all who serve God are in the same marching order: their "left, right, left" is in rhythmic harmony.

Nothing ever happens here!

Dr Billy Graham tells the story about the day Abraham Lincoln was born. A neighbour hailed a man from town and said, "Any news down at the village, Ezra?"

"Well, Squire Maclean's gone to Washington to see Madison sworn in, and old Spellman tells me that this Bonaparte fellow has captured most of Spain. What's new out there neighbour?"

"Nothing at all, nothing at all, except a new baby down at Tom Lincoln's house. Nothing ever happens out here."

NOTHING? That baby changed the face of American history, preserved the unity of that great nation, abolished slavery, left an example of integrity and purpose - call that nothing!

Many years ago a baby was born in an obscure little town in an obscure little land, and in an obscure dwelling - a stable. Apart from stories of stars and shepherds, of angels and astronomers, no one took the slightest notice. To the world it was a non-event, "the world knew Him not" (John 1:10). But that Babe was Jesus, whose life and death affected and still affects the whole of civilisation. On that first Christmas Day "the Word became flesh" to bring salvation to a fallen race.

Thanksgiving day

But every day should be a time of thanksgiving, and if we think aright, it will, for we owe everything to God, "for in Him we live and move and have our being" (Acts 17:28).

What, then, should be my catalogue of appreciation? For a start, take the following:

Thank God for the good earth,
For healthful sunshine's warming rays,
For refreshing showers,
For the principle of life in growing things,
For the gloom of night,
For the glow of day,
For the changing seasons,
For the year's full round,
And for a heart to appreciate the care of God
For our needs of body, mind and soul.
For all the gifts that fall within the bounds
Of his bountiful providence.

Above all, for putting up with us sinners for so long, for extending His love to us in the gift of His Son, for so directing our affairs that we were eventually faced with the great decision of accepting His proffered mercy and forgiveness - and for the divine impulse that led us to accept His pardon freely offered.

Since then have come "all spiritual blessing in Christ" (Eph 1:3). Surely we can say "Thanks be to God for His unspeakable gifts" (2 Cor 9:15).

9 October

Reaping!

One of the surest things in nature and in grace is that if we sow we shall reap. In both spheres three principles apply.

First, we reap if we sow - as Paul said, "In due season we shall reap, if we faint not" (Gal 6:7-9). This is an encouragement to those who sow good, but a threat to those who sow evil. Reward or retribution will come - it is a cosmic law.

Secondly, we reap what we sow. To do the will of God is to sow righteousness and reap happiness. To practise evil is to sow present gratification and reap future woe. When a friend visited financial swindler Horatio Bottomley in prison, he found him sewing mail bags.

"Ah, Bottomley," he said, "Sewing?"
"No, reaping," replied the once powerful journalist.

Thirdly, we reap more than we sow. Who can measure the harvest of a noble or kindly deed!

An obstinate, ragged boy was graciously treated by his Sunday School teacher. In spite of his bad behaviour, she persisted to give him clothes as well as the Gospel. She conquered her discouragement and eventually won him over. Who was he? He became one of the greatest missionaries to China - Robert Morrison.

But to sow the wind of dissolute living is to reap the whirlwind of shame and remorse. So keep up the good sowing - the harvest will come.

A preacher's "in-fit"

We often hear of a preacher's outfit, but what of its essential counterpart - the "in-fit", without which no preacher of Christ's gospel can be effective. May we suggest three essential elements?

First the preacher's own nature. Paul spoke of being "separated (by God) from his mother's womb" (Gal 1:15). Is it possible that the very make-up of our being - our temperament, tastes and tendencies - are indicative of what God planned us to be? According to Hebrews 5:1-3, a priest's own humanity is essential to his being a humane minister.

Secondly, the preacher's experience. God often puts His servants "through the mill" in order to grind them into shape. His own experience of life adds reality and authenticity to his message. Every preacher should be "a witness unto Me" (Acts 1:8), and no-one can be a witness without experience.

The famous artist, J M W Turner, once had himself lashed to the mast of a ship during a storm. His subsequent painting of the elemental forces of nature amazed his fellow-artists. It was real: so should preachers preach from life.

Thirdly, the preacher's vision. True and edifying ministry can only come from one who has seen God, and by Spirit-anointed ministry, reveals Him.

11 October

Every day is a bonus

On visiting an old member of my congregation, I found her in tears. I asked her what was the matter. She replied, "I'm 70 years old today. I've reached the allotted span. This is the end." I reassured her, reading to her that relevant passage in Psalm 90:10, and pointed out that "threescore years and ten" was indeed "the days of our years", but told her of God's added bonus - "they may be fourscore years." She was pacified.

But is not every day a divine bonus, a gift from God? Old Jacob must have felt so when he spoke to Pharoah of his age as "the days of the years of my pilgrimage are an hundred and thirty years" (Gen 47:9). They were often tough ("evil") and hurtful, but he pressed on his pilgrim way "a day at a time", and now this nomadic shepherd is blessing the mightiest monarch of the day: a pinnacle of achievement.

Each day a bonus? Yes, a gift of grace. As Jeremiah put it, "It is of the Lord's mercies that we are not consumed, because His compassions fail not. They are new every morning; great is Thy faithfulness" (Lam 3:21, 22). Thank God for the refreshing dew of His presence that makes each passing day a revelation of His unfailing love.

12 October

Room for the sky

That superb English landscape painter, John Constable, wrote: "That landscape painter who does not make his skies a very material part of his composition neglects to avail himself of one of his greatest aids. The sky is the source of light in nature, and governs everything."

And so with life. All that the sky represents - heaven "beyond the blue" - is essential to a full-blown maturity. Take spiritual hopes and values out of our experience, and what's left?

Bunyan, in his peerless "Pilgrim's Progress", gives a picture of a man raking in the rubbish tip and reaching out after a bubble. Above his head hangs a glorious crown, but he has no eyes for that. And so many grovel in earthly pursuits, and fail to see the heavenly glories within their grasp.

In all our living we must find room for the sky to complete the picture; in all our preaching we must never neglect the ultimates of other-worldly ideals. Leave out the sky and life's perspective lacks reality; leave out the sky, and hope's expectations become dim. "Set your affection on things above," counselled Paul. In other words, "make room for the sky" (Col 3:2).

13 October

Just passing by

When Mary of Bethany anointed the feet of Jesus, "the house was filled with the fragrance of the perfume" (John 12:3). She, in her embarrassment, "wiped His feet with her hair". For long after, her perfumed life - the same that anointed Jesus - would remind people of this act of worship. Her very passing by would be redolent of that fragrant moment.

May not we, too, distil the sweet fragrance of Christ as we pass by (cf 2 Cor 2:14,15)?

A rose crossed my path.
How did I know?
A fragrance sweet
Assailed my sense,
Proof of its gladdening presence.
A godly life was lived.
How did I know?
The fragrance of love
Assailed my heart
Pervading my spirit with peace.

Our fellowship with Christ, augmented by prayerful devotion and attested by deeds of kindness, can shed a holy fragrance that our very presence can be a benediction, and our mere passing by, like Peter's shadow (Acts 5:16) bring healing to wounded hearts, and consolation to tired minds.

14 October

Sad-you-see

An old friend of mine, in punning mood of the Sadducees, who say "that there is no resurrection, neither angel nor spirit" (Acts 23:8), remarked "That is why they are sad-you-see." And he was right, for to cut out the possibility of a future life of joy and peace is to make this dark world darker still.

"Neither angel nor spirit" robs our lives of the fact of a spiritual world, a host of helpful agencies that "minister for them who shall be heirs of salvation". (Heb 1:14).

The unseen world is as real and as relevant as the world we see. But it requires the eye of faith to behold this realm of bright spirits. To take into consideration this invisible creation (Col 1:16) does much for us.

First, it delivers us from MATERIALISM. There is more to existence than things within the scope of sense. Secondly, it helps us to realise that our great Creator has more than one mode of activity. He is boundless in His creative force. Thirdly, it adds to the life of believers a heavenly outlook. The "invisible" makes the "visible" meaningful and relative. Life is more than we can see. (2 Cor 4: 17,18).

15 October

A nifty nephew

Paul had a sister whose son was finishing his education in the centre of Jewish learning, Jerusalem. He secretly admired his notorious uncle Paul, and when he overheard a plot to assassinate him, he reported it to the Roman commander who held the apostle in custody. His nifty act saved the life of his intrepid uncle. What a nephew! (Acts 23:16-22).

<u>Divine providence</u>. God uses many means to preserve His servants. Here a close relative (for "blood is thicker than water") at great personal risk plays an important role in this drama of apostolic life.

<u>Divine promise</u>. The Lord had given His word that Paul would testify in Rome, and no machinations of men could break that holy promise.

<u>Divine purpose</u>. The presence and testimony of Paul in Rome, the centre of the Gentile world, was part of God's plan. No plot of alien Jewry, no force of stormy nature could frustrate God's will. When the Lord plans His people's lives neither earth nor hell can prevail against it.

16 October

A fighting spirit

At the end of his days Paul could write: "I have fought a good fight" (2 Tim 4:7); and so he had! He departed leaving a string of churches in the Middle East and Europe, a catalogue of epistles that still form the essence of New Testament theology, and an example of the fighting spirit that advances the cause of Christ.

In his last public address at the Royal Albert Hall, London, on 9 May, 1912, the intrepid William Booth, founder and first general of the Salvation Army, concluded in the following words: "While women weep, as they do now, I'll fight; while little children go hungry, as they do now, I'll fight; while men go to prison, in and out, as they do now, I'll fight; while there is a drunkard left, while there is a poor girl lost upon the streets, while there remains one dark soul without the light of God, I'll fight - I'll fight to the very end."

Such words make me feel ashamed that I have done so little for the souls of men, for the service of God. The Lord help us to "fight the good fight of faith" (1 Tim 6:12) and vanquish sore.

17 October

Men and mountains

Have you ever read William Blake's lines:

> "Great things are done when men and mountains meet
> which are not done by jostling in the street."

How impressive a concept, and, in their way, how inspiring! But how do we react to the "mountains" that often tower menacingly above us in our Christian life. Do we regard them as impediments or challenges?

James says that testings are benefits. "When all kinds of trials and temptations crowd into your lives, my brothers, don't resent them as intruders, but welcome them as friends." (James 1:2, J B Phillips).

The big things we face are not looming terrors, they are calls to endeavour. Planned by God, they test our stamina and challenge our stability. To climb them is to gain a higher experience and a wider vision. To exploit them is to become stronger in God. Do not whinge about them, welcome them. They are meant for our development.

A balanced life

The Christian virtue of "TEMPERANCE", wrought in us by the Holy Spirit (Gal 5:23) is really the balance-wheel of spiritual life, that self-control that releases what is good and restrains what is evil.

William Penn, the emigrant Quaker, founder of Pennsylvania, put it delightfully well thus:

"Be reserved, but not sour; grave, but not formal; bold, but not rash; humble, but not servile; patient, but not insensible; constant, but not obstinate; cheerful, but not light; sweet, rather than familiar and intimate with very few."

But such balance needs help in its progressive production. In mechanics we meet with "a parallelogram of forces", where energies are balanced to form a state of equal power. So a Christian life may be reinforced and regulated by the parallel forces of doctrine and devotion, submission and service, enterprise and endeavour. Or, to put it in the words of Oswald Chambers: "My utmost for His highest!"

19 October

"He that keepeth Israel"

The second "Song of Degrees" has this assuring note: "Behold, He that keepeth Israel shall neither slumber nor sleep." (Psalm 121:4). This precious promise to earthly Israel may be extended to "the Israel of God" - the Church (Gal 6:16). What a message to all believers!

<u>We have a keeper</u>. When we need help we look not to the "hills" of escape or worldly cover, we seek Him "which made heaven and earth". The God of creation is our mighty Redeemer.

<u>He is our gracious guardian</u>. He does not "suffer our foot to be moved". By his help, we can stand our ground against all opposition - man or devil.

<u>He is our sleepless sentinel</u>. Human guards may suffer from fatigue, and in a long night of temptations grow weary of watching, but our God "neither slumbers (in fitful inattention) nor sleeps (in total subjection to weakness)", His watchful attention is ever alert.

The story is told of Bishop William Quayle, who was awake one night fruitlessly worrying, when he heard God say to him, "Quayle, you go to bed - I'll sit up the rest of the night." So why worry? If God is looking after us we are safe night and day.

20 October

Acceleration

T Sharper Knowlson in his book, "Put on Your Thinking Cap" (pg 156) quotes philosopher Schills as saying: "We may detect a law of acceleration pervading history." He believed that the rate of change in evolution is clearly increasing, and that such changes issue at shorter intervals.

This seems manifest in modern times. Within this twentieth century knowledge burgeoned so rapidly that it is difficult for normal folk to keep abreast of developments. Computers have speeded up our acquisition of data. Internet now links millions of enthusiasts to cosmic-wide information - science has delved into nature's secrets more deeply, astronomers probe further and further into space, seeking the origin of the universe in which we live. And there seems no end to what may increasingly be discovered.

What the next century will reveal (or even the next decade) is mind-boggling.

Does all this give deeper meaning to the words of Jesus - "Behold, I come quickly" (Rev 22:7,12,20). The rapid acceleration of historical events may reach that divine climax sooner than some may expect. At least we can "speed its coming" (2 Pet 3:12 NIV) by holy living and fervent anticipation. Speed on the day; our hearts are ready!

21 October

The forward look

Soren Kierkegaard, patron saint of existentialism, said: "Life can only be understood backwards, but it must be lived forwards."

Looking ahead. History is behind us, mystery is before us, but reality is with us. While memory is an aid to guide us and vision a hope to spur us, yet we are "now-people". But, if we had nowhere to go, no good or goal to anticipate, life would be a dreary drag, a dour and deadly plod. We look ahead to live. Though "now we see through a glass darkly", it is balanced by the "then" of future glory. At least, so affirms the apostle Paul (1 Cor 13:12)

Looking back. Even in this life we look back and see how God has graciously led us. We are where we are because we have been where we have been. The past has helped to create our present, and like Samson who drew honey from the remnants of a former conquest - a dead lion - so we taste sweetness from trials overcome. This will be our rich experience when we meet our Lord "face to face". So until then we travel in hope, when: "I'll bless the hand that guided, I'll bless the heart that planned, when throned where glory dwelleth in Emmanuel's Land."

"There's plenty left . . . "

Little Timothy was enjoying his first visit to the seaside. His mother had helped him to build a sand-castle, and round it had formed a ditch. "That's the moat," she said, "Now fill it with water." The toddler took his bucket to the water's edge, filled it, and came back. But he stumbled, and lost most of the bucket's contents. "Now look what you've done," chided mother, "You've spilled it." "Never mind, Mummie," was the reply, "there's plenty left". And went back for a refill.

Plenty left! He could never exhaust the ocean. And we can never exhaust the grace of God - His love in acts of goodness and mercy.

John states, "And of His fullness have all we received and grace for grace" (John 1:16). A T Robertson, an outstanding Greek scholar, points out that "grace for grace" contains the picture of an incoming tide where one wave bounds over another to reach the shore. So we may receive "grace upon grace" from the ocean of God's love. Again and again we can return for more, for there's always PLENTY LEFT. We cannot exhaust God.

23 October

The underrower

Ancient triremes had three banks of oarsmen to provide the necessary propulsion. The lowest tier were called "the underrowers". They could not see where they were going, but rowed their rhythmic strokes at the drum-beat of the director above. To use the Greek word, they were hyperētēs - under-rowers.

Paul uses this word in 1 Corinthians 4:1, when he speaks of Apollos and himself as "ministers of Christ". What a vivid term for Christian service. As underrowers we receive our directions from above, and pull our spiritual oars together at our Captain's command. We cannot always understand the way we are going, but we trust our Pilot and give our strength and attention to His will.

It may seem undignified so to serve, but our trust is in our Lord and Master. We are ready to serve Him whether seen or unseen, whether regarded or disregarded by men. And it is our confidence in our heavenly Guide that enables us to bend our strength to the progress of God's "Ship of State" - His Church on earth.

Things God cannot do

The exam is over. A tired little examinee prays at bedtime: "Please God make Copenhagen the capital of Japan - even if it is only for a week or so."

So relates Rita Snowden, well-known Christian writer, who adds: "She will not have learning enough for life, till she understands that there are some things that even God cannot do."

God cannot deny himself (2 Tim 2:13). He is constant, He is consistent, He is changeless. No disbelief of man can affect divine immutability. "I am the Lord, I change not" (Mal 3:6). If He is God He cannot change: He cannot improve, for perfection admits of no degrees; He will not grow less, for Deity denies deterioration. He will ever remain true to Himself.

God cannot contradict himself. His promises remain secure, His precepts are sure. God does not "repent": He may change His methods in dealing with man (Gal 6:6), but He never changes His mind (1 Sam 15:29).

All this has a two-fold meaning for us. It is a consolation, for God will always have mercy on a penitent sinner; it is a challenge, for no man can oppose God and win: He is both Rewarder and Retributer.

25 October

Unnoticed

"If you are a good interpreter," says one of the top-flight interpreters of Geneva, "nobody notices you, nobody ought to notice you. It is only when you slip up that you become noticeable."

And so with Christians, who are interpreters of Christ to the world. Some preachers, to their shame, parade themselves, but a true witness to Jesus is ready to seek the shadows as they speak of their Lord and Saviour.

Have you noticed that none of the four Gospel writers appends his name to his work. We may only arrive at the identity of Matthew, Mark, Luke and John by a method of induction. In any case, the glory of the Christ so inspiringly presented to us is so majestic that we forget that it is penned by humans. Even when we feel we have discovered the writers, we do not praise them, we are blinded to earthly sources by the glory of the Christ of God presented to us.

A visitor to Edinburgh sought to hear two reputed ministers. His comment was that the first impressed him as a gifted orator, but the second with a sense of God's presence and reality. May our impacts on others lead them to lose us in the vision of the Saviour we acclaim.

Theology of failure

Haddon Robinson, senior editor of "Christianity Today", once penned a remarkable concept. He wrote:

> "Anyone can put together a theology of success. It is not hard to celebrate men and women who are winners, and explain what makes them great. The tough work lies in constructing a theology for failures. Perhaps because I have failed so often in my life I look for the word from God that will help me keep going when I feel I've let God and everyone else down."

We may write the theology of failure ourselves, but God can edit it and expand it into a higher philosophy. In fact, He can take those very failures we moan about and make them a basis for success. The fact I may have failed so much is because I have attempted so much. Some folk never fail because they never try to succeed. They never fall because they never try to climb.

But God has a word for us: "Fear not, thou worm Jacob . . . I will help thee . . . thou shalt thresh the mountains" (Isa 41:14,15). The original Jacob seemed a failure until God took hold of him. But out of this frail, fickle and feckless man came blessings massive and eternal.

27 October

Gospel of the second chance

The story is told of Roy Riggles, an American athlete, who on a New Year's Day football match in 1929, collected the ball, ran 65 yards in the wrong direction and scored for the wrong team. He was devastated - nay more, positively humiliated.

But, to his amazement, the coach put him on for the second half. "Roy," he said, "Get up and go back. The game is only half over." He went and played a magnificent game. So says the record.

Jonah the prophet must have felt humiliated when the Lord thwarted his plans to escape an onerous task. He, from patriotic bias, felt he could not preach to Nineveh, potential enemy to Israel, lest they repent and escape judgement. He ran away, but God ran faster and caught him up. Jonah was deposited into the foaming deep, and, delivered by a monstrous fish. That'll teach you, Jonah, to disobey God!

A disobedient prophet! A pitiful wreck of a man! But did God cast him off? No! "And the word of the Lord came unto Jonah the second time" (Jonah 3:1).

This is the Gospel of the Second Chance. Have you fallen short of your expectations or failed to fulfil your obligations? Don't give up, trust in God and have another go. The game is not over yet!

What is a humbug?

Darwin was once accosted by two young practical jokers. They had artificially contrived a strange creature made up from parts of different insects, and presented it to the great naturalist for identification. Darwin inspected it closely. "Did it hum when you caught it?" he asked. "Yes, it did," they replied. "Well, then, it is a humbug," he concluded grandly.

Life is full of humbugs of various kinds, but the worst human humbug is one who is a fake - and does not know it. Jesus met them. He called them "hypocrites" - play-actors, people who put on a mask Are they ashamed of their real selves? As we read their encounter with our Lord we are led to conclude that they acted the part so much that they ended up really believing what they fancied themselves to be.

A humbug has all the trimmings of piety, but not its reality; he claims a spirituality he does not possess; he "hums" of religious correctness, but his real life denies it. No wonder Jesus excoriated them so severely. "Be not deceived, God is not mocked" (Gal 6:7) - you can fool men, but not God.

29 October

Excelsior!

"Excelsior - higher, higher!" cried the young enthusiast of Longfellow's poem of that name. His trouble was that he started to climb a mountain in the worst season and in failing light. He heeded not the advice of experience, though he spurned the blandishments of beauty.

He failed: but his spirit was right. If only his enthusiasm had been matched by good sense!

As Christians we must ever press on to higher things. Our "excelsior" is to ever seek greater and richer experiences in God: as the hymn-writer puts it:-

> "I'm pressing on the upward way,
> New heights I'm gaining every day;
> Still praying as I onward bound,
> 'Lord plant my feet on higher ground'."

But, unlike the hapless youth of "Excelsior" fame, we have the Spirit of God to gird us and the Word of God to guide us. With these our holy ambition to reach the heights can be fulfilled. Yet not completely, for there will always be more of God to know. After a miraculous ministry, after "visions and revelations of the Lord" (2 Cor 12:1), Paul still felt he had not "attained" (Phil 3:12). In his declining years he felt there was so much more to know of Jesus - and he still pursued that prize.

Bubbles

Paul warned his converts of the force of "philosophy and vain deceit" by which their minds could be assaulted and their lives become a prey to "intellectualism or high-sounding nonsense" (Col 2:3, J B Phillips). The Greek for "vain" is <u>Kenos</u>, meaning "empty". Much of human philosophy is like a bubble, attractive but empty, beautiful but liable to burst.

Millai's famous picture of his grandson blowing bubbles (later used as an advert for Pear's soap) is pretty, but conveys the concept of childhood dreams that are pretty but ephemeral.

Bunyan's "Pilgrim's Progress" gives us a more sinister portrait of "bubble-mindedness". An old man is grasping at a pretty bubble, while a golden crown is just above his head.

To young and old are presented ideas that are attractive but empty. Man's concept of beauty and goodness fall short of divine truth. Yet again and again the human mind prefers man's fumblings to God's realities.

In a day of many superficial dogmas and phrenetic ideas, we need to discover and dwell on the wholesome and soul-building truth revealed in the Scriptures, the inspired and profitable Word of God (2 Tim 3:16,17).

31 October

The age of noise

Aldous Auxley once commented: "The twentieth century is among other things the 'Age of Noise'. Physical noise, mental noise and noise of desire . . . All the resources of our miraculous technology have been thrown into the current assault against silence."

Unwanted noise, often merely a cacophony of senseless sound, is an assault on our privacy. Homes are no longer a sanctuary, they have become a sounding board for raucous music. Even churches are no longer an escape from the clashing cymbals of pop-designer music. Public address systems magnify often unwanted noise-forms into our worship. Why all this thunder of sound?

First, the devil does not want us to think. If he can fill our ears with ballad and chorus, he can close it to "the still small voice" of deeper and loftier things. Read 1 Kings 19:12; Psalm 104:34.

Secondly, human nature does not pause to think. To a quiet mind comes unsolvable problems: the world has gone mad, what can I do about it? Nothing! - so shut it out. But noise not only damages hearing, it deadens our sensibilities and dulls our thinking.

Christians must ever find a quiet corner in which to listen to God.

1 November

Three looks

The Christology of Hebrews is superb. No other New Testament scribe speaks so fully and so nobly of Jesus - the God-Man. Three times we are exhorted to look to Him.

In Hebrews 2:9 we see Jesus factually. Where Adam failed, our Lord triumphed. As we gaze upon Him "crowned with glory and honour", we see the divine fulfilment of what God intended the human race to be. Redemption is a fact, salvation is ours.

In Hebrews 9:28 we see Jesus forwardly. He came once to save our souls from sin, "unto them that look for Him shall He appear the second time without sin unto salvation." Our present experience is to be saved from sin's PENALTY and POWER; then we shall be saved from its very PRESENCE.

In Hebrews 12:2 we see Jesus focally. The Greek word translated "looking" means "to look away, fix one's eyes trustingly on someone". It is as we focus our gaze on Jesus, turning our eyes from surrounding circumstances to Him, that we can run the Christian race - and obtain the prize of eternal salvation. So keep on looking, brother, to Jesus.

2 November

Rainless clouds

Jude 12

Clouds may take various forms - the high and horizontal STRATUS, the glowing halo of NIMBUS, or the thundery darkness of CUMULUS - but all are linked with moisture and the possibility of its precipitation in rain: God's method of irrigation.

Clouds are part of the meteorological cycle that sustains nature (cf Eccles 1:3-7). <u>Sun</u> draws up moisture from the sea; <u>wind</u> drives the <u>clouds</u> thus formed over the land to be deposited in refreshing <u>rain</u>, rain flows in <u>streams</u> and rivers to the ocean whence it came - the cycle is complete. But what a vital contribution to earth's ecology!

So spiritually, the <u>sun</u> of God's love, the <u>wind</u> of God's Spirit combine to send blessings to men. Our heartfelt response in praise and thanksgiving complete the cycle of divine purpose.

But "clouds without water" are not only a disappointment, they are an anomaly. Clouds are meant to be vessels of blessing. But Jude speaks of certain intruders into early Church fellowship who made a profession of faith, but ministered nothing good. They made a show of piety, but all they did was to darken the sky, hiding the light of God's Truth, empty shams, rainless clouds.

3 November

Upside downness

Isaiah chided Israel with perverting truth. "You turn things upside down," he wrote, "as if the potter were thought to be the clay" (Isa 29:16 NIV).

Do we not see this today in much of Christendom? Things are upside down:-

<u>When experience takes precedence over the word of God</u>, when deeds direct doctrine, when systems outweigh Scripture. It is good to "taste and see that the Lord is gracious" - but He is gracious whether we taste or not. Priority belongs to the Bible: the final arbiter is the inspired Word.

<u>When finance becomes more important than faith</u>. "Silver and gold have I none," said Peter (Acts 3:6). The Church started with an empty purse - but a mighty faith. If we believed more we would need to beg less.

<u>When we let the world set our agenda</u>. Yes, we must adjust some things to current culture, but the will of God must take precedence to the whims of the times. "Be not conformed to this world" (Rom 12:2). The modern age must not direct us, nor even a former age control us. Whether it be tradition or fashion, nothing must supersede God's revealed will.

The apostles were described as "These that have turned the world upside down" (Acts 17:6). Actually, they simply sought to put it right-side up. That is what the Gospel does. When we accept Jesus as Saviour and Lord, our concept of right and wrong is often reversed - and revived.

4 November

The genetic fallacy

Since the discovery of DNA, that marvellous intricate system that patterns our lives, many claims have been extended as to the power of this genetic code.

Suggestions are made that what we have hitherto considered immoderate, and even immoral behaviour are merely molecular mishaps, therefore excusable.

This is nonsense, and makes a mockery of ethics, both natural and Biblical. Because I have a natural tendency does not mean I must indulge it. I can discipline myself.

It may surprise you to know that DNA is spoken of in the Bible: read Psalm 139:13-16. "I am fearfully and wonderfully made . . . my substance curiously wrought . . . in Thy book all my members were written." The language is not scientific, but who could have put it better?

In the same Psalm it says - "Search me . . . see if there be any wicked way in me, and lead me in the way" (vs 23,24). Genetics does not eliminate ethics. The grace of God can subdue and direct into ways of truth and righteousness all those innate energies of nature.

5 November

Hot-air balloons

The park near where I lived was a lifting-off point for hot-air balloons. As I watched the process of preparation I saw a large inert mass of material stretched out on the grass. Then fire was directed through an orifice into this lifeless form. Gradually it filled up with hot air, and was soon a living orb straining at its guy ropes. It was released, it rose with its basket into the sky - a majestic sight.

Is this how a Christian should be? In ourselves we are earth-bound, tied by gravity and nature to these lower regions. We need something to lift us, to break the laws of nature. We may have it. "Be filled with the Spirit" wrote Paul (Eph 5:18), the result is that we soar into a new experience of life. We see things from a different angle, we do things from a different motive, we enjoy things in a fuller way.

Our spiritual life is exhilarated, our life becomes filled with holy melody. It transforms our worship, it enhances our domestic relations, it helps us to fulfil our social duties with joy and gladness, it lifts us above earthly woes.

But the balloon is only kept aloft by continuous supplies of that which lifted it up. So we must be continually filled.

6 November

The chariot rolls on

In the earliest days of the Christian Church believers could be counted - 120 (Acts 1:15), 3,000 (Acts 2:41), 5,000 (Acts 4:4). But growth was so rapid that numbers were swallowed up in terms like "numbers multiplied" (Acts 5:14, 6:7), "Churches . . . multiplied" (Acts 9:31) , "increased in number daily" (Acts 16:5). What an advance from digital reckoning to computer assessment.

Three reasons account for this.

First, they were full of life. Their new experience of God was evident in the joyful, almost frisky, activity. If a church is alive, it will grow. The life of Christ, both in its quality and abundance, led to bounding experience. "Joy of the Lord" overflowed.

Secondly, they were fed. The Word of the Lord was multiplied (cf Acts 12:24, 19:20). Nourished on "all the counsel of God" (cf. Acts 20:27,28), they developed energies that were released in service. "The word of His grace" (Acts 20:32) not only builds up the Christian life, it nerves the saint for sanctified activity.

Thirdly, they were fired. The Holy Flame of Pentecost, like the fire of the Levitical altar, was never allowed to go out (Lev 6:12). Fed by holy devotion, the early Church continued to glow with sacred fire throughout the era of The Acts.

The chariot of God - "chariot of fire" - may still roll on if we let God have His way.

7 November

Vindication

When Paul speaks of "Great is the mystery of Godliness" He emphasises the essence of the Gospel story as summed up in the life and experience of the Lord Jesus. He was manifested in Incarnation, justified by the Resurrection, under constant angelic observation, world-wide declaration, universal acceptation and eternal glorification.

The phrase "justified in the Spirit" (1 Tim 3:16) is rightly translated in the NIV by "vindicated by the Spirit", a fact endorsed by His resurrection, as Romans 1:4 also indicates.

The whole ministry and mission of Jesus, apparently terminated by His crucifixion, is shown to be totally vindicated as His declared life-purpose.

His Gospel was shown to be true. In raising Him from the dead, the Father declared His total acceptance of His Son as the Saviour of men, as the Mediator of His covenant, and as the Consummator of eternal purpose to "gather my saints together unto Me; those that have made a covenant with Me by sacrifice" (Psalm 50:5).

Jesus is the fulfilment of Old Testament precept and promise, the realisation of its types and shadows, the representation of its ideals and covenants. And all this is confirmed and assured by His resurrection.

8 November

Beyond the blue

The glory of the Gospel is that it not only enhances this side of living, but it also reveals the other side of dying.

And no richer expression of this theme is given than the vision of John in The Revelation 7:9-17, where "a great multitude which no man could number, of all nations, and kindred's, and people, and tongues, stood before the Throne."

Heaven's negatives. No more loneliness, distress, dire experience, privation or sorrow. And that most tender of promises: "God shall wipe away all tears from their eyes."

Heaven's positives. The ecstasy of God's presence, the thrill of worship, the joy of holy service, the satisfaction of being led and fed by our everlasting Shepherd - the Lamb of God. "Day and night" we will "serve Him". This expression - "day and night" is but a human term for eternal continuity. We shall have new bodies that do not need to be recuperated by sleep, and renewed spirits that never tire of holy eternal exercises. Worship will be our dominating activity. Our work will be worship.

And Paul had a glimpse of this glorious realm (2 Cor 12:2-4), so that he could say, "our light affliction, which is but for a moment, worketh for us a far more exceeding weight of glory." The vision of glory to come brightens the gloom of earthly trials.

David's mole

1 Chron 6:8

When Absalom rebelled against his father in an attempt to seize the throne, David was beset with hurtful experiences. One of the most painful was the defection of Ahitophel.

This aristocrat, revered for his wisdom, was not only the king's counsellor, he was a personal friend (Psalm 41:9). They were closer than brothers, they even shared their spiritual devotions as they "walked into the house of God in company" (Psalm 55:14). David was deeply wounded, more than that, the sagacity and perception, of him whose word "was as if a man had inquired at the oracle of God" (2 Sam 16:23) was now at the disposal of Absalom.

In despair David cried, "O Lord, I pray Thee, turn the counsel of Ahitophel into foolishness" (2 Sam 15:31). The Lord did just that! Hushai, one of David's leading men, became a "mole", insinuating his way into the confidence of Absalom. He did stretch the truth a bit, but, playing on the rebellious son's pride (and fear of defeat) he persuaded him to abandon the wise strategy of the senior politician and adopt a more ostentatious scheme. The ensuing delay gave David time to recuperate his forces. Ahitophel anticipated the future result - and hung himself.

Lesson! For every "Ahitophel" of treachery, there is a "Hushai" of loyalty. The Lord so balances our lives that intended evil is transmutted into good (see Rom 8:28).

10 November

The abiding spirit

Jesus promised His disciples "another Comforter . . . even the Spirit of Truth", and said that He would "abide with you for ever". As the Author of the New Dispensation, our Lord Himself enjoyed the experience of "the Spirit descending and remaining on Him" (John 1:33).

This was to be the mark of the dispensation about to be established. In Old Testament times the Holy Spirit came upon selected servants of God for certain tasks within a limited period, but now God's people are to enjoy the abiding Spirit as long as the time should last.

And what a blessing His coming was (and still is) to the Church of Jesus Christ!

The abiding Spirit is an animating presence. At His coming on the day of Pentecost, the waiting group of 120 were filled with new energy: wind represented driving force, fire spoke of dynamic fervour.

The abiding Spirit was an activating power, driving the early disciples "into all the world". This expulsive energy made the disciples missionaries.

The abiding Spirit proved to be an arresting personality. His holy temperament breathed into their lives, coloured their prayers, directed their preaching, gave miraculous support to all their witnessing for Jesus. He still does.

11 November

Rosemary for remembrance

"There's rosemary, that's for remembrance," said demented Ophelia, fair fiancee of Hamlet. But rosemary speaks more to me than Shakespeare's lovelorn maiden.

An inclined cobble road in Folkestone leads down to the embarkation-point where troops in World War I took off for France. It is lined with "rosemarie for remembrance", lest we forget those who sacrificed their all to preserve our liberty and honour as a nation. My own father must have trod that way as he was among some of the first draughts sent to the continent. He came back: many didn't. Shall they be forgotten? It is well that Remembrance Day still marks a nation's gratitude for those who paid the price of our freedom. The two-minute silence speaks our thanks.

But there was a greater sacrifice some 2,000 years ago, when Jesus died on the Cross for our salvation. "Greater" because He had more to lose - He was God's beloved and only Son; "greater" because He had more to give, He laid down His pure and spotless life as "the Lamb of God" as a sacrifice for our sins; "greater" because the effect has been a way opened back to God for alienated and sinful mankind.

Before He suffered on the Tree our Lord, at the Last Supper, instituted the sacred ceremony we call "Holy Communion". "Do this in remembrance of Me" He asked. And to the dawn of eternal day His faithful saints will ever remember Him in "The Breaking of Bread" as He wished.

12 November

Children are persons

The Book of Jonah ends with a remarkable statement: "More than 120,000 persons that cannot discern between their right hand and their left hand" (Jonah 4:11).

These are evidently young children as yet lacking the basics of knowledge. But (and this surprised me) they are called "persons", that is, individuals, descendants of Adam - for so is the Hebrew word used. So then, children have distinctive personality. Girls are not "Little Women", as Louisa M Allcott affirmed, they are girls, and can only be understood as such. Boys and girls may be adults in the making, but they are adolescent, both physically and mentally, before then (and perhaps spiritually also). We should respect their dignity as "persons". Children also have hidden potentialities. The aim of education should not be to fit them into a preconceived uniformity, though basic learning (such as the four 'Rs' - reading, (w)riting, (a)rithmetic and religion) are important for all, but to discover their possibilities and make room for their genetic energies to be released.

They also have their real perplexities. It is not easy growing up. Although the adult world is life's object, yet the steps to attain it are often puzzling and difficult. Parents, teachers and friends may help by applying essential disciplines, setting worthy examples and imparting needed encouragement, advice, opportunities and trust. Let children be children while they can.

What a ministry!

James Moffatt translates Job 4:3,4 thus: "You . . . put strength into feeble souls; your words have kept men on their feet". The words of Eliphas to Job give us an ideal of what inspired preaching can accomplish.

Ian Maclaren said, "The chief end of preaching is comfort. Never can I forget what a distinguished scholar, who used to sit in my church, once said to me: 'Your best work in the pulpit has been to put heart into men for the coming week'." The stormy winds of life can be strong to violent, but God-directed ministry can help people to stand, nay more, even make progress in the pilgrim life when sorrow, stress and strife would tend to blow them off their feet.

When Isaiah began his second great period of ministry, he opened with the exhilarating words, "Comfort ye, comfort ye my people, saith your God" (Isa 40:1). These words, set to noble music, and incorporated into Handel's "Messiah", echo this message of hope and consolation to God's people.

Our Lord was Prime Minister of Good Cheer. His words were heart-warming and mind-reassuring - and still are. Read them, and find comfort.

Speed is the essence

"Prime Minister Harold Wilson gives a clue to his technique of government in his explanation of how the Labour Party is like an old stage-coach: 'If you rattle along at a great speed, everybody inside is either too exhilarated or too seasick to cause any trouble. But if you stop, everybody gets out and argues about where to go next'." So writes his biographer, Leslie Smith.

And so with spiritual life. It is only as we "run the way of Thy commandments" (Psalm 119:32) that we can maintain spiritual progress. Anything less than hearty and complete involvement in God's ways is dangerous. As the Nile Delta teaches us, it is as a river slows down that it deposits impeding mud, and divides the full-flow into many driblets.

It is so with corporate churchlife. When we lose our spiritual impetus there comes danger of schism, of false doctrine, or carnal intrusions. This was so in the early Church. This God-born society started off in a burst of energy that quickly spread the testimony through the civilised world, but the later apostles show the intrusion of false prophets and false teaching.

And so today. When the Church of God loses its momentum, it deposits debris that impedes its progress. We need a continuous surge of Spirit-led activities to enable us to flow fresh and free.

15 November

Two mighty mites

Luke 21:1-4

The mite was one of the smallest coins ever minted. It took two to make a farthing (Mark 12:42). Yet this minute gift has brought in millions to church coffers as its story is related in multitudinous sermons and appeals. The "poor widow" became an example of what giving can be.

"Two mites". God's estimate of values is different from ours. We count giving by quantity, He by quality; we reckon by amount, He by cost; we estimate by what is given, He by what is left.

"Two mites". Rabbinical law decreed that nothing less than two mites should ever mark a Temple-offering. But what the church treasurer counted unworthy to grace the ledgers of the Holy Place, God has recorded in His Book. The anonymous widow has achieved eternal fame. We will seek her out in heaven to thank her.

"Two mites". In giving to God or man, it is the heart that counts. A willing offering is always acceptable to the Almighty, not that He needs our gifts, for "the cattle on a thousand hills are His", but it is the love, the reverence and the thankful heart that He looks for and appreciates.

Giving to God does not depend on the amount for its value, it is the unseen purpose and love of heart and mind that God weighs and assesses.

"Out of the mouth of babes"

Psalm 8:2

The Bible makes it clear that children and young people can enjoy deep experiences of God. We may not go all the way with Wordsworth, who spoke of new-born babes as "Trailing clouds of glory", but Jesus certainly recognised the praises of "children crying in the Temple" as echoes of worship (Matt 21:16).

Such a deep moment of a young teen-ager is described thus:

"I praise Thee because I know that thou art in me, and I am in Thee. I was by myself in the school playground at the back of the house last night, looking at the stars, and I don't know why, but suddenly all the walls of everything seemed to be taken away: the walls of my body were not there; the walls of the distances which separate me from other things were not there. Everywhere was Here, and Here was Everywhere. There was no time, there was no distance, there were no walls, but just Thou and Me, and we were One together in eternity".

Powerful stuff! But how easily we abandon the simplicities of soul-life, overwhelmed by the de-spiritualising sophistication of civilised behaviour.

When Jesus spoke of receiving the Kingdom of God "as a little child" (Mark 10:15) He intimated the sublime simplicities of an unspoilt infant, whose trust is so appealing that nothing binds its richness. To such "babes" are God's secrets revealed that are hidden from the self-sufficient know-alls. May we ever retain our simple faith.

Do you ever get angry?

"Be angry, and sin not," counselled Paul (Eph 4:26), and in this terse advice stresses two points. First, it is not always a sin to be angry. Second, but anger, like fire, must be kept within limits.

William Barclay puts it thus: "Anger is one of God's greatest gifts to men. But anger is like a strong medicine, which if it is used in the right way, can do infinite good, and which, if used in the wrong way, can do infinite harm. What then, is the rule for anger? When anger is for our own sake, it is always wrong. When anger is for the sake of others, it is often divine right".

How our Lord, with blazing fury, drove out the corrupting merchandise of the Temple! And later, how he, with caustic words, excoriated the hypocritical leaders of the Jews! Paul could say, "who is offended, and I burn not"? (2 Cor 11:29). When his converts were stumbled in their Christian way, he became all "hot and bothered" to help them regain their feet. And the epistles of 2 Peter and Jude show how mad these men of God felt at the inroads of false teachers.

Yes, my friend, it is not always sinful to be angry, in fact it is sinful not to be angry at the atrocities of evil men and the vicious antics of the devil. The world has been blessed by angry men and women who became all fired-up in good causes.

But be careful. Let your personal irritations be blotted out by twilight lest Satan use our overwrought emotions to perpetuate evil.

18 November

Have a good sing

Wherever the Spirit of God outflows there is "thanksgiving and the voice of melody" (Isa 51:3). This fact is stressed by Paul, he describes what follows when believers are "filled with the Spirit" (Eph 5:18-20). The initial effect is "speaking to yourselves in psalms and hymns and spiritual songs, singing and making melody in your heart to the Lord".

But such inspired song is varied, "psalms" (ie Old Testament scripture put to music), "hymns" (ie compositions of spirit-filled believers), "spiritual songs" (ie inspired impromptu utterances under divine anointing). They are also deeply emotional, heart-felt and heart-meant. They are congregational, a joint-worship in fellowship with other believers, often accompanied with instruments. They are edifying - "teaching and admonishing one another" (Col 3:16), and are an inspired and inspiring form of vocal worship.

John Wesley gives sound advice on the public enjoyment of joint-praise "Beware of singing as if you were half dead or half asleep. But sing modestly; do not bawl as if to be heard above or distinct from the rest of the congregation. Sing in time. Do not run before nor stay behind. Take care not to sing too slow. This drawling way naturally steals on all who are lazy; and it is high time to drive it out from among us, and sing all our tunes just as quick as we did at first. Amen!" So urges the Apostle of Good Sense.

So then, have a good sing. It not only fills the lungs and expands the mind it also can prove a holy exercise, an act of devotion to God, and a means of enjoying communal praise and fellowship.

19 November

The Great Attractor

A recent news-flash states: "Astronomers may have solved the mystery of The Great Attractor, a hidden force that has been tugging stars across the universe from behind the milky way. It has been identified as a cluster of galaxies billions of miles out in space".

What a picture of the vast cosmos around us! Immense galaxies, each with billions of stars. And who knows what galaxies may be behind them? It is mind-boggling!

What is behind them all? What infinite mind or power sets and keeps all in motion and being? What links them all together in one Universe? Three elemental forces seem effective throughout the vast Cosmos. Illumination, we know heavenly bodies because they emit light. Then comes radiation, heavenly bodies are detected by energies radiated from their active explosive constituents; and gravitation expressed in the influence of the mass of such bodies. But what is behind it all?

The Bible offers a rational and sufficient explanation. "In the beginning God created the heavens and the earth" (Gen 1:1). The binding force, the first great cause of all, is GOD. The rest of the Bible follows this.

The New Testament speaks of another great attractor. Jesus said: "And I, if I be lifted up from the earth, will draw all men unto me" (John 12:32). In the ethical universe of right and wrong, the Cross of Jesus is still, and ever will be, the great attracting power, drawing men from their sins unto God, leading fallen humanity to the source of forgiveness, of grace and of love.

20 November

The kiss in the window

Rita Snowden tells of young Stevie, too young to write letters himself, yet written to by his grandma, who always ended with a cross, which he was told was a kiss for him. With his mother he attended St Andrews Presbyterian Church, whose stained-glass window contained the symbol of their patron-saint, a St Andrew's cross, to him, the form of a kiss, shaped in an 'X'. When asked, "which church do you go to?" He answered, "The church with the kiss in the window".

What a parable! To us a kiss is a token of love. Every church should have "a kiss in the window" metaphorically. At the door it should be seen in the hearty welcome, in the pew it should be clear in the sincere fellowship, in the pulpit it should show itself in courage-building and comfort-laden preaching.

The father's kiss of the prodigal son was the kiss of pardon, a reflection of the love which receives the penitent sinner (Luke 15:20); the symbol of Christian fellowship is the kiss of charity (1 Peter 5:14) - does our "British hand-shake" fulfil all that this implies? The acknowledgement of the Lordship of Jesus is seen in the kiss of submission (Ps 2:12). "Kiss the Son" which all who love the Saviour gladly do.

To define a kiss is not easy: "to smack with the pursed lips" shows how vain are words to describe this act. A kiss can only be fully appreciated in action, even as the forgiveness of God can only be known by personal experience.

21 November

"I am a voice....."

So said John the Baptist when pressed to identify himself and his mission (John 1:23), and in doing so bequeathed to us a superb definition of a preacher of the Gospel.

But such definition reflects others. There are, then, three kinds of effective preacher.

He is not a noise "Pharaoh king of Egypt is but a noise" (Jer 46:17) - all wind but no worth, sound without sense. To use the words of Shakespeare, such preaching is "full of sound and fury, signifying nothing". Or as Mark Twain once observed; "Words, words, nothing but words".

He is not merely an echo, as Jesus said this of Pilate: "Sayest thou this of thyself, or did others tell thee?" (John 18:34). Effective preaching is not merely a reflection of what others think or say, but of personal conviction: as Paul said, "I believed, and therefore have I spoken" (2 Cor 4:13). We may learn much from others, but we must not let books think for us, or consider mere quotations as proofs.

He is a voice. That is, his ministry is personal; a voice-print is as unique as a finger-print; so should our preaching be our own, an expression of self. It is also articulate, not a mumble nor an ear-splitting blast, but a clear expression of thought and emotion. Greatest of all, it is meaningful. A true sermon is a message. A man of God does not merely use words, he says something, and when that something is based on Scripture and inspired by the Spirit it does something. Such a "voice" can become the voice of God.

22 November

"*When I was a child......*"

1 Cor 13:11

The full force of these words is often over-looked. Some adults forget that they were ever children. They judge the actions and words of young folk by their own grown-up (and sometimes cynical) standards.

Paul was more realistic. "I talked like a child, I thought like a child, I reasoned like a child" (NIV). The Greek word for child here is nēpios, like our term "nipper".

A child is not a miniature adult. Louise M. Alcott's classic, "Little Women", is a misnomer. Girls are girls and boys, boys. They live in their own world, have their own wants, and need to be understood. Potential is there: but childhood has limitations as well as possibilities.

Peter Parson tells the story of a boy who was asked, "What are you going to be when you grow up?" He answered, "I'm going to be possible". The perplexed question, "Possible? What do you mean?" "Well, every day my mother tells me I am impossible".

And every child needs to have extended to that patience, understanding and encouragement that makes the "impossible" become "possible". Imagination, so rich in early childhood, can closer approach reality if we older ones remember what it was like to be young, and give guidance and scope (with directive and controlled discipline) to those younger ones who, though they may not always realise it, need us as much as we need them.

23 November

"When I became a man....."

1 Cor 13:11

Some people never grow up. At 50 they are as self-centred as a child of five. The Corinthian church had many "babes in Christ" (1 Cor 3:1). Again and again Paul urges them to be men, "perfect", mature, fully grown (cf 2:6). "In understanding be men" he says (1 Cor 14:20), "Quit you like men", he urges (1 Cor 16:13). In other words, "Expand your spiritual minds", "Exercise your spiritual muscles" - use your brains, use your brawn, be thoughtful and active.

Childhood has its weaknesses. First, children (even babies) are supremely <u>self-interested</u>. They have to be to survive. But adulthood expands that interest to others - "Thou shalt love thy neighbour as thyself". In fact, the whole purpose of Christian ethics is to change from being egocentric to becoming Christocentric - a gradual, but necessary process.

Again, childhood has a limited conception of values or of occasions. A girl will break her heart over a battered doll. "Save your tears for greater sorrows", chided a father I know; but it is all so real and hurtful at the time. Contrariwise, a little gaudy gift often seems to a child like a wealthy bounty. Adults usually have wider interests and truer valuation.

Also, a child finds it difficult to wait, they have "give-it-me now" minds. But a grown-up has learned that there are some things we must work and wait for. It is by "faith and patience that we inherit the promises" (Heb 6:12). But good things are worth waiting for.

24 November

"We see Jesus....."
Heb 2:9

But it is <u>how</u> we see Him that matters.

Some see Him as just a <u>MYTH</u>, a product of someone's imagination, a "cunningly devised fable". But what genius could conceive such a character?

Others say He was a mere <u>MAN</u>, a product of evolution, perfect but human. But those that knew Him best know Him as the unique Son of God.

Others concede Him to be a great <u>MORALIST</u>, but come short of regarding Him as divine.

Then there are those who describe Him as a <u>MARTYR</u>, a witness unto death of the principles He stood for: a saintly man in a sinful world.

But the Bible declares Him to be a <u>MEDIATOR</u> (1 Tim 2:5) who was at the same time God and man. His incarnation enabled Him to be what Job called for, "a daysman" who, because He was both human and divine could "lay his hand upon both" (Job 9:33).

Because Jesus Christ is God He can represent both sides of the human/divine dilemma. By the sacrifice of Himself He satisfied God's justice and purchased mercy and forgiveness for all who trust Him. So to see Jesus is salvation.

"My cup runneth over"
Ps 23:5

So wrote David in his best-known of all psalms. And what a statement it is! From this brief text I draw three thoughts.

First, the privilege of knowing God, thus emphasising what pervades the whole of Scripture - the personalism of God's salvation. He loves me as an individual - it is "my cup". I am not just a number, I am a name, an intimate of God, not just a digit in a census, but a distinct personality.

Secondly, the pleasure of enjoying God. "My cup runneth over". The bountiful munificence of God not only fills me with His love, He overflows my heart with benefits. And all God's people can say the same. The Lord is not exhausted by His abundant giving, He overflows to each trusting saint. When the Lord is our Shepherd, "I shall not want".

Thirdly, the possibility of containing God - "My cup". God made man with a capacity for Himself, an innate ability to absorb spiritual things. We do not just have a body, we are also "spirit and soul" - a pneumatico-psycho-somatic entity. More simply, we have a physical life - "body", a mental life, - "soul", and a spiritual life - "spirit". It is only when each part is active that we really live. It is then that "my cup runneth over".

26 November

The love of Christ

In Ephesians 3:18 Paul speaks of "the breadth, and length, and depth, and height" of the love of Christ. Then he poses a paradox - "to know the love of Christ which passeth knowledge". What a contradiction? yet true! No human thought or language can grasp or explain Christ's love - it is, as far as human knowledge is concerned, ultradimensional.

But what we cannot explain we can experience; what the mind cannot grasp, the heart can know. The love of Christ is as spacious as the universe, it extends in all directions. It is more lasting than time, it is redolent of eternity, it is the very nature of God Himself.

It is <u>broader than liberalism</u> and embraces all mankind: it is <u>longer than traditionalism</u>, and extends beyond all man's conceptions, for it is truth: it is <u>deeper than fundamentalism</u>, for it is the basis of all bases, no emotion can plumb deeper depths, here is the mystery of God: it is <u>higher than mysticism</u>, for man's quest for "the beatific vision" is more than fulfilled in Jesus, the Son of God, the glorified Christ.

The love of Christ is a spiritual reservoir we can never exhaust, a potent passion we can never fully absorb, an ideal we can never completely grasp. But we can accept it, we can enjoy it, and by His help, reflect it in our daily living.

27 November

Moral sustenance

"Your words have kept men on their feet" said Eliphaz to Job (Job 4:4. Moffat's version). What was meant as a criticism was really a compliment.

A business-man who regularly attended the ministry of Dr. Alexander Whyte once said to him: "your greatest work has been to put heart into men to face the coming week". This is the test of preaching: does it inspire the hearers?

Doctrine has its place in preaching ministry, for it is scriptural exposition that gives it its authority; delivery is vital, for what is not heard and understood is lost; but what gives preaching a prime place in Christian worship is not only authority and acceptance, it is also, and greatly, appeal - the Holy Spirit impacting on the human spirit inspiring courage, assurance and moral animation.

In a hard, cynical and difficult world, we all need the sound of words that give us strength and hope. Remember the great speeches of Winston Churchill in the last war? His "bulldog growl" his indomitable faith in the cause of right, his word of defiant courage put heart into a struggling nation.

So should preaching speak to those who wait upon such ministry. We should leave a divine service with a determination to triumph over evil, inspired by the mighty concept that God is over all.

28 November

Cracked - but useful

The most popular, and best known of all bells must be "BIG BEN", the hour-bell of the clock of Westminster Houses of Parliament. Sir Benjamin Hall, who had charge of the building project, addressed parliament in a rambling search for a name for the bell. A bored waggish member shouted out "Call it Big Ben, and have done with it!" The house rocked with laughter. The name stuck.

Soon after the bell was cast in 1858 it cracked, causing a shrill, unpleasant tone when it was struck. The crack was filled and smoothed down, leaving "Big Ben" with a distinct quality of sound that was unique. It's chimes have become familiar the world over. None other could take its place in the affections of the British race.

You don't have to be perfect to be useful. "But we have this treasure (that is, the joy and light of the Gospel) in earthen vessels" (2 Cor 4:7). God uses human-nature, with all its foibles, faults and frailty, to perfect his saving plans. He could have selected angels - in fact, He has done on special occasions - but has decided to employ men to reach men. How wise! Angels would scare us, but fellow-man, whose lives are changed by God, can woo us to the Lord. The very fact that they are of us is an effective starting point.

And when God wished to effect His Redemptive Plan, He sent His Son, "made of a woman" (Gal 4:4). He "became flesh and dwelt among us" - He is one of us, He became a Son of Man that we, by His grace and mercy, might become Sons of God.

Let the master take over

Beethoven, out walking one day, heard his "Moonlight Sonata" being pounded out on an old piano. He looked through the open door of the cottage and saw a blind girl trying to finger this wonderful melody. He tapped the door, walked in - "Move up", he said, "let me have a go"; and played as only he could His own composition.

"Marvellous!" said the enraptured maiden. "The master himself could not have done better!" "I am the master", said Beethoven, and quietly slid away.

We sometimes fumble our way in our endeavour to live the Christian life. But often it doesn't sound right. What should be melody seems tuneless. What shall we do? Struggle on, and hope for the best?

Paul found a better way. He said, "I live, yet not I, but Christ liveth in me" (Gal 2:20). What human nature could not produce, the life of Christ could. As he yielded himself by faith to a living Lord, the harmonies of spiritual life became possible.

Even so we may find melody and harmony. The "score" of holy living may seem difficult to interpret in the music of godly experience, but if we let the Master take over it can be done.

30 November

Vantage point

Deut 34:1-7

From the top of Pisgah Moses viewed the Promised Land. In the clear air he saw as far as the Mediterranean Sea, taking in his panoramic scope of vision the hills and plains of this "land of milk and honey".

But, alas, he would not enter this Holy Land (at least, not in this life). First, he had fatally flawed his hopes by a temporary lapse, secondly, God's holiness must be honoured. Even spiritual leaders are not exempt from discipline when they let God down.

However, "mercy rejoiced against justice" when nearly 1,500 years later, Moses appeared with Elijah as they met Jesus on the Mount of Transfiguration.

But may we not be granted vantage points in our Christian experience? Moses was 120 years old before Canaan was spread before him like a living atlas. How much better when youth sees "the Promised Land" in spiritual vision. What prospects lie before us as we consider the possibilities outlined in Holy Scripture! The Bible presents to all believers - young and old - a picture of sublime possessions. Treasures of wisdom and knowledge are hid in Christ, priceless blessings are available to faith and glorious prospects to hope. When we become sons of God by faith in Christ, "all things are ours",

We need not wait, for our Lord has made all this available. But we must needs ascend our "Pisgah". The discipline of discipleship will lift us to a vantage point from which we can see the fullness of our salvation.

Spiritual myopia

Short-sightedness can impair vision, both in the natural and spiritual realms. Peter speaks of those who, failing to develop their spiritual lives become myopic. They "cannot see afar off" (2 Peter 1:9). This defective vision applies three ways.

Backward – having "forgotten that he was purged from his old sins". To forget "the pit when we were digged" is to lose any sense of gratitude for the grace that saved us. Paul never forgot the time when Jesus met him on the Damascus road. Neither should we forget our beginnings.

Inward – myopics find it difficult to focus on near things, their peripheral vision is often misty. If our spiritual vision is well-focused we will understand God's present dealings and his ways. They may be "past finding out", but we will see the outline with clarify, and grasp His purposes.

Forward – the short-sighted person is blind to distant vision; even so, the spiritual myopic loses his grip on the Bible revelation of things to come. Eschatology, the doctrine of the last things, becomes a vague hope rather than a living expectation – the "now-world" takes precedence.

Jesus exhorted the "blind" Laodiceans to "anoint thine eyes with eye-salve, that thou mayest see" (Rev. 3:18). Our heavenly Optician can not only diagnose our complaint, he can cure it. Come to Him and your vision can be restored.

Christ is risen

Why confine our thoughts of the resurrection of Jesus to Easter? "NOW is Christ risen from the dead", wrote Paul (1 Cor 15:20) and this "now" is an eternal now fixed in the Chronicles of Heaven and not confined to the almanac of earth. He IS risen!

Dr Billy Graham in his book WORLD AFLAME (pg 133) relates the following: "When I was in Russia, I heard a story about a Russian village. After the Bolshevik revolution, the local Communist leader had been sent to tell the people the virtues of Communism, and to take their minds away from religion which Karl Marx called "the opium of the people". After the Communist had harangued them for a long time, he said to the local Christian pastor rather contemptuously, "I will give you five minutes to reply". The pastor replied, "I do not need five minutes, only five seconds". He came to the platform and gave the Easter greeting "The Lord is risen!" As one man the villagers thundered back, "He is risen indeed!""

And that is the answer. What no political system, philosophical concept or earthly power can do, Jesus can. He is alive today to meet our needs, forgive our sins, reconcile to God, teach us to love our neighbour. Above all, because He is alive He is able to give us power to accomplish these things - because He lives we too can live the life that pleases Him.

Shining mirror

In 2 Corinthians 3:13-18, Paul cites the Old Testament story of Moses veiling his face to hide its shining glory from the people. He turns it into an allegory.

When they of Israel read "Moses" (the written law of God) all they see is "letters" – the real glory of the divine mind and purpose is hidden from them, their minds are "veiled" from the glory of God's plan of salvation. But it is not the same for Christians. We read of the word of God with clear vision, the "face" of Christ is unveiled, His glory shines forth from the word of the Gospel.

He later speaks of our "beholding as in a mirror the glory of the Lord". If we liken this with James 1:23 we see the scriptures likened unto a looking-glass. In James we see ourselves reflected - the Bible shows us what we are. From Paul we see the same "mirror" reflecting God, a shining mirror bright with heavenly glory. As we gaze into it our own faces, not veiled with unbelief but open with simple faith, are lit up with the glory of God, a glory which transforms us into its own likeness.

"The glory of God in the face (or character) of Jesus Christ" shines brightly in the Holy Book. As our faith in Him is stimulated by this vision, the Holy Spirit, whose power is latent in the Book, transforms us into the image of Christ "from glory to glory". As we see Jesus with believing eyes we become like Him.

4 December

Sunshine is energy

Solar energy is becoming an increasing reality in commercial and domestic spheres. Solar panels transform light into energy.

This is no new thing. From the beginning of creation plant-life, by means of photo-synthesis, has turned light into life. The chlorophyll that resides in green vegetation turns the light of day into life-sustaining elements that feed and sustain plant life.

And here is an ecological miracle. In this process green vegetation absorbs carbon dioxide and exudes oxygen. We live by breathing in oxygen and breathing out carbon dioxide. What a wonderful balance - a God-arranged pattern of life. That is why we must preserve tropical rain-forests, and maintain our green zones.

The sun is our life. It keeps our earth in orbit, it establishes and regulates our times and seasons, it orders our tides and weather. Its warmth sustains us, its light promotes growth, its actinic rays produce chemical changes. We could not exist without it.

And Jesus is "the Sun of Righteousness with healing in His wings (or rays)" (Mal 4:2). He is "the Light of the world (John 8:12) beaming blessings upon men. To those who accept His saving grace there dawns a new day. As old Zacharias said "the Dayspring from on high has visited us" (Luke 1:78). What a blessed experience to feel the warmth of His love, the radiance of His presence, the "health of His countenance". To be in the orbit of His will is "life more abundant".

5 December

Too busy ?

Men who have made their mark are mostly noted for periods in solitude – either voluntarily or obligatory. Mohammed wrote the Koran in exile, Luther translated the Bible in prison, Marx penned "Das Capital" in the British Museum library, Hitler wrote "Mein Kampf " in gaol. Jerome translated the Vulgate in his cell, Bunyan dreamed "Pilgrims Progress" in Bedford prison. All had solitary experiences in which were birthed written works of force and vast influence.

Look also at the Bible. Moses had 40 years in Midian, Paul a period in Arabia, John in exiled loneliness on Patmos. Above all, our blessed Lord Jesus was for almost 30 years shut away in Nazareth, an out-of-the-way town in Judea. All had periods when reflection was possible. And indeed, for any great work time is needed to brood, to consider, and (for a Christian) to wait on God.

We all need the silence of solitude to assess our ways, to reflect on our works, to seek heavenly guidance for our earthly task.

From the very beginning of time God set the standard. He rested (Gen 2:2). Not that He was weary or bereft of creative ideas, but to witness to all his creation that six days toil should be followed by one day's rest. Human nature is built on this six to one ideal. The seventh day, cut off from normal rush and bustle, should be set apart for recreation, contemplation and worship. It is a special day, and to keep it such commands God's blessing, promotes health and prosperity.

Thread of hope

Tormented Job complained "My days are swifter than a weaver's shuttle, and are spent without hope" (Job 7:6). Dr John Parkhurst points out that the Hebrew for "hope" – an extended period of time, could also be rendered "thread" – an extended form of fibre. He translates thus ".... and they are finished for want of thread". Truly in the loom of life the <u>warps</u> are the days that pass so swiftly, and the <u>weft</u> are the experiences woven into the web.

Accepting this, Job felt that his days were empty of meaning. In this mood he could have sat down with "the Preacher" and cried thus in his pitiful dirge : "VANITY OF VANITIES; ALL IS VANITY" (Eccles. 1:2).

Life without hope is mere existence: the past a painful memory, the present a pitiful misery the future a tormenting mystery. Thank God Pandora, out of whose opened coffer fled many benefits, still closed the lid on hope. In more than one sense "we are saved by hope".

Christianity restores hope to mankind. It is one of the abiding virtues to essential happiness (cf 1 Cor 13:13). When our despairing hearts turned to Jesus, He banished our gloom and gave us a glowing expectation of blessing that would extend through time and leap the barrier of the grave into eternity.

This hope, like a binding thread, takes up the fruitful experiences of our past, the ongoing days of our present, and assures us of "a bright tomorrow". Our whole life becomes bound together in a meaningful whole – the web of life.

7 December

Fragments

"Gather up the fragments", said Jesus after feeding 5,000 with bread and fish, "that nothing be lost" (John 6:12). Why should He who fed a multitude with miracle food care for crumbs? But He does.

And what benefits come from fragments! First, we learn from this to make the best of what God gives. He is prodigal in His supply, but we must be provident in our service.

"Fragments" If we utilised our wasted seconds how soon would they add up to hours? If we mark our spending, how soon could "a penny well spent be a pound saved"?

"Fragments" Some of the most beautiful relics of Ancient Rome are mosaics. Have you ever examined excavated remains of Roman architecture? Mosaics were a prominent feature. Yet they are composed of tiny scraps of pottery. Broken bits of smashed-up urns and other vessels – useless cast-offs – are patterned into exquisite forms. Portraits and designs are fixed by cement into delightful pictures. What a parable! God is taking up scraps of "broken earthenware" to build up a marvellous Temple for Himself. And the cement is His love and grace.

"Fragments" A Salvation Army Corps made a special effort to support a mission station in Africa. A grandma made a patchwork quilt – bits of cloth sewn together. Smilingly the Captain sent it without other gifts. A troublesome chief chose it as his robe of honour. And so my friend stitch your bits together with skill and charity, and who knows what those fragments will do?

Role model

Adolescence, that borderland between infancy and adulthood, is often subject to emotional turmoil. Not yet totally free of childhood ways, nor able to adopt adult attitudes, they follow role models in a kind of hero-worship. The actions of “heroes” (sometimes notorious or outlandish) are imitated in action, in attitude, in dress, in fashion. How important it is for youngsters to have set before them noble examples! And TV does not help much at times. Teachers, leaders and people of prominence should seek to present moral patterns. On the highest plane Paul commented: “Be ye followers of me, even as I also am of Christ,” where the term “followers” really should be “imitators”, (Greek mimetes – or mimics) (1 Cor 11:1). Here’s a personal question: “If somebody followed me, where would they end up?”

But this imitating works more than one way. A father takes his small son to bed. “Dear God, make me like my Daddy,” he prays. Tucking him in, the father breathes a prayer “O God, make me like my little boy.” What a combination when the simplicity of childhood is joined with the strength of manhood!

May nothing in my life ever hinder or debase the seeking of youth after the satisfying model of manhood. The ideal role model is Jesus, in whom meekness and majesty, humility and grace unite. Let us seek to be like Jesus all day long.

9 December

Listeners

"Who hath ears to hear, let him hear" (Matt. 13:9). These words of Jesus tell us that ears are for listening with.

But there are KINDS OF LISTENERS, as our Lord makes clear in the Parable of the Sower. There is the casual listener, who does not let the words sink in; there is the shallow listener, who takes little notice of the word, it sinks in, but not very far; there is the biased listener, who is distracted by other issues that stifle the word; but there is the attentive listener who takes the word to heart. This is the productive kind.

There are also KINDS OF LISTENING. With some it is just a physical act – the vibrations of sound are conveyed to the brain, and that seems the end of it. They "hear", but it is merely a reaction to noise. With others it is a psychological impression, they hear and understand; but with the real hearers it is a pneumatological event, a working of the Holy Spirit by spoken words through the mind to the heart. And it is this listening that counts.

As our Lord said in His closing appeal in The Sermon on the Mount: "He that heareth these sayings of Mine, and doeth them ….." (Matt. 7:24). Responsive hearing results in action, and to respond to the teaching of Christ is to build one's life and destiny on a solid foundation.

10 December

Human rights

The American Declaration of Independence has these powerful words: "We hold these truths to be self-evident, that all men are created equal, that they are endowed by their Creator with certain unalienable rights, that among these are life, liberty and the pursuit of happiness."

Every clear, unbiased thinker must accept this concept. It banishes oppression, slavery and a multitude of impediments that ignorant, ignoble or iniquitous men would throw into the path of the personal progress to fulfilment of individuals or nations. There is a sense in which all men are brothers, for "God .... hath made of one blood all nations of men" (Acts 17:26). Our Lord, as Son of Man, could trace his genealogy back to Adam – and so could all of us if we had the knowledge. From a common source spring common rights – inalienable rights.

But with rights also come responsibilities. "Am I my brother's keeper? said the petulant man-slayer Cain (Gen 4:9). The answer must surely be, now as ever, "If he is thy brother, thou art his keeper".

Those who clamour for "human rights" should balance that act by an equally vociferous and practical clamour for "human responsibilities". Only thus can the balance of life be achieved.

11 December

"Toil on ...."

Paul has a remarkable link of life-enhancing virtues in 1 Thessalonians 1:3 "Work of faith ...... labour of love ...... patience of hope". What a trio! And what a pragmatic effect of inner spiritual force! Christianity is nothing if not practical. Our service for God finds its inspiration and fulfilment in these three graces in action.

Work of faith. Faith is not a matter of words, it is a source of works: doctrine finds its fulfilment in deeds, the practical proof of faith's reality. We toil incessantly when we work at faith's bidding.

Labour of love, takes us even further. By faith we "spend" for God, giving all we've got; but by love we are "spent" in His service, not counting the cost.

Patience of hope. Hope can be an inspiring expectation of the fulfilment of God's rich plans for a glorious future. By it we endure to the end.

Paul speaks of Christian service as "labour" (1 Cor 15:10, 16:16). The Greek word for "Labour" is Kopiaw, "to toil to the point of weariness", to exert oneself to the full. Service for God is often hard work, but it can be joyful and is certainly rewarding. So:

> "Toil on, and in thy toil rejoice,
> For toil comes rest, for exile home;
> Soon shalt thou hear the Bridegroom's voice,
> The midnight peal, "Behold, I come".

12 December

Books

"What thou seest, write in a book", said "the great Voice as of a trumpet" to John (Rev. 1:11). And aren't we glad that the vision was so recorded!

While it is true that the most impressive form of communication is speech, yet, though oral presentation may make an immediate impact, frail memory can either forget or embellish the original expression. Three things give written matter a tremendous advantage.

First, permanence. Not only may we refer to the written word again and again, it also passes on from generation to generation. Thus knowledge is preserved for all time.

Secondly, penetration. A book can infiltrate into society. It can go where the spoken word cannot be communicated. My written word can reach lands to which I may never go, and though I die, my words "yet speaketh".

Thirdly, proliferation. Although modern technology makes speech more widely disseminated and preserved, yet books and pamphlets can be multiplied by the million to reach the whole world.

"Of making many books there is no end", said the preacher (Eccles. 12:12), but one book outstrips (and will outlast) them all – the Bible, "the world of God, which liveth and abideth forever" (1 Peter 1:23). But no book can contain or explain all the glories of Jesus (John 21:25). He, the WORD, is beyond words. But what literature fails to do, love can accomplish.

Love yourself

"For no man ever yet hated his own flesh", commented Paul (Eph 5:29). There is a legitimate self-love, wherein we nourish and cherish ourselves. A pride in one's appearance, an endeavour to be one's best, a joy in one's personal achievements is natural and allowable.

But this can be marred by three things. First, inordinate self-esteem, where we count ourselves above others. Secondly, a self-neglect that reduces our well-being and debases our humanity. Thirdly, a lack of self-discipline that makes us slaves of vicious habits and attitudes.

Gluttony, drugs, smoking and drinking can deface the image of God in us.

But self-love should become a pattern of neighbour-love "thou shalt love thy neighbour as thyself" (Lev 19:18). God, who made us, knows what will make us nearest the divine will for our well-being and happiness. To be wrapped up in ourselves cripples our moral potentiality; to extend to others what we devote to ourselves brings a complacency and a maturity that words cannot tell. "The Golden Rule" of Jesus (Matt. 7:12) leads to a life of tranquillity and fulfilment.

But how can I fulfil such a lofty ideal? The answer is in Luke 11:9. If we ask our heavenly Father to help us, He will give us His sustaining, enabling Holy Spirit.

14 December

Face to face

Nothing can take the place of personal presence. Letters, cassettes, videos, even "virtual reality" fall short of that immediate contact. It brings more than the sound of voice, or the vision of form. There is a kind of aura of presence, when we are in one another's company that no other media can minister.

So John felt. He writes to "the elect lady" (who was possibly Martha of Bethany) "I would not write with paper and ink: but I trust to come unto you, and speak face to face, that our joy may be full" (2 John 12).

And so, visit your friends as much as is possible. Letters and phone-calls are a blessed substitute when we cannot meet face to face: but nothing equals the warm embrace of those we love.

James, in his usual down-to-earth manner, examples a special case for visiting: "to visit the fatherless and widows in their affliction" (James 1:27). This is "pure religion", this is practical Christianity, this is love in action.

And the word "visit" has a special meaning in the Bible. Take Naomi's case. She "heard that the Lord had visited His people in giving them bread" (Ruth 1:6). However, we may not always present gifts, but we can minister comfort and sympathy "face to face".

15 December

So this is love

Paul ended his first Epistle to the Corinthians with the words, “My love be with you all in Christ Jesus” (16:24).

This is surprising! He had just torn strips off them, excoriating them with blistering words. They were a backslidden group of immature believers, unsteady in their beliefs, unsafe in their moral standards and unsure in their attitudes. He rebukes them; and yet he loves them.

But is not that true love? “Faithful are the wounds of a friend”, says Proverbs 27:6. The greatest enemy of real love is sentimentality that reduces this primal emotion to mere feeling. Yes, this love can be passionate, but it is also practical; it can experience the richest rapture, but it also sacrifices one’s own interests for the loved one. It is the very opposite of selfishness. It does not evaporate in feelings or vanish with absence. Real love will, if necessary, “lay down its life for the brethren” (1 John 3:16), a sacrifice of “no greater love” (John 15:13).

But how can human nature rise to such heights? Paul himself gives the answer. “In Christ Jesus”. Our Lord is the shining example of what love can mean – He is also the inspiration to act as He did, to “follow His steps” (1 Pet. 2:21).

16 December

Faith's laboratory

Spurgeon once said, "Our beliefs should be tested in the laboratory of experience before we preach them". And this conforms with Psalm 34:8, "O taste and see that the Lord is good: blessed is the man what trusteth in Him". It is very difficult to explain a taste, it can only be truly appreciated by experience.

This vitally affects the force of our Christian testimony. Cesar Ritz, one-time owner of the Ritz Hotel in Paris, is said by his son to himself try out every new mattress he ordered by sleeping one night on it. If he didn't sleep well, the mattress was returned. There are some things we must test for ourselves before we can recommend them.

When I attended my oculist for an eye-test I was asked if I would prefer plastic lenses. "I use them myself," said the lady assistant. That persuaded me – and I found them equal to glass, and safer.

So Paul could present a gospel he had "tasted". "I believed, and therefore I have spoken", he wrote (2 Cor 4:13), and goes on to show the effects of such belief on his life and ministry. To personally experience the grace of God is not only a strong convicting agency, but a powerful tool in our presenting Christ to others.

Open it – and see

Joseph Conrad, an expatriated Pole whose literary genius earned him a knighthood, almost missed it.

A long blue official envelope was delivered to him marked "On His Majesty's Service". It lay for several weeks unopened on his desk, until the Prime Minister was gravely embarrassed and sent a messenger round to see what had happened. Then the truth came out. Conrad had not dared to open it – he thought it was about his income tax.

What deters you from opening the Bible? Does the title "Holy Bible" put you off? Of course many differently titled modern versions are now available. You can even read this Book of God openly, and nobody could detect the fact.

But more are deterred from reading the Scriptures for fear of finding out their own state of heart and mind. They respect the book, but relegate it to oblivion by neglect. Yet it contains the most enriching news and views ever put into print.

In fact, the story of your destiny is clearly outlined for your information and warning. To believe it is to become a "Son of God", to deny it is to wallow in eventual eternal misery. But open the Book – it could change your life.

18 December

Microscopic vision

During his spare time, Antony Van Leeuwenhoek (1632-1723) laboriously ground tiny lenses and mounted them to make crude microscopes. Squinting through these lenses, this 17th century draper of Delft, Holland, became the first man to observe and report upon the activities of "animalcules" – the protozoa and bacteria of the microscopic world. He also confirmed by direct observation the circulation of the blood. His reports to London's Royal Society represent a milestone in scientific development. So inform Parker Davis, the American drug company.

By this aid to natural vision the laws of light were so adjusted as to open up a new world, a process still going on.

There is a sense in which the Bible is a spiritual microscope whereby God shows us things beyond the scope of natural reason and philosophy to discern. It penetrates into the inner recesses of human nature, and is "a discerner of the thoughts and intents of the heart" (Heb 4:12). When we diligently study it a new world of truth is opened up to us. Hidden truth is so magnified that our searching minds cannot but grasp the significance of God's purposes, and our yearning hearts cannot but be moved and warmed by revelations of God's love and mercy.

By this Holy Book we can learn of God and of human nature to such a degree as gives us deeper understanding of life. So "read, mark and inwardly digest" its message.

A telescopic view

The astronomer Galileo found that the telescope opened to him a vast universe. The star-spangled sky became to him a fuller realm of wonder. His vision was extended manifold – but even then the boundaries of the cosmos were beyond his view (and in spite of advanced modern technique, they still are).

His discoveries changed his whole concept of God's creation, and eventually of scientific outlook universal. He endured much criticism and opposition, especially from theologians, but truth prevails, and Galileo now stands as a pioneer of astral progress, while his detractors are forgotten as a bad joke.

The Bible is a spiritual telescope. It makes distant ideas come closer, it peers into the unknown future. In its functioning the vast universe of truth becomes more clear to us; still a wonder, but less a mystery.

The Preface to the Revised English Bible closes with these words: "God has yet new light and truth to break forth from his word. The Committee prays that the new version will prove to be a means to that end". In other words, an instrument to penetrate into the cosmos of wisdom and understanding of life's meaning and destiny.

"I have more understanding than all my teachers; for Thy testimonies are my meditation." (Ps 119:99). The word of God gave the psalmist vision beyond what tradition or philosophy could.

20 December

Bring it back

"Of making many books there is no end," wrote the Preacher (Eccles 12:12). Thank God for the preservation of knowledge accomplished by literary works.

But to build up one's own library can bring problems. One is that people borrow, but fail to bring back. It almost amounts to theft, sometimes even to villainy.

How is it that normally honest folk, who keep their own accounts with integrity, sometimes are less than correct about books? Any lending librarian will convey to you a pitiful account of books taken out but not returned. Forgetfulness, carelessness, irresponsibility? Who knows!

I have a bookmark with the following inscription quaintly put:

> "He that doth this book borrowe
> And doth not bring it back,
> Certes he shall have sorrowe,
> And comfort he shall lack."

But it is more like a lament than a proposed corrective.

The sharing of literature can bring help to those who cannot afford expensive books, or whose searching cannot locate desired volumes. But a Christian conscience should register alarm if a book is held longer than contemplation requires. "Restore to me my long lost friend," is often the futile prayer of the book-lender. It should not be so. A book lover should also be a lover of the lender.

21 December

What preaching should be

"Then spake Haggai the Lord's messenger in the Lord's message" (Haggai 1:13). On this brief statement we have three essential elements of effective preaching.

First, vocation. "The Lord's messenger".
A sense of divine calling to deliver a divine message adds conviction, and indeed authority, to the preacher's words. "How shall they preach, except they be sent," wrote Paul (Rom 10:15). All who preach should give God's word at God's bidding – or feel so.

Second, vision. "The Lord's message".
Every preacher should worship at the shrine of Holy Writ, "trembling at the Word of God", (Isa 66:2), lest he should misrepresent it or misapply its intent. While we must use sanctified sense and sensibility in presenting the word of the Lord, our message must be more than mere opinion or conjecture, it should have the touch of the anointing of the Spirit. An effective sermon is more than political opinion or even credal correctness, it is a "message," a divine medium of conveying the will of God to His people.

Thirdly, voice. "Then spake Haggai".
A sermon should be expressed audibly, articulately and simply. Phillip Brookes described preaching as "truth flowing through personality". This voice was Haggai's voice: there is nothing like one's voice for revealing one's personality. Don't imitate other preachers, be your honest, educated, disciplined self when you preach. Nothing else will do.

22 December

Hallelujah chorus

The Triumphal worship of Revelation 19:1-7 is punctuated with four "ALLELUIAS" (the Greek spelling of the Hebrew Hallelujah). It is a regular "Hallelujah Chorus".

And yet it is surprising that the Greek New Testament should use a Hebrew praise-word. In fact, this is the only place in the text of Revelation where this word occurs.

What a period of praise this is! First, a great multitude in heaven, rejoicing in the justice of God in destroying Babylon. His righteous work becomes the theme of their rejoicing worship. They say again "Hallelujah!" Their act of worship is bounded by this "Praise ye the Lord." Then again, stirred by a "Voice.... out of the Throne" they thunder another shout of praise. A fourth "Hallelujah" extols the majesty of God and anticipates the greatest event of this new age, "the marriage of the Lamb".

But why use a Hebrew term in this setting? It is like a hand reaching back into ancient times to grasp the hand of expectation implicit in the Old Covenant. All that when the promises, the hopes, the anticipations encouraged by the Holy Spirit's nature.

What is implicit in "Hallelujah" is that JAH, the Eternal, will always be with us, and for us. His grace and mercy will always merit our "hallelu".

Stillness

Here is a trio of delightful texts:

"Sit still, my daughter" (Ruth 3:18)
"Lie still, and let Him mould thee" (a modern translation of Psalm 37:7)
"Be still, and know that I am God" (Psalm 46:10)

Modern life is full of rush and noise. There seems "no time to watch and stare". We have lost the art of waiting; every thing must be "instant", whether it be coffee or cures. We even pack the Sabbath with mundane activities. No wonder society is sick – physically, mentally and spiritually sick.

How often we fail to "sit still" and let God work out His purposes for us. And to "lie still" and give God a chance to mould us after the fashion of His will seems an impossibility – we prefer to fume and fret rather than rest in the Lord.

But to "be still" is an essential element in learning God's ways. Sometimes it is wisdom to stand back and watch the Lord at work. "The battle is the Lord's". His strategy and tactics are often beyond our understanding, but He is ever at work countering evil and promoting good. Relax brother, "He holds the whole world in His hand".

Give Him time to speak to you and space to work for you. Learn to know the stillness of faith, the rest of hope.

Euclid was wrong

Outside his geometrical proposition that "the whole is equal to the sum of all its parts", the dictum does not hold.

Man is a complicated arrangement of nerve and muscle, bone and flesh, blood and water. But mere addition of parts does not make a man. He is all that – plus the principle of life.

This "more than parts" is seen in Genesis chapters one and two. After each day's activity "God saw that it was good", but when creation was complete, "God saw everything that He had made, and behold it was very good." It was not until all creations parts were completed, <u>and in action</u>, that perfection was acknowledged.

It is like a Swiss-made watch; each part is perfect, but it is not until they work together that it tells us the time.

Analysis has its place in scientific research, but it does not represent reality. Even synthesis may fall short of real explanation. It is like the chemist who saw his wife in tears and exclaimed, "I have analysed tears; they contain a little phosphate of lime, chloride of sodium, mucous and water". Enough to give her greater pain and bigger tears.

When we regard a person we should be slow to criticise, for we know but little of each other. Indeed, "we know in part", so let us be gracious and tolerant.

Psychoanalysis

Many have been helped by the services of psychoanalysts, but their ministrations are often limited, and their conclusions fall short. You see, with all their knowledge, they are still human, therefore fallible. They cannot divest themselves of their own nature. I've often wondered, "who analyses the analysts?" Its like arguing in a circle: no finality.

In fact human judgement, even when well-informed, can be flawed and feeble. Someone put the work of the analyst thus:

> "He takes the saints to pieces
> And labels all their parts,
> He tabulates the secrets
> Of loyal loving hearts.
> He probes their selfless passion,
> And shows exactly why
> The martyr goes out singing,
> To suffer and to die .....
> His reasoning is perfect,
> His proofs as plain as paint,
> He has but one small weakness,
> He cannot make a saint."

But God can. As we put our case in His hands we can "become partakers of the divine nature" (2 Peter 1:4). And, as the conversion of Saul of Tarsus proves, it can happen in a moment (Acts 9:2-6). To become a saint we do not need long sessions on the psychoanalyst's couch, all we need is faith in a living Saviour (Acts 16:31).

26 December

The brains' trust

Do you remember this popular radio programme of long ago? A select group of notables – Commander Campbell, Dr Huxley and Professor C E M Goad – who commented on topical issues with entertaining openness?

Colourful figures all, especially Dr Joad with his philosophical approach to the subjects discussed. Here is one of his expressive statements: "If I were allowed to interview one famous personage and ask him one question only, I would choose Jesus Christ, and ask, 'Did you, or did you not rise from the dead?'"

But, Dr Joad, the answer was given long before you asked the question. Jesus "showed himself alive after His passion by many infallible proofs" (Acts 1:3). He said to John of Patmos: "I am He that liveth, and was dead; and, behold, I am alive forevermore. Amen!" (Rev 1:18).

We need not qualify for "A Brain's Trust" to accept this answer, all we need to do is to believe this divine affirmation. Something will happen to us. We will feel the power of the Living Christ as He regenerates us. It is "heart-faith" that does it (Rom 10:9) not mere "head-faith".

Dead – alive

“Don’t tell anybody,” said Charles Lamb, clutching a friend’s arm as they walked down Fleet Street, “But I have been dead for years and nobody knows it”. But he himself did, and that proved he still had a modicum of real existence.

But there are those who are dead and don’t know it. Jesus told the church at Sardis, “Thou hast a name that thou livest, and art dead” (Rev 3:1). Paul speaks of “dead-alive” women, who gratify the flesh but neglect the spirit (1 Tim 5:6).

It is good to build up a reputation for being spiritually alive: (“Thou hast a name that thou livest”). Provided our good name is grounded on solid achievement, we can exert a benign influence on others.

But such a reputation must be sustained by living testimony. How we can deceive ourselves! Jesus told Sardis they were dead – but they failed to know it. Spiritual deadness is insensitivity to our condition, living too much on the past, and satisfied complacency respecting our reputation.

Whatever whimsical Lamb meant, it is true that to confess our “deadness” can be a vital preliminary to our seeking new life in Christ.

What to do when troubles come

The writer of Hebrews stresses the need of a spiritual approach to our afflictions and distresses. These persecuted souls were exhorted to be "followers of them who through faith and patience inherit the promises" (Heb 6:12). In other words "stick it out: the Lord is with you". Here are two things to help us through such times.

First, we should <u>believe our beliefs</u>. Trials are a test of our faith. It is not enough to have a creed, we must have a conviction. When trouble comes we are thrown back on the promises of God. Will they work? Faith says, "Yes!" and hold on until God gives deliverance. Times change, circumstances change, we change – but God never changes, His word cannot fail.

Secondly, we must learn to <u>doubt our doubts</u>. With the Psalmist we may be constrained to say "How long, O Lord," or even to moan, "Hath God forgotten to be gracious" (Ps 77:9). To sink a little under our load is not sinful, it is natural, but to wallow in our woe is sinful. Have you doubts, face them with God's faithful word, declare that irrationality, banish them with a determined effort of will and let there dawn a new day of faith. In such a situation deadly doubt is dead.

The speaking clock

In a London Church I once attended was a clock which, instead of the usual figures one to twelve, had in their place the words GOD IS LOVE. This, with three large dots between the words, made up the twelve points of a normal clock face.

What a message! Each time we looked at the clock it spoke of God's love, reminding us of the timeless and timely care of God for His people. Each hour, each minute, is a fresh revelation of His mercy and grace. Think of it like this:-

> "God is love at midnight chill
> When the world is dark and still;
> God is love through all the night
> Keeping saints within His sight.
> God is love at dawn's first light,
> With the darkness put to flight.
> God is love at high mid-day,
> When we pause from work to pray;
> God is love through afternoon.
> Growing weary? None too soon
> Comes evening with its soft twilight,
> Then gently falls the shades of night –
> And 'God is love', still glad we say,
> Through the night and through the day."

The love of God preceded time, for before the ages began to unfold He had planned their ultimately happy course. The love of God pervaded time, for, in spite of all that a sin-troubled world endures, the grace of God still conquers evil. The love of God will persist to and through eternity for He can never change. The great thing that makes Heaven so alluring and acceptable is the unchangeable fact that GOD IS LOVE.

30 December

Fossils

Archaeology, the study of beginnings, is a fascinating science. It digs into the geological past to discover relics of early life, often different, yet related to modern existence.

Someone, whether wiseacre or wag we cannot judge, has likened Church History as a similar pursuit – the unearthing from time the fossilised remains of ecclesiastical structures that once played a vital part in their contemporary scene, with relics of such forms existing today.

How true is this? And what effects do such survivals have on present church life. It is true that the present exists because of the past; but can former conventions be an impediment to present progress?

Let us note three things about fossils.

1. They are dead. Often beautiful, they show adaptation to their own time – but they are dead. Within the strata of their own time they reveal much – but they are dead.

2. They are dated. By various scientific considerations, the past is divided into "ages" with specific characteristics. But how much applies to our modern scenario?

3. There is the alarming suggestion that DNA – the life-pattern of such dead creatures may be revived, and these long defunct life-forms recovered.

Be this as it may. Applied to ecclesiology – can ancient forms be resuscitated to meet our modern needs. Some things will never die – like the scriptures – and when these form our lives, we, too live cf Rev 21:5.

The "eyes" have it

Hebrew is a colourful language. Its vivid terms often need paraphrase to bring the full meaning into our mother tongue. Take for instance the terms "a bountiful eye" (Prov 22:9) and "an evil eye" (Prov 23:6). The former is literally a <u>good</u> eye; the latter a <u>bad</u> eye. Does this indicate an outlook on life?

<u>The good eye</u>- "giveth of his bread to the poor." That is, it sees a need and seeks bountifully to meet it. The good eye is unselfish, nay more, liberal.

<u>The bad eye</u> – is niggardly. "Neither desire thou his dainty meals," because though he may invite you to dinner to gain reputation for a quality he does not possess, he actually begrudges you every crumb you eat. He is selfish.

This aspect of "evil" as selfishness is developed by Dr Edwin Hatch in his "Essays in Biblical Greek". He applies it to the words of Jesus in Matthew 7:11, "If ye being evil ...." and shows how our Lord understood the basic element of human nature – selfishness. This is original sin, in fact, the essence of all sin; putting self before God and men. This egoism, the enthronement of self, must be overcome if we are to enjoy life at its best. The prime purpose of "true religion" is to turn the ideas and ideals, the deeds and the doctrines from oneself. Ego must give way to Christ.

THE LAST THOUGHT

Say amen!
1 Corinthians 14:16

This Hebrew word, which has its origin in the concept of stability, is transliterated in many languages. "Amen!" is a universal term, a fragment of cosmic lingua franca. Heavenly worship is full of "Amens!"

Affirmation. When I say "Amen" to another's prayer I not only express my agreement, I adopt the prayer as my own – "So be it" is my endorsement.

Acceptation. When I say "Amen!" to a preachers word, I express my conviction of its truth, and confirm its worthiness to be accepted.

Anticipation. This term, applied to the promises of God (2 Cor 1:20) implies our firm anticipation of their fulfilment. "It shall be done," we affirm in faith. One of the last words in the Bible is "Amen (even so) come Lord Jesus" in response to the Saviour's assurance of His return.

Jesus is called, "the Amen" in Revelation 3:14. His name is the divine signature to His cheque-book of promises. His name is the affirmation of all God's precepts, His name is the assurance of destiny. He began the programme of salvation, He will finish it (Heb 12:2).

Epilogue

The complete guide to living

Isaac Walton's "The Compleat Angler" is a literary classic. But it is not to be compared with the inspired Scriptures, which are "invaluable to teach us what is true and to make us realise what is wrong in our lives; it straightens us out and helps us to do what is right": (2 Tim 3:16, Living Bible).

How strong are the commands not to add to or take away from God's word! (Deuteronomy 4:2, 12:32, Prov 30:6, Rev 22:18).

To ADD to God's word is an insult to the Almighty. It is as if we feel He does not know enough or understand our call. Paraphrase - yes! Comment - yes! But only so long as the sense is not missed. Translation has its problems, but that version is best which conveys most clearly the original thoughts of God.

To TAKE AWAY from God's word is to set our opinion against His, or ignore what He would have us know. We can "take away" from God's word by neglect, and condemn it by not reading it. The ministry of a servant of God is to "Preach the Word" (2 Tim 4:2).

The foregoing series of "Just a Thought" is well worth the toil of writing if they inculcate respect for the word of the Lord and reverence for the Lord Himself.